AGI: Reasoning Intelligence

How Intelligent Systems Think, Solve Problems, and Make Better Decisions

By

Susie Hala

IntelliGloss AI Education Series

Module 2: Artificial General Intelligence (AGI)

Legal Disclaimer

Educational Purpose Disclaimer

"This publication is part of the IntelliGloss AI Education Series, a structured curriculum support system for AI literacy in grades 6–12."

The information presented in this publication is provided for educational and informational purposes only. This book is intended to support educators, administrators, parents, and learners in understanding the concepts, opportunities, and challenges associated with artificial intelligence in education. It is not intended to serve as legal, technical, policy, cybersecurity, or professional advice.

Readers should consult qualified professionals, institutional guidelines, and local regulations before implementing any educational programs, technologies, or policies described in this book.

Technology and Accuracy Disclaimer
Artificial intelligence is a rapidly evolving field. While every effort has been made to ensure the accuracy and reliability of the information presented at the time of publication, technologies, policies, research findings, and best practices may change over time. The author and publisher make no guarantees that all information will remain current or applicable in future technological environments.

Readers are encouraged to verify tools, platforms, and recommendations independently before using them in educational settings.

Implementation Responsibility
Schools, educators, and institutions are solely responsible for determining how and whether to implement artificial intelligence tools, strategies, or classroom activities discussed in this book. Educational environments vary widely, and policies regarding technology use, student privacy, and curriculum development differ by district, state, and country.

The author and publisher assume no responsibility for outcomes resulting from the implementation of ideas, examples, or frameworks described in this book.

Student Safety and Data Privacy
Artificial intelligence tools may involve the collection or processing of data. Educators and institutions are responsible for ensuring that any technology used complies with applicable student privacy laws, data protection regulations, and school policies, including but not limited to FERPA, COPPA, GDPR, or other relevant regulations depending on jurisdiction.

The author and publisher are not responsible for the privacy practices, security policies, or data handling procedures of third-party platforms or software mentioned in this book.

Third-Party Tools and References
This book may reference third-party technologies, organizations, research studies, or platforms for illustrative and educational purposes. Such references do not constitute endorsements or guarantees regarding the performance, reliability, safety, or suitability of those tools for educational use.

Educators and institutions should conduct their own evaluations and risk assessments before adopting any technology.

No Professional Liability
The author and publisher shall not be held liable for any direct, indirect, incidental, or consequential damages resulting from the use or misuse of the information contained in this book. This includes but is not limited to decisions related to curriculum design, technology adoption, classroom instruction, institutional policies, or educational outcomes.

Educational Interpretation
The concepts and examples provided in this book are intended to support discussion and learning. They should not be interpreted as official standards, mandatory guidelines, or universally applicable policies for artificial intelligence education.

Schools and educators are encouraged to adapt the ideas presented here according to their local policies, cultural context, educational standards, and student needs.

Author's Intent
The goal of this book is to promote responsible AI literacy, thoughtful discussion, and ethical awareness as schools prepare students for a world increasingly shaped by intelligent technologies.

The author encourages readers to approach artificial intelligence education with curiosity, caution, and a commitment to responsible learning.

Title: AGI: Reasoning Intelligence How Intelligent Systems Think, Solve Problems, and Make Better Decisions

ISBN: 978-1-972925-30-0

Published by
IntelliGloss Press
United States of America

Dedication

This book is dedicated to the next generation of learners—
the students who will grow up in a world shaped by intelligent technology,
and who deserve to understand it with clarity, confidence, and purpose.

To the educators who show up every day with dedication and heart,
guiding students through a rapidly changing world—
your role has never been more important.

To the parents and families who support learning at home,
encouraging curiosity, responsibility, and growth—
you are the foundation of every child's success.

And to my granddaughters,
whose curiosity, imagination, and future inspire me to do this work—
this book is for you.

May you not only learn how to use technology,
but understand it, question it, and shape it for the good of others.

About the Author

Susie Hala
Founder of the IntelliGloss AI Education Series

Susie Hala is an author, educator, and curriculum developer dedicated to advancing artificial intelligence literacy in education. Her work focuses on helping schools, educators, and students understand how intelligent technologies are shaping modern society—and why that understanding is essential for the next generation.

Hala is the creator of the IntelliGloss AI Education Series, a comprehensive and growing collection of educational books designed to make complex artificial intelligence concepts accessible, structured, and practical for classroom use. Her work emphasizes clarity, organization, and responsible implementation, enabling schools to introduce AI literacy without requiring advanced technical backgrounds.

In addition to her work in education, Hala brings hands-on experience working with artificial intelligence systems, including early exposure to rule-based AI technologies during her time working with AT&T. She has also developed modern digital platforms that integrate artificial intelligence, automation, and online systems, building e-commerce solutions and AI-driven applications that connect payment platforms, hosting environments, and conversational AI tools into real-world, functional systems.

This combination of foundational understanding and practical experience allows her to translate complex AI concepts into clear, accessible language for both educators and students.

Recognizing that artificial intelligence is rapidly transforming how information is created, interpreted, and used, Hala advocates for equipping students with the ability not only to use AI tools, but to understand, question, and evaluate them. Her work emphasizes critical thinking, ethical awareness, and responsible digital citizenship.

The IntelliGloss AI Education Series supports schools in teaching key areas such as artificial intelligence foundations, algorithms, machine learning concepts, and AI ethics, as well as the broader evolution of intelligent systems—from Artificial Narrow Intelligence (ANI) to Artificial General Intelligence (AGI) and Artificial Superintelligence (ASI). These resources are designed for students in grades 6–12 and for educators seeking structured, classroom-ready approaches to AI literacy.

In addition to her work in education publishing, Hala has a strong background in entrepreneurship, having built and managed multiple businesses and educational initiatives. Her experience across industries reinforces her belief that technology education must remain grounded in human values, critical thinking, and ethical responsibility.

Her mission is clear: to ensure that the next generation understands intelligent technology—not just how to use it, but how it truly works.

Preface

Two Students. Two Paths. One Future.

Before we begin, it is important to understand why learning how artificial intelligence works—not just how to use it—matters for every student.

Imagine two students who have just graduated from high school and are preparing for a job interview. The first student knows how to use artificial intelligence tools. This student can generate answers, complete assignments quickly, and rely on AI to assist with tasks. However, this student does not understand how artificial intelligence works behind the scenes.

The second student also knows how to use AI tools, but in addition, understands the foundational concepts behind them. This student has learned about data, algorithms, tokens, models, and how intelligent systems are trained and operate. This student can think critically about AI, recognize its limitations, and adapt when needed.

At first, the first student may appear faster and more efficient. However, over time, the second student demonstrates a deeper level of understanding, independence, and problem-solving ability. The second student is not only able to use artificial intelligence but also to question it, improve it, and grow with it.

This book is written for the second student.

In a world where artificial intelligence is becoming part of everyday life, students must not only learn how to use intelligent systems—they must learn how they work. True understanding leads to confidence, responsibility, and the ability to lead in an AI-driven future.

This perspective is not just theoretical—it is personal.

There was a time when I was the first student.

I knew how to use systems. I followed processes, completed tasks, and worked within structured environments that required accuracy and consistency. At the time, I did not think of these systems as artificial intelligence. They were simply part of the job—tools that had to be learned, followed, and mastered.

But looking back, I now understand something much deeper. I was working within rule-based systems—the earliest foundation of what we now recognize as artificial intelligence.

That realization changed everything.

As I began studying modern AI, including machine learning, deep learning, and intelligent systems, I started to see a clear connection between the past and the present. The structured systems I once worked in, the logic behind decision-making, and the step-by-step processes all still exist today. They have simply evolved.

Artificial intelligence did not appear overnight. It grew from rule-based systems into systems that can now learn, adapt, and assist in ways we never imagined.

I made a decision to move from simply using systems to understanding them.

That journey—from student one to student two—is the reason these books exist.

My mission is to help others bridge that same gap.

I believe that artificial intelligence should be understandable for everyone. It should not feel intimidating or out of reach. Students should feel confident exploring it. Teachers should feel prepared to introduce it. Everyday learners should have access to clear, structured explanations that make sense.

You do not need a background in technology. You do not need to know how to code. You only need the right explanation.

A Note from the Author

AI Is a Tool — Not a Decision Maker

Artificial Intelligence is becoming part of everyday life. Students use it to complete assignments, teachers use it to support instruction, and businesses use it to improve efficiency. While these tools are powerful and useful, there is an important truth that must remain clear from the very beginning:

Artificial Intelligence does not make decisions—people do.

One of the main purposes of this book is to help readers understand how AI works, what it can do, and—just as importantly—what it cannot do. AI systems are designed to process information, identify patterns, and generate responses based on data. They can assist with thinking, but they do not think independently. They can provide answers, but they do not understand consequences. They can suggest ideas, but they do not choose actions.

Every outcome that involves AI begins and ends with human involvement. A person asks the question. A person reviews the response. A person decides what to do next. Responsibility does not transfer to the machine.

In today's world, it is easy to confuse speed with intelligence and automation with authority. Because AI can respond quickly and confidently, it may appear as though it is making decisions. In reality, it is performing a task based on patterns it has learned—not exercising judgment.

This distinction matters. When people begin to rely on AI without understanding its role, they risk misunderstanding information, misusing technology, or placing trust in a system that is not capable of accountability. Clear understanding leads to responsible use.

This book was written to remove confusion and provide clarity. It is designed to help students and educators move beyond simply using AI tools and begin understanding the structure behind them. By learning how AI supports human thinking—rather than replacing it—readers can approach technology with confidence, awareness, and responsibility.

Artificial Intelligence is a powerful assistant. It can enhance learning, support creativity, and improve productivity. But it remains a tool.

The decisions, the actions, and the responsibility will always belong to the human.

— Susie Hala

Bringing Clarity to Artificial Intelligence

During a recent meeting with a school district, it became clear that one of the biggest challenges in artificial intelligence education is not the technology itself—but the way it is explained.

In that discussion, terms such as **chatbots, generative AI, agentic AI, autonomy, tools, hallucinations, and AI usage levels** were all mentioned together. While each term represents a distinct concept, they were often blended into one conversation without clear distinctions. The result was confusion, even among those who were actively trying to understand and make informed decisions.

This experience revealed an important truth:
Without clear definitions and structure, artificial intelligence becomes difficult to teach, difficult to learn, and difficult to use responsibly.

This book is designed to provide that structure.

Understanding the Core Concepts

To build a strong foundation, it is essential to separate and define the key ideas that are often confused.

Chatbot
A chatbot is a conversational interface that allows users to interact with an AI system through questions and prompts. It responds to input but does not act beyond what is directly requested.

Generative AI (Gen AI)
Generative AI refers to systems that create new content, including text, images, audio, and code. These systems generate outputs based on patterns learned from large datasets. While powerful, generative AI does not truly understand information and may occasionally produce inaccurate results.

Agentic AI
Agentic AI describes systems that can take action toward a goal. Rather than responding to a single prompt, these systems can plan, make decisions within defined limits, and carry out multi-step tasks. This introduces a higher level of functional independence.

Autonomy
Autonomy refers to how independently an AI system operates. Some systems require constant human guidance, while others can perform multiple steps with minimal input. Autonomy is not a separate type of AI, but a measure of how much control the system has in completing tasks.

Additional Terms That Shape Understanding

AI Tools
AI tools are the applications people use to interact with artificial intelligence, such as writing assistants, design platforms, and data analysis systems. These tools make AI accessible in everyday tasks.

Hallucination
A hallucination occurs when an AI system generates information that appears correct but is inaccurate or unsupported. This is a known limitation of generative systems and highlights the need for human verification.

The AI Use Continuum

Another important concept is how AI is used at different levels. Rather than viewing AI as a single capability, it is more accurate to understand it as a continuum of use:

Assistive Use
AI supports simple tasks such as answering questions, correcting grammar, or providing suggestions.

Augmented Use
AI helps expand human capability by generating ideas, organizing content, and assisting in problem-solving.

Agentic Use
AI begins to take on multi-step responsibilities, planning and completing tasks with reduced human input.

This continuum shows that AI can range from a helpful assistant to a more independent system, depending on how it is applied.

The Moment Everything Sounded Like One Conversation

During a recent discussion on artificial intelligence, I listened closely as different experts spoke about the future of AI. One referenced advanced systems beyond human intelligence, another discussed goal-driven AI systems, and the conversation shifted quickly between topics like autonomy, tools, and system behavior. At first, it sounded like a single, unified discussion. But the more I listened, the more I realized something important.

They were not all talking about the same thing.

One part of the conversation focused on future possibilities—high-level systems that do not yet exist. Another part focused on current technologies that are already being used today. At the same time, different terms were being used to describe how AI behaves, how it makes decisions, and how much independence it may have. These ideas were layered together in a way that made them sound connected, even when they were not.

This experience revealed a major challenge in understanding artificial intelligence today. Many discussions combine different types of AI, different levels of intelligence, and different behaviors into one conversation. Without clear structure, these ideas begin to blur together. For someone trying to learn, this can feel overwhelming and confusing.

This book is built to solve that problem.

Artificial intelligence is not one single concept. It is a system made up of multiple layers. Some layers describe how intelligent a system is. Other layers describe how the system behaves. Still others describe how much control or independence the system has. When these layers are separated and explained clearly, AI becomes much easier to understand.

The goal of this book is to bring clarity where confusion often exists. Instead of mixing everything into one explanation, each concept is presented in a structured and organized way. This allows students, educators, and readers to see how the pieces fit together without losing sight of what each part actually means.

Understanding artificial intelligence begins with understanding its structure.

Once that structure is clear, the conversation becomes clearer as well.

Why Clarity Matters

When these concepts are not clearly defined, they merge into what can be described as a "conceptual blur." This can lead to misunderstandings about what AI can and cannot do, as well as unrealistic expectations or misuse in educational settings.

Clear understanding helps ensure that:

Students remain active learners, not passive users

Educators maintain control over instructional outcomes

AI is used as a support tool rather than a replacement for thinking

The Purpose of This Book

This book is built on a simple but essential principle:

Students should not only use artificial intelligence—they should understand it.

By clearly defining core concepts such as chatbots, generative AI, agentic AI, autonomy, and the continuum of AI use, this curriculum provides a structured pathway for developing both technical understanding and critical thinking.

Artificial intelligence is not a single tool or system. It is a collection of capabilities that must be understood in context.

Clarity is the foundation of responsible innovation.

Structuring Artificial Intelligence to Create Clarity and Understanding

Why Structure Is Necessary

Artificial intelligence is often presented as one unified concept. In many discussions, different ideas such as intelligence level, system behavior, and autonomy are combined into a single explanation. This can make AI appear more complex and confusing than it actually is.

Clarity begins when these ideas are separated and organized.

Structuring artificial intelligence allows each concept to be understood on its own before being connected to the larger system.

The Problem Without Structure

When AI is not structured, conversations may include multiple terms that sound related but describe entirely different things. For example, a discussion may move quickly between advanced future systems, current tools, and system behaviors without clearly distinguishing between them.

This creates the impression that all forms of AI operate at the same level and in the same way, which is not accurate.

Without structure, understanding becomes difficult.

The Solution: A Structured Approach

Artificial intelligence becomes clearer when it is organized into distinct categories.

Level explains how intelligent a system is.
Behavior explains how the system operates.
Control explains how much independence the system has.

Each category answers a different question. Together, they form a complete picture of how AI systems function.

Clarity Through Separation

A system can operate at a current level of intelligence while demonstrating different behaviors or levels of independence. For example, a system that generates responses and a system that takes steps toward completing a task may operate at the same intelligence level but differ in how they behave.

This distinction becomes clear only when structure is applied.

Instructional Insight

When teaching artificial intelligence, it is important to avoid presenting all concepts at once. Separating ideas into categories allows learners to focus on one dimension at a time, building understanding step by step.

Structured learning leads to deeper comprehension.

Key Takeaway

Artificial intelligence is not one single idea. It is a system made up of multiple parts. Structuring those parts creates clarity, improves understanding, and allows learners to see how the system truly works.

Reflection Question

How does separating intelligence level, behavior, and control make artificial intelligence easier to understand?

The IntelliGloss Instructional Approach

The IntelliGloss AI Education Series is designed to help students move beyond simply using AI tools and begin understanding artificial intelligence as a complete system.

Students learn how AI is built, how it operates, and how it connects to the real world.

A Message to Students and Readers

If you have ever felt that technology was too complicated…
If you have ever been confused by systems that were never clearly explained…

I want you to know:

You are capable of understanding artificial intelligence.

Sometimes, the challenge is not the concept itself—it is how it has been presented.

This series was created to change that.

A Message to Educators

To the educators using this material:

These books are designed to support you in introducing artificial intelligence in a way that is clear, structured, and meaningful for students.

AI is becoming part of every industry, and students deserve more than just exposure to tools—they deserve understanding.

This series aims to provide that foundation.

Final Reflection

Every experience we have—especially the challenging ones—prepares us for something greater.

The systems I once worked in taught me discipline, structure, and attention to detail. Today, those same lessons allow me to break down complex ideas and make them understandable for others.

That is what this series represents:

Turning complexity into clarity.

Why Artificial Intelligence Education Matters for Every Student

Why AI Literacy Is Essential for Every Student

Artificial intelligence is no longer a future concept or a specialized technology used only by experts. It is already part of everyday life for students of all ages. From smartphones and search engines to navigation apps, social media, streaming platforms, and educational tools, AI systems influence how information is accessed, decisions are made, and learning takes place.

Because AI is embedded in daily life, understanding it is no longer optional. It is a foundational skill, similar to digital literacy and critical thinking. Students do not need to become programmers or engineers, but they do need to understand what AI is, how it works at a basic level, and how it affects their lives.

AI education should not be limited to computer science classrooms. Every student interacts with AI systems daily. Teaching students how these systems function empowers them to become informed users rather than passive consumers of technology.

This book is designed to make artificial intelligence understandable, approachable, and relevant. It focuses on clarity, responsibility, and real-world understanding to help students prepare for a future where humans and intelligent systems work side by side.

IntelliGloss AI Education Series

Teaching how AI actually works—from hardware to power to global systems.

Why AI Education Matters

Artificial intelligence is already shaping how students learn, write, research, and solve problems.

Yet many students—and educators—are using AI tools without understanding how these systems actually work.

Schools need more than access to technology.
They need structured, responsible AI education.

Our Approach

The IntelliGloss AI Education Series is designed to help students move beyond simply using AI tools and begin understanding artificial intelligence as a complete system.

Students learn how AI is built, how it operates, and how it connects to the real world.

The IntelliGloss Framework

Our books introduce AI through a clear and connected system:

Chip Family — the hardware that powers AI

Watts Family — the rate at which AI uses power

Energy Family — the total power AI consumes over time

Infrastructure Family — the global systems that support AI

This framework helps students understand AI from the inside out.

Built for the Classroom

Each book includes:

- Structured chapters aligned with semester learning
- Clear explanations designed for student understanding
- Reflection sections with learning objectives
- Worksheets, quizzes, and answer keys
- Teacher Implementation Guides

Supporting Schools and Educators

The IntelliGloss series supports:

- Responsible and ethical AI use
- Student data awareness and safety
- Critical thinking and digital literacy
- Classroom-ready instruction for grades 6–12 and beyond

What This Book Is—and What It Is Not

Many people today are becoming familiar with artificial intelligence through tools like ChatGPT, Microsoft Copilot, Canva, and other AI-powered applications. These tools can help with writing, answering questions, creating images, and completing everyday tasks.

In addition to these tools, you may also hear terms such as **AI agents, agentic AI, autonomous systems, and generative AI**. While these may sound complex, they are all part of the same evolving landscape of artificial intelligence technologies.

This book is not a guide on how to use those tools.

Instead, it explains what makes those tools possible.

Behind every AI tool is a system made up of multiple layers working together. At the most basic level, information is represented as bits and processed through powerful computer chips. That information is organized into data, broken into tokens, and then processed by algorithms and models that allow the system to recognize patterns, generate responses, and perform tasks.

These components—chips, bits, tokens, data, algorithms, and models—work together as a complete system. While users may only see the tool, the real intelligence comes from how these underlying parts interact behind the scenes.

Artificial intelligence can also be understood in terms of different levels of capability. Most of the AI systems used today fall under **Artificial Narrow Intelligence (ANI)**, which is designed to perform specific tasks, such as answering questions or generating content. More advanced forms, such as **Artificial General Intelligence (AGI)** and **Artificial Superintelligence (ASI)** represent future possibilities where AI could match or exceed human-level thinking. While these advanced levels are still theoretical, understanding the differences helps provide a broader view of where AI is today and where it may be heading.

For students, parents, and educators, this distinction is important. Learning how to use AI tools is helpful, but understanding how they work—and where they fit within the larger AI landscape—builds stronger thinking, better decision-making, and more responsible use.

Most importantly, artificial intelligence does not make decisions on its own. It does not take responsibility for actions or outcomes. AI systems generate responses based on data and patterns, but it is always the human who decides what to do with that information.

This book is designed to make these underlying systems clear and accessible, even for readers who are new to artificial intelligence.

Artificial intelligence is still in its early stages of development. As these technologies continue to grow, those who understand the foundation behind them will be better prepared to adapt, question, and use them wisely.

Who This Book Is For

This book is designed for educators, school leaders, and curriculum developers guiding students in an age of rapidly advancing technology.

Artificial intelligence is already influencing how students learn, research, and communicate. Yet many educators have not received formal training in how these systems work or how they should be addressed in the classroom.

This book helps bridge that gap by providing clear explanations and practical frameworks for understanding artificial intelligence in an educational setting.

How Schools Can Use This Book

This book supports schools in developing a structured approach to artificial intelligence literacy.

It can be used for:

Professional development for educators

Classroom discussions and activities

Curriculum support across subject areas

Policy and academic integrity conversations

Rather than focusing on specific tools, this book emphasizes lasting principles that help students understand, evaluate, and use AI responsibly.

Closing Perspective

Artificial intelligence will continue to evolve. With the right knowledge and leadership, schools can ensure that students not only use these technologies, but understand them, question them, and apply them responsibly.

IntelliGloss is more than a book series. It is a structured approach to preparing students for a future shaped by artificial intelligence.

Rather than focusing only on how to use AI tools, this series helps students understand how AI actually works—from its foundational building blocks to real-world applications.

“Before exploring the technical structure of artificial intelligence, it is equally important to understand the human principles that guide its use.”

Human Values Family

Definition

The Human Values Family in artificial intelligence represents the guiding principles that shape how AI systems are created, used, and integrated into society. These values include ethics, responsibility, trust, and human well-being.

Artificial intelligence may be built on data, algorithms, and computational systems, but its true impact is measured by how it affects people. For this reason, AI is not only a technical system—it is a human-centered system.

Key Concepts

The Human Values Family exists to ensure that artificial intelligence serves humanity in a positive and responsible way. While AI systems can process information and generate outcomes, they do not possess judgment, empathy, or moral understanding.

This means that human values must guide every stage of AI development—from design to deployment.

AI reflects the intentions, decisions, and assumptions of the people who build and use it. If those values are not carefully considered, AI systems can unintentionally produce biased, harmful, or misleading results.

Understanding human values in AI is not optional—it is essential.

Core Elements of the Human Values Family

Ethics
Ethics in AI refers to making decisions that are fair, just, and respectful of human rights. This includes minimizing bias, protecting privacy, and ensuring transparency in how systems operate.

Responsibility
Responsibility means that humans remain accountable for AI systems. Developers, educators, organizations, and users must take ownership of how AI is used and the outcomes it produces.

Trust
Trust is critical for the successful adoption of AI. People must feel confident that AI systems are reliable, safe, and aligned with their best interests.

Human Well-Being
AI should enhance human life—not replace, harm, or diminish it. This includes supporting learning, improving access to information, and creating opportunities while maintaining human dignity.

Real-World Connection

Artificial intelligence is already influencing how people learn, communicate, and make decisions. From search engines to classroom tools, AI is shaping daily experiences.

Without clear human values guiding these systems, there is a risk of reinforcing misinformation, bias, or unrealistic expectations.

For students, this means learning not only how to use AI tools, but how to question them, evaluate their outputs, and understand their limitations.

Applications in Education

In the classroom, the Human Values Family helps students develop critical thinking and ethical awareness. Teachers can use this framework to guide discussions about fairness, responsibility, and the impact of technology on society.

Students can explore questions such as:

How should AI be used responsibly?

What makes an AI system fair?

How does technology influence human behavior?

This approach supports both technical understanding and responsible decision-making.

Benefits

Teaching human values in AI helps students:

Develop ethical awareness

Strengthen critical thinking

Understand the societal impact of technology

Become responsible users and future creators of AI

It ensures that learning about AI goes beyond functionality and includes responsibility.

Challenges

Human values are not always universal. Different cultures, communities, and individuals may have different perspectives on what is considered fair or ethical.

Additionally, AI technology is evolving rapidly, often faster than policies and guidelines can keep up. This makes it essential for educators and students to stay informed and adaptable.

Summary

The Human Values Family reminds us that artificial intelligence is not just about machines—it is about people.

By focusing on ethics, responsibility, trust, and human well-being, students can learn to use AI thoughtfully and responsibly.

Understanding these principles helps prepare learners to navigate a world where artificial intelligence plays an increasingly important role in everyday life.

Executive Summary

IntelliGloss AI Education Series

Teaching How Artificial Intelligence Actually Works

Artificial intelligence is already shaping how students learn, write, research, and make decisions. Yet in many classrooms, students are being introduced to AI tools without understanding how these systems actually function.

This creates a critical gap.

Students may become efficient users of technology, but without foundational knowledge, they are not equipped to think critically, evaluate outputs, or use AI responsibly. As AI continues to expand across every industry, this gap will only grow more significant.

The **IntelliGloss AI Education Series** was created to address this challenge.

The Problem

Most current approaches to AI in education focus on tool usage rather than system understanding. As a result:

- Students rely on AI without understanding its limitations
- Educators lack structured frameworks for teaching AI concepts
- Key terms such as generative AI, agentic AI, and autonomy are often introduced without clear definitions
- Responsibility and ethical use are not consistently emphasized

Without clarity, artificial intelligence becomes difficult to teach, difficult to learn, and difficult to manage in a school environment.

The Solution

The IntelliGloss AI Education Series provides a structured, classroom-ready approach to artificial intelligence literacy for grades 6–12.

Rather than focusing on individual tools, this series teaches students how AI works as a complete system—from foundational components to real-world applications.

Students learn to move beyond surface-level interaction and develop true understanding.

The IntelliGloss Framework

The series introduces AI through a clear and connected structure, including:

Foundational building blocks such as data, algorithms, tokens, and models

System-level understanding through categories such as intelligence level, behavior, and control

Real-world context through applications, limitations, and responsible use

Human-centered learning through ethics, responsibility, trust, and student safety

This structured approach transforms artificial intelligence from a confusing concept into an understandable system.

Instructional Design

Each book in the series is designed for practical classroom use and includes:

Structured chapters aligned with instructional pacing

Clear, student-friendly explanations

Reflection sections to reinforce understanding

Worksheets, quizzes, and answer keys

Teacher implementation support

No prior technical background is required for educators or students.

Guiding Principle

A central message of the IntelliGloss series is:

Artificial Intelligence is a tool—not a decision maker.

Students learn that while AI can support thinking and provide information, all decisions, actions, and responsibilities remain with humans. This principle reinforces critical thinking, accountability, and responsible technology use.

Why It Matters

AI literacy is no longer optional. It is a foundational skill.

Students who understand how AI works will be better prepared to:

- Think critically about information
- Adapt to emerging technologies
- Use AI responsibly and ethically
- Succeed in an increasingly AI-driven world

Our Goal

The IntelliGloss AI Education Series is designed to help schools move beyond simply using artificial intelligence tools and toward a deeper understanding of how these systems actually work.

By providing clear structure, defined concepts, and real-world context, this series equips students and educators with the knowledge needed to think critically, evaluate information, and use AI responsibly.

The goal is not just to introduce technology—but to build understanding, confidence, and accountability in an AI-driven world.

This is not just about learning to use AI—it is about preparing students to understand it, question it, and lead with it.

Clarity leads to confidence.
Understanding leads to responsible use.

Mission Statement

The mission of the IntelliGloss AI Education Series is to make artificial intelligence clear, structured, and accessible for every student and educator.

In a world where AI is rapidly transforming how information is created, used, and understood, this series is designed to move beyond surface-level interaction and provide a deeper understanding of how intelligent systems actually work.

Through clear explanations, organized frameworks, and real-world context, IntelliGloss equips learners with the ability to think critically, evaluate information, and engage with technology responsibly.

This mission is grounded in a simple belief:
students should not only learn how to use artificial intelligence—they should understand it.

By building both technical awareness and human-centered understanding, the IntelliGloss AI Education Series prepares students to navigate, question, and shape a future increasingly influenced by intelligent technologies.

The goal is not just to keep up with artificial intelligence—but to understand it, guide it, and use it responsibly.

Vision Statement

The vision of the IntelliGloss AI Education Series is to create a future where artificial intelligence is clearly understood, responsibly used, and thoughtfully integrated into education and everyday life.

In this future, students are not passive users of technology, but informed thinkers who understand how intelligent systems work, recognize their limitations, and apply them with purpose and responsibility.

Educators are equipped with clear frameworks and structured resources that make artificial intelligence accessible, teachable, and meaningful across all subjects—not just in technical fields.

Schools become environments where technology is not simply adopted, but understood—where students are encouraged to question, evaluate, and engage with AI in ways that support learning, creativity, and ethical awareness.

As artificial intelligence continues to evolve, this vision supports a generation that is prepared not only to adapt to change, but to lead it with knowledge, confidence, and integrity.

The future of artificial intelligence will not be defined by technology alone—but by the understanding and responsibility of those who use it.

Connecting AI Understanding to Cybersecurity Awareness

Definition

Understanding artificial intelligence is the first step toward understanding cybersecurity. While cybersecurity focuses on protecting systems, data, and users, artificial intelligence explains how those systems are built, how they function, and where they may be vulnerable.

The Connection

Every AI system is made up of components such as data, algorithms, models, and infrastructure. These same components are also the targets of cybersecurity threats.

When students understand:

How data is collected and stored

How algorithms make decisions

How AI models process information

How systems operate across frontend and backend layers

They begin to recognize where risks can exist and how systems can be misused.

Why This Matters

In today's digital world, students are not just users of technology—they are participants in complex systems powered by artificial intelligence.

Without understanding how these systems work:

Technology becomes something they trust without question

Risks become harder to recognize

Decisions are made without awareness of consequences

With understanding:

Students become more aware of how their data is used

They recognize how systems can be manipulated

They make more informed and responsible choices

Building Digital Readiness

Digital readiness is not only about using tools. It is about understanding the systems behind those tools.

By learning how AI works, students develop:

Awareness of digital environments

Confidence in navigating technology

A foundation for future learning, including cybersecurity

Conclusion

Cybersecurity begins with understanding.

Before students can protect systems, they must first understand how those systems are built and how they operate. This is why learning artificial intelligence is not only about innovation—it is also about responsibility.

The Foundation of Artificial Intelligence

Definition

The foundation of Artificial Intelligence (AI) refers to the core building blocks that allow AI systems to function. These building blocks work together to help machines learn from information, recognize patterns, and make decisions. AI is not magic—it is a system built on structured components that operate behind the scenes.

Understanding the Foundation in Simple Terms

Artificial Intelligence can be compared to a house. Before a house is complete, it must be built on a strong foundation. This foundation includes concrete, wiring, plumbing, and support structures that are not always visible but are essential for the house to function properly.

In the same way, AI systems rely on foundational components that are not visible to users but are necessary for AI tools to work. When people use AI applications such as chatbots or design tools, they are interacting with the surface. The true power of AI comes from what is underneath.

Key Components of the AI Foundation

1. Data (The Information)

Data is the starting point of all AI systems. It includes text, images, numbers, audio, and other forms of information. AI systems learn by analyzing patterns within this data.

2. Algorithms (The Instructions)

Algorithms are step-by-step instructions that tell the AI system how to process data. They guide how the system learns, identifies patterns, and produces results.

3. Models (The Trained System)

A model is created when data and algorithms are combined through a training process. The model acts as the "brain" of the AI system, allowing it to make predictions and generate responses.

4. Computing Power (The Engine)

AI systems require powerful computers to process large amounts of data. This includes specialized hardware such as processors and graphics processing units (GPUs) that allow AI to function efficiently.

5. Infrastructure (The Environment)

Infrastructure refers to the systems that support AI operations, including servers, storage, networks, and energy systems. Data centers are a key part of this infrastructure, providing the physical space where AI systems operate.

How These Components Work Together

AI systems function by combining all foundational components into a single process. Data is collected and analyzed using algorithms. This process creates a model that can recognize patterns and make decisions. The entire system is powered by computing machines and supported by infrastructure.

Why Understanding the Foundation Matters

Many people use AI tools without understanding how they work. This can lead to confusion, misuse, or over-reliance on technology. By understanding the foundation of AI, students and educators can:

Develop critical thinking skills

Use AI tools more responsibly

Recognize the limitations of AI systems

Build a deeper understanding of modern technology

Real-World Example

When a student asks a chatbot a question, the response does not come from "thinking" like a human. Instead, the AI system uses a trained model that has learned patterns from large amounts of data. It follows algorithms to predict the most appropriate answer, using powerful computers and infrastructure to deliver the response quickly.

This process is also influenced by how the question is asked. The words, structure, and clarity of a question—often referred to as a *prompt*—can affect the quality of the response. Learning how to communicate effectively with AI systems is an important skill known as prompt engineering. For further understanding, students and educators may explore *What to Say When You Talk to Yourself: A Guide to Prompt Engineering* by Susie Hala, which explains how carefully structured prompts can guide AI responses more effectively.

Conclusion

The foundation of Artificial Intelligence is built on data, algorithms, models, computing power, and infrastructure. These components work together to create systems that can learn, predict, and assist humans. Understanding this foundation helps students move beyond simply using AI tools and toward truly understanding how artificial intelligence works.

The Foundational Families of Artificial Intelligence

Introduction

Artificial intelligence is often described as a powerful technology, but in reality, it is not a single system. It is a combination of multiple components working together to create intelligent behavior.

To better understand how artificial intelligence works, it is helpful to break it down into organized groups. In the IntelliGloss framework, these groups are called **Foundational Families of Artificial Intelligence**.

Each family represents a key part of how AI systems are built and operate. Some families focus on how information is created and stored. Others focus on how machines learn, make decisions, process language, or perform tasks. Additional families represent the physical hardware, energy systems, and global infrastructure that make artificial intelligence possible.

When these families work together, they form a complete AI system.

This approach allows students and educators to move beyond simply using artificial intelligence tools and begin to understand what is happening behind the scenes. Instead of viewing AI as a mystery, learners can see it as a structured system made up of clearly defined components.

The diagram on the next page provides a visual overview of these families and how they connect to form the foundation of artificial intelligence.

By learning each family step by step, students develop a deeper understanding of how AI systems process information, learn from data, and interact with the world.

Understanding the Foundational Families of Artificial Intelligence is the first step toward true AI literacy.

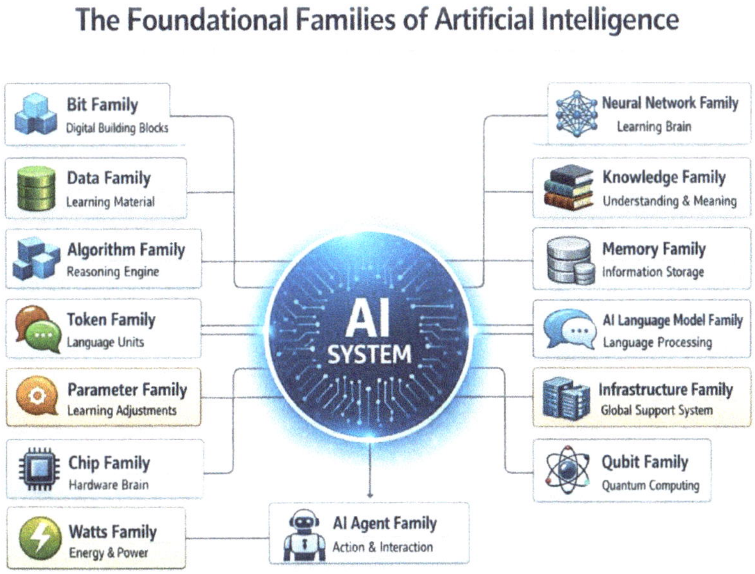

The Foundational Families of Artificial Intelligence

Family	Role	Description
Bit Family	Digital Building Blocks	The smallest unit of digital information (0 or 1). All computing systems begin with bits.
Algorithm Family	Reasoning Engine	Step-by-step instructions that tell computers how to solve problems and process information.
Token Family	Language Units	Pieces of text used by AI models to understand and generate human language.

Family	Role	Description
Parameter Family	Learning Adjustment System	Adjustable numerical values inside AI models that allow them to learn patterns from data.
Data Family	Learning Material	The information AI studies in order to learn patterns, relationships, and knowledge.
Logic Family	Decision Rules	The reasoning structures that allow AI systems to make decisions and evaluate conditions.
Memory Family	Information Storage	Systems that store and retrieve information so AI models can access past knowledge and context.
Knowledge Family	Understanding & Meaning	Structured information that allows AI to represent facts, relationships, and concepts.
Neural Network Family	Learning Brain	Interconnected layers of artificial neurons that enable AI systems to recognize patterns, learn from data, and make predictions.
AI Model Family	Intelligence Engine	The trained system that uses data, parameters, and neural networks to perform tasks such as prediction, classification, and generation.
AI Translator Architecture Family	Language Conversion System	Systems that transform input into output, enabling AI to convert text, speech, or images into meaningful responses.
AI Agent Family	Action and Task Execution System	AI systems designed to perceive information, make decisions, and carry out tasks autonomously or semi-autonomously.
Chip Family	Hardware Brain	Physical processors (GPUs, TPUs, CPUs, NPUs) that perform AI computations.
Watts Family	Energy Power	The electrical power required to run AI hardware and data centers.
AI Energy Family	Energy Source System	The total energy consumed over time to operate AI systems, including training and real-time usage.
Infrastructure Family	Global Support System	Data centers, internet networks, cloud systems, and global infrastructure that allow AI to operate and scale.
Ingredient Family	System Composition	The essential components that come together to create an AI system, including data, algorithms, models, hardware, and energy.
Qubit Family	Quantum Information Units	Quantum bits that can represent multiple states simultaneously, forming the foundation of quantum computing.

The Bit Family

Introduction

The Bit Family represents the starting point of all digital technology. Every computer system, application, and artificial intelligence model is built from bits—the smallest unit of information in computing.

A bit can hold one of two values: 0 or 1. While this may seem simple, these two values form the foundation of everything digital. When bits are combined and organized, they create larger units of data that allow computers to store text, display images, play videos, and run complex systems.

From a single bit to massive data systems, all digital information follows this same structure. This is how computers are able to represent and process the world in a form they can understand.

In artificial intelligence, bits are essential because they store the data that models learn from, process the calculations that drive decision-making, and support the systems that generate responses.

Understanding the Bit Family helps students see how simple binary signals grow into powerful technologies. It reveals that behind every advanced AI system is a foundation built from the most basic building blocks of information.

Bit Family — Visual Understanding of Data Size

How Much Data Can Each Unit Hold? (Simple Examples)

Unit	Size	Photos (Approx.)	Video (Approx. Hours)
Bit	1 bit	N/A	N/A
Byte	8 bits	1 character	N/A
Kilobyte (KB)	~1,000 bytes	Part of a paragraph	N/A
Megabyte (MB)	~1,000 KB	~1 photo	~1 minute of video
Gigabyte (GB)	~1,000 MB	~250 photos	~1–2 hours of video
Terabyte (TB)	~1,000 GB	~250,000 photos	~1,000–2,000 hours of video
Petabyte (PB)	~1,000 TB	~250 million photos	~1–2 million hours of video
Exabyte (EB)	~1,000 PB	~250 billion photos	~1–2 billion hours of video
Zettabyte (ZB)	~1,000 EB	~250 trillion photos	~1–2 trillion hours of video
Yottabyte (YB)	~1,000 ZB	~250 quadrillion photos	~1–2 quadrillion hours of video

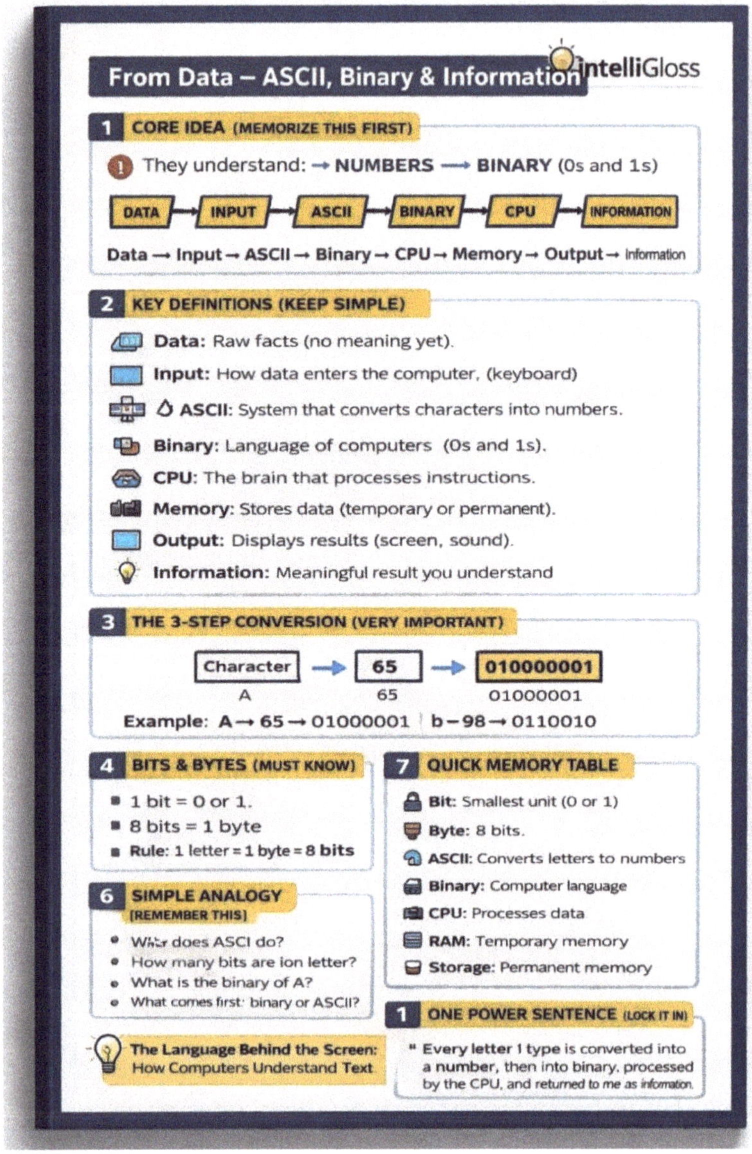

The Algorithm Family

Definition and Overview

The **Algorithm Family** represents the *thinking engine* of artificial intelligence — the set of mathematical instructions that guide how AI analyzes data, learns patterns, and makes decisions.

An **algorithm** is a sequence of steps designed to solve a problem or complete a task. In AI, algorithms tell the system *how to learn*, *how to predict*, and *how to improve* with every iteration.

In simple terms:

The Algorithm Family is the *logic of intelligence* — the invisible code that transforms data into decisions and predictions into progress.

How Algorithms Power AI

Every AI system — from simple chatbots to large-scale deep learning models — relies on algorithms as its foundation.
They determine how the model:

- Processes and cleans data,
- Identifies relationships between variables,
- Learns from feedback, and
- Improves over time.

Without algorithms, even the most powerful dataset or neural network would remain static and lifeless.

In essence, **algorithms are the teachers** that train AI how to think.

Why the Algorithm Family Matters

Algorithms are what separate automation from intelligence.
They allow machines to **reason**, **adapt**, and **learn** — not just follow commands.
For prompt engineers, understanding algorithmic behavior helps explain *why* AI sometimes misunderstands a question, repeats patterns, or changes tone after feedback.

Every AI response you receive follows an underlying process — a pattern recognition journey from input to output.

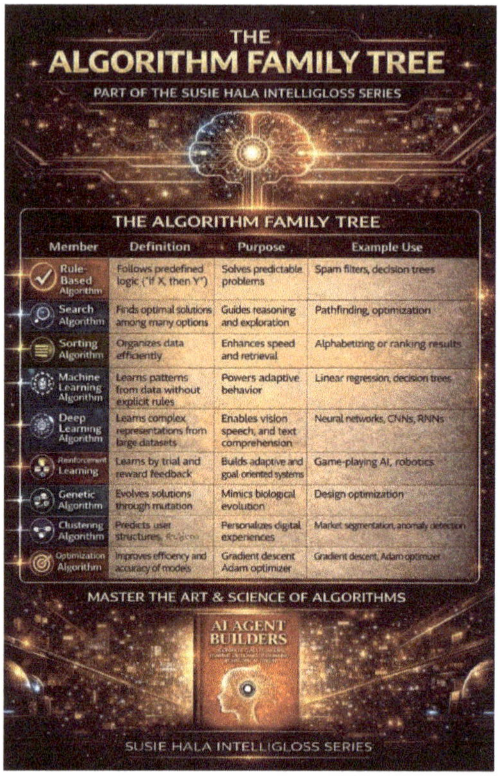

Analogy for Everyday Readers

Imagine AI as a chef in a kitchen:

The **Data Family** provides the ingredients.

The **Knowledge Family** gives the recipes.

The **Algorithm Family** is the *cooking process* — mixing, heating, tasting, and adjusting until the dish is perfect.

Just as cooking methods determine the quality of food, algorithms determine the quality of intelligence.

Algorithm Efficiency and Energy Use

Not all algorithms are equal.
Some are **fast but shallow**, while others are **deep but energy-intensive**.
Training large AI models requires algorithms that can handle billions of calculations per second — powered by the **Watts Family** (energy) and executed through the **Chip Family** (hardware).

The design of efficient algorithms directly affects sustainability in AI — minimizing power consumption while maximizing accuracy and speed.

Algorithms and Prompt Engineering

For prompt engineers, algorithms explain *how* the AI arrives at its answers.
When a model gives inconsistent or off-topic results, it's often due to:

Misinterpretation of input signals (input encoding),

Bias in training algorithms, or

Overfitting to certain data patterns.

Knowing this helps you craft prompts that guide the AI's decision-making — not just its output.

Quick Takeaway: The Algorithm Family is the reasoning heart of AI.
It transforms information into understanding and enables machines to think, learn, and evolve like digital problem-solvers.

Token Family Introduction

The Token Family represents one of the most important bridges between human language and artificial intelligence. While humans communicate using words, sentences, and meaning, AI systems do not understand language in the same way. Instead, they rely on tokens—small units of text that allow machines to process, analyze, and generate language step by step.

A token can be a word, part of a word, a character, or even punctuation. When a student types a sentence into an AI system, that sentence is not read as a whole idea. It is first broken down into tokens. These tokens become the input that the AI model uses to recognize patterns, predict outcomes, and generate responses.

The Token Family works closely with several other foundational families in artificial intelligence. It connects directly with the Data Family, which provides the text used for training, and the Neural Network Family, which processes token patterns to produce intelligent outputs. It also plays a key role in the AI Translator Architecture Family, where tokens are transformed, analyzed, and reassembled into meaningful responses.

Understanding tokens helps students see what is happening behind the scenes when they interact with AI tools. Instead of viewing AI as a "magic system," they begin to understand that every response is built from sequences of tokens processed through mathematical models.

In simple terms, if language is what humans speak, tokens are what AI understands.

Token Family Breakdown Chart

Component	Role	Description	Example
Tokenization	Input Conversion	The process of breaking text into smaller units (tokens) that AI can process	"Artificial Intelligence" → "Artificial" + "Intelligence"
Tokens	Language Units	The individual pieces of text used by AI models for understanding and generation	"AI", "learn", "ing", "."
Subword Tokens	Efficiency Units	Words split into smaller parts to handle unknown or complex vocabulary	"unbelievable" → "un", "believ", "able"
Character Tokens	Fine-Grained Units	Text broken down into individual characters for detailed processing	"AI" → "A" + "I"
Vocabulary (Token Set)	Token Library	The complete set of tokens an AI model recognizes and uses	GPT models have thousands to millions of tokens
Encoding	Token Mapping	Converting tokens into numerical representations for computation	"AI" → [1234, 5678] (example IDs)
Decoding	Output Reconstruction	Converting numerical outputs back into readable text	[1234, 5678] → "AI system"
Context Window	Memory Limit	The number of tokens an AI can process at one time	Example: 8,000 tokens ≈ several pages of text
Token Embeddings	Meaning Representation	Mathematical vectors that capture relationships between tokens	"king" and "queen" have similar embeddings
Token Prediction	Language Generation	The process of predicting the next token in a sequence	"AI is" → predicts "powerful"

The Token Family reminds us that behind every intelligent response is a structured sequence of tokens working together. What feels like natural conversation to humans is, for AI, a carefully processed stream of language units transformed into meaning.

The AI Ecosystem Family

The AI Ecosystem Family is a connected group of artificial intelligence technologies, systems, behaviors, and applications that work together to help machines perform intelligent tasks. This ecosystem includes core AI systems, AI agents, agentic AI, AI autonomy, autonomous AI workers, and generative AI. Each part plays a different role in how modern AI systems think, learn, create, make decisions, solve problems, and interact with the world.

At the center of the ecosystem is artificial intelligence itself — the broad field focused on building machines and software that can perform tasks that normally require human intelligence. AI agents act as the systems that carry out goals and actions. Agentic AI describes the ability of

AI systems to plan, reason, adapt, and pursue objectives with limited human guidance. AI autonomy represents the level of independence an AI system has while making decisions and taking actions. AI autonomous workers apply these capabilities to perform real-world tasks like digital employees or assistants. Generative AI adds the ability to create new content such as text, images, music, video, code, and designs.

The AI Ecosystem Family demonstrates that modern artificial intelligence is no longer just one single technology. Instead, it is an interconnected environment of systems, tools, intelligence, automation, creativity, and human collaboration. As AI continues to evolve, these technologies are becoming increasingly integrated into education, business, healthcare, communication, cybersecurity, research, and everyday life.

Understanding the AI Ecosystem Family helps students, educators, and readers see how the different parts of AI connect together to shape the future of intelligent systems and the digital world.

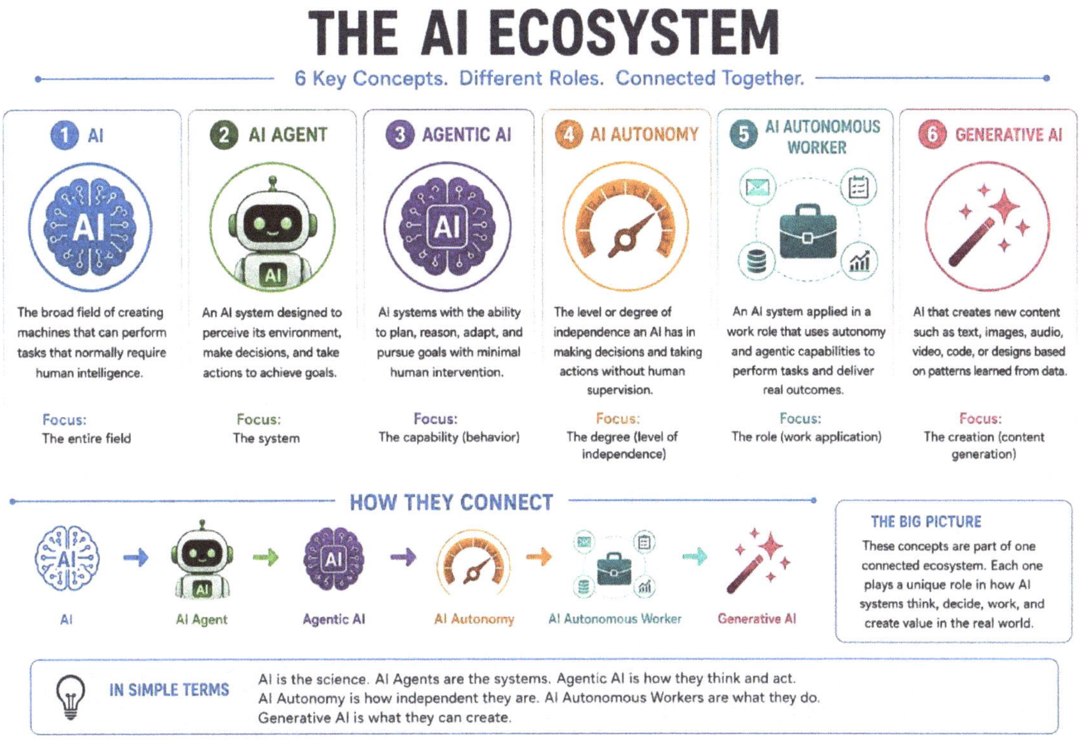

Parameter Family Introduction

The Parameter Family represents the internal learning system of artificial intelligence. While tokens provide the language and data provides the learning material, parameters are what allow AI systems to adjust, improve, and make intelligent decisions over time.

In simple terms, parameters are numerical values inside an AI model that change as the system learns. These values are not visible to users, but they play a critical role in how the model understands patterns, relationships, and meaning. Every time an AI system is trained, it adjusts its parameters to better predict outcomes and generate accurate responses.

Parameters exist throughout neural networks, where they act as the connections between artificial neurons. Each connection has a weight, which determines how important a particular piece of information is. During training, these weights are continuously adjusted based on data, allowing the system to improve its performance.

The Parameter Family works closely with the Data Family, which provides the information needed for learning, and the Neural Network Family, which organizes how parameters are structured and applied. It also supports the Token Family by helping the model interpret and predict sequences of language.

Understanding parameters helps students recognize that AI is not simply programmed with fixed rules. Instead, it learns by adjusting internal values that guide how it processes information. These adjustments are what allow AI systems to evolve from simple pattern recognition to complex reasoning and decision-making.

In essence, if data is what AI learns from, parameters are how AI learns.

Parameter Family Breakdown Chart

Component	Role	Description	Example
Parameters	Learning Values	Numerical values inside an AI model that are adjusted during training	Millions or billions of values inside a model
Weights	Connection Strength	Values that determine how strongly one neuron influences another	A higher weight = stronger influence
Bias	Adjustment Factor	A value added to help the model shift and fine-tune outputs	Helps improve accuracy in predictions
Training Process	Learning Mechanism	The process of adjusting parameters using data to improve performance	Model improves after analyzing many examples
Loss Function	Error Measurement	Measures how far the model's prediction is from the correct answer	Lower loss = better performance

Component	Role	Description	Example
Optimization Algorithm	Adjustment Strategy	Method used to update parameters efficiently	Gradient Descent adjusts weights step by step
Gradient	Direction of Change	Indicates how parameters should change to reduce error	Shows whether to increase or decrease a value
Backpropagation	Learning Process	System that sends error signals backward to update parameters	Adjusts earlier layers based on output error
Hyperparameters	Control Settings	External settings that guide how training happens (not learned)	Learning rate, batch size
Model Size	Capacity Indicator	The total number of parameters in a model	Larger models = more learning capacity

The Parameter Family is the hidden engine of learning in artificial intelligence. While users interact with outputs, it is the continuous adjustment of parameters behind the scenes that makes intelligent behavior possible.

Data Family Introduction

The Data Family represents the foundation of learning in artificial intelligence. Every AI system depends on data to develop knowledge, recognize patterns, and make decisions. Without data, artificial intelligence cannot learn, adapt, or function effectively.

Data can take many forms, including text, images, audio, video, and numerical information. These inputs provide the raw material that AI systems analyze during training. By studying large amounts of data, AI models begin to identify patterns, relationships, and structures that allow them to make predictions and generate responses.

The quality and diversity of data play a critical role in how well an AI system performs. Accurate, balanced, and relevant data helps models produce reliable results, while poor or biased data can lead to incorrect or unfair outcomes. This is why data collection, preparation, and evaluation are essential steps in the development of responsible AI systems.

The Data Family works closely with the Parameter Family, which adjusts internal values based on data, and the Neural Network Family, which processes and organizes data through layers of computation. It also supports the Token Family when dealing with language, as text data is converted into tokens for analysis.

Understanding the Data Family helps students recognize that AI does not "know" things on its own. Instead, it learns from the information it is given. The more meaningful and well-prepared the data, the more capable the AI system becomes.

In simple terms, data is the source of knowledge, and it is the starting point for all artificial intelligence.

Data Family Breakdown Chart

Component	Role	Description	Example
Data	Learning Material	Raw information used by AI systems to learn patterns and relationships	Text, images, audio, numbers
Dataset	Organized Collection	A structured group of data used for training and evaluation	A folder of labeled images
Training Data	Learning Input	Data used to teach the AI model during training	Thousands of sentences for a language model
Validation Data	Performance Check	Data used to tune the model during training without directly learning from it	Helps prevent overfitting
Test Data	Final Evaluation	Data used to measure how well the model performs after training	New unseen examples
Structured Data	Organized Format	Data arranged in tables with clear categories	Spreadsheets, databases
Unstructured Data	Flexible Format	Data without a predefined structure	Text documents, images, videos
Labeled Data	Guided Learning	Data tagged with correct answers to guide training	Image labeled "cat" or "dog"
Unlabeled Data	Self-Learning Input	Data without labels, used in unsupervised learning	Raw text without categories
Data Quality	Accuracy Measure	The reliability and correctness of data	Clean, complete, and consistent data
Data Bias	Imbalance Issue	When data does not represent all groups fairly	Skewed or incomplete datasets
Data Preprocessing	Preparation Step	Cleaning and organizing data before training	Removing errors, formatting text

The Data Family reminds us that artificial intelligence is only as strong as the information it learns from. High-quality data leads to meaningful insights, while poor data can limit or misguide intelligent systems.

Memory Family Introduction

The Memory Family represents how artificial intelligence systems store, retain, and retrieve information. Just as humans rely on memory to recall past experiences, learn new concepts, and make decisions, AI systems depend on memory to access previously processed information and maintain context.

In artificial intelligence, memory is not a single component but a collection of mechanisms that allow systems to handle information over time. Some forms of memory are short-term, holding information temporarily while a task is being completed. Other forms are long-term, storing learned knowledge that can be used across different tasks and interactions.

Memory plays a critical role in enabling AI systems to understand sequences, maintain context in conversations, and improve decision-making. For example, when a user interacts with a language model, the system uses memory to keep track of previous words, sentences, or prompts in order to generate coherent and relevant responses.

The Memory Family works closely with the Data Family, which provides the information to be stored, and the Parameter Family, which encodes learned knowledge within the model. It also supports the Neural Network Family by enabling systems to process sequences and retain important patterns over time.

Understanding the Memory Family helps students see that AI is not simply reacting to individual inputs in isolation. Instead, it relies on stored information and contextual awareness to produce meaningful and consistent outputs.

In simple terms, if data is what AI learns from, memory is how AI remembers and uses what it has learned.

Memory Family Breakdown Chart

Component	Role	Description	Example
Memory	Information Storage	The ability of an AI system to store and access information	Retaining previous inputs in a task
Short-Term Memory	Temporary Storage	Holds information for immediate processing	Keeping track of words in a sentence
Long-Term Memory	Persistent Storage	Stores learned knowledge for future use	Knowledge embedded in model parameters
Context Memory	Conversation Tracking	Maintains information within a specific interaction	Remembering earlier parts of a prompt
Working Memory	Active Processing	Handles information currently being used in computation	Processing a sequence step by step
External Memory	Extended Storage	Memory stored outside the model for retrieval	Databases, vector stores
Internal Memory	Embedded Knowledge	Information stored within the model itself	Learned patterns inside neural networks
Sequence Memory	Order Awareness	Tracks the order of inputs over time	Understanding sentence structure

Component	Role	Description	Example
Retrieval Mechanism	Access System	Retrieves stored information when needed	Searching relevant past data
Attention Mechanism	Focus System	Highlights important parts of memory for processing	Focusing on key words in a sentence
Memory Capacity	Storage Limit	The amount of information the system can handle at once	Context window size

The Memory Family shows that intelligence is not just about processing information in the moment, but about retaining, organizing, and using knowledge over time to create meaningful understanding.

Knowledge Family Introduction

The Knowledge Family represents how artificial intelligence organizes, connects, and uses information to create understanding. While data provides raw information and memory stores it, knowledge is what gives that information meaning and structure.

In artificial intelligence, knowledge is not simply a collection of facts. It is the result of identifying relationships, patterns, and connections within data. AI systems use knowledge to recognize concepts, make decisions, and generate meaningful responses. This allows machines to move beyond simple data processing and toward more intelligent behavior.

Knowledge can be represented in different ways within AI systems. Some forms are structured, such as databases and knowledge graphs, where relationships between concepts are clearly defined. Other forms are learned implicitly through neural networks, where patterns are encoded within parameters and used to guide predictions.

The Knowledge Family works closely with the Data Family, which provides the information needed to build knowledge, and the Memory Family, which stores and retrieves that information. It also connects with the Parameter Family, where learned knowledge is embedded within the model, and the Neural Network Family, which processes and organizes that knowledge.

Understanding the Knowledge Family helps students recognize that AI systems do not simply memorize information. Instead, they learn how pieces of information relate to one another, allowing them to interpret meaning, solve problems, and respond intelligently.

In simple terms, if data is information and memory stores it, knowledge is the understanding that makes it useful.

Knowledge Family Breakdown Chart

Component	Role	Description	Example
Knowledge	Understanding System	Organized information that allows AI to interpret meaning and make decisions	Recognizing relationships between concepts
Facts	Basic Information	Individual pieces of information stored within a system	"Water freezes at 0°C"
Relationships	Connection Mapping	Links between pieces of information that create meaning	"Teacher teaches student"
Knowledge Representation	Structure System	Methods used to organize and store knowledge in AI	Knowledge graphs, semantic networks
Knowledge Graph	Network Mapping	A structured representation of entities and their relationships	Google Knowledge Graph
Semantic Understanding	Meaning Interpretation	The ability to understand meaning behind words and data	Understanding synonyms and context
Inference	Reasoning Process	Drawing conclusions based on known information	If A = B and B = C, then A = C
Rules	Decision Framework	Logical guidelines used to make decisions	If temperature < 0°C → freeze
Ontology	Concept Framework	A structured system defining categories and relationships	Classification of animals
Explicit Knowledge	Direct Information	Clearly defined and stored knowledge	Rules, databases
Implicit Knowledge	Learned Patterns	Knowledge learned through experience and data	Patterns learned by neural networks
Knowledge Integration	System Coordination	Combining information from multiple sources	Merging text, images, and data

The Knowledge Family transforms information into understanding, allowing artificial intelligence to move beyond data and memory into meaningful reasoning and intelligent decision-making.

AI Model Family Introduction

The AI Model Family represents the core system within artificial intelligence that performs tasks such as prediction, classification, and content generation. It is the part of AI that users interact with, whether they are asking questions, generating images, or analyzing data.

An AI model is a trained system that has learned patterns from data. During training, the model processes large amounts of information and adjusts its internal parameters to improve accuracy. Once trained, the model can take new input and produce meaningful output based on what it has learned.

AI models can take many forms depending on their purpose. Some models are designed to recognize images, others to understand language, and others to make decisions or predictions. Large Language Models (LLMs), for example, are designed to process and generate human language by predicting sequences of tokens.

The AI Model Family works closely with the Data Family, which provides the learning material, and the Parameter Family, which stores learned patterns. It also relies on the Neural Network Family for structure and the Chip and Infrastructure Families for execution and deployment.

Understanding the AI Model Family helps students see that AI is not just a concept, but a working system that has been trained to perform specific tasks. It is the engine that transforms input into output.

In simple terms, if AI is the system, the model is the part that actually does the thinking and producing.

AI Model Family Breakdown Chart

Component	Role	Description	Example
AI Model	Core System	The trained system that performs tasks	Chatbot, image generator
Training	Learning Process	Process of teaching the model using data	Learning from datasets
Inference	Output Generation	Using the trained model to produce results	Answering a question
Model Architecture	Structural Design	Defines how the model is built	Neural networks, transformers
Parameters	Learned Values	Internal values adjusted during training	Billions of weights
Input Data	Entry Information	Data provided to the model for processing	User prompt
Output Data	Result	The response or prediction generated	AI-generated text
Model Types	Functional Categories	Different kinds of models for different tasks	Classification, generation
Fine-Tuning	Model Adjustment	Improving a model for specific tasks	Custom-trained AI
Pretrained Model	Base System	A model trained on large datasets before use	General-purpose AI
Evaluation	Performance Check	Measuring how well the model performs	Accuracy, loss metrics

The AI Model Family represents the working core of artificial intelligence, where learned patterns are transformed into meaningful actions, predictions, and responses.

Neural Network Family Introduction

The Neural Network Family represents the structural foundation of how artificial intelligence learns and processes information. Inspired by the human brain, neural networks are systems of interconnected units, often called neurons, that work together to analyze data, recognize patterns, and make decisions.

In artificial intelligence, a neural network is made up of layers. The input layer receives data, the hidden layers process that data, and the output layer produces a result. As information flows through these layers, the network applies mathematical transformations that allow it to detect patterns and relationships within the data.

Neural networks rely heavily on the Parameter Family, where weights and biases determine how strongly information flows between neurons. During training, these parameters are adjusted to improve the network's performance. The more the network learns, the better it becomes at recognizing patterns and making accurate predictions.

The Neural Network Family works closely with the Data Family, which provides the information needed for learning, and the Memory and Knowledge Families, which help store and organize learned information. It also supports the Token Family when processing language, allowing AI systems to interpret sequences of tokens in meaningful ways.

Understanding neural networks helps students see that AI is not simply following instructions. Instead, it is learning from examples and improving over time through layered processing and pattern recognition.

In simple terms, neural networks are the systems that allow AI to think, learn, and make sense of information.

Neural Network Family Breakdown Chart

Component	Role	Description	Example
Neural Network	Learning Structure	A system of interconnected neurons that processes data and learns patterns	Image recognition system
Neuron (Node)	Processing Unit	A basic unit that receives input, processes it, and passes output forward	A single calculation point

Component	Role	Description	Example
Input Layer	Data Entry Point	The first layer that receives raw data	Pixels of an image
Hidden Layers	Processing Layers	Intermediate layers that transform data and detect patterns	Feature detection layers
Output Layer	Result Generator	The final layer that produces predictions or decisions	"Cat" vs "Dog" classification
Weights	Signal Strength	Values that determine how strongly inputs influence outputs	Higher weight = stronger impact
Bias	Adjustment Value	Helps shift outputs to improve learning accuracy	Fine-tuning predictions
Activation Function	Decision Function	Determines whether a neuron should activate based on input	ReLU, Sigmoid
Forward Propagation	Data Flow	The process of passing input data through the network to produce output	Input → Hidden → Output
Backpropagation	Learning Process	Adjusts weights and biases based on error to improve performance	Correcting mistakes
Loss Function	Error Measurement	Calculates how far the output is from the correct answer	Prediction vs actual
Deep Neural Network	Advanced Structure	A network with many hidden layers for complex learning	Deep learning models

The Neural Network Family provides the structure that allows artificial intelligence to transform data into understanding, making it possible for machines to learn from experience and improve over time.

Dual Language System in Artificial Intelligence

Definition

The Dual Language System in Artificial Intelligence refers to the way AI communicates using two different forms of language at the same time: human language for interaction and machine language for internal processing.

Key Components

Human Language (Natural Language)
This is the language people use to communicate with AI, such as English, Spanish, Tongan, or Fijian. It includes words, sentences, and questions that users type or speak.

Machine Language (Numerical Representation)
This is how AI understands information internally. Words are converted into numbers called tokens and processed using mathematical models and algorithms.

How It Works (Step-by-Step)

A user enters a question in human language

The AI converts the words into numerical tokens

The AI processes the tokens using a neural network

The AI generates a response based on patterns and probabilities

The response is converted back into human language

Example

User Input:
"What is Artificial Intelligence?"

AI Process:

Converts words into numbers

Analyzes patterns from training data

Predicts the best possible answer

Output:
"Artificial Intelligence is the ability of machines to perform tasks that normally require human intelligence."

Why This Matters

Understanding the dual language system helps students realize that:

AI does not "think" like humans

AI translates language into math and back into language

Every interaction with AI is based on patterns, not emotions or understanding

Applications

Chatbots and virtual assistants

Language translation systems

Search engines

Voice recognition tools

Challenges

Misinterpretation of human language

Bias in language data

Lack of true understanding or reasoning

Summary

Artificial Intelligence works by translating human language into machine-readable data and then converting the results back into human language. This dual system allows AI to interact with people while operating through mathematical processes behind the scenes.

AI Translator Architecture Family Introduction

The AI Translator Architecture Family represents the system that transforms input into meaningful output in artificial intelligence. It acts as the bridge between what humans provide and what AI produces. Whether a user types a question, uploads an image, or speaks a command, this architecture is responsible for interpreting that input and generating a response.

In artificial intelligence, translation does not only mean converting one language to another. It refers to the broader process of transforming one form of information into another. For example, text can be translated into a response, speech can be converted into text, and images can be interpreted into descriptions. This transformation process is at the core of how modern AI systems function.

The AI Translator Architecture is built on multiple foundational families. It relies on the Token Family to break input into manageable units, the Neural Network Family to process patterns, and the Parameter Family to guide learning. It also uses knowledge and memory to maintain context and produce coherent results.

At the center of this architecture is the ability to encode and decode information. Encoding transforms input into a format the model can understand, while decoding converts processed information back into human-readable output. This continuous transformation allows AI systems to interact with users in a natural and meaningful way.

Understanding the AI Translator Architecture Family helps students see that AI is not simply responding randomly. Instead, it is systematically translating input into output through structured processes and learned patterns.

In simple terms, if tokens are the language pieces and neural networks are the brain, the AI Translator Architecture is the system that turns understanding into communication.

AI Translator Architecture Family Breakdown Chart

Component	Role	Description	Example
AI Translator Architecture	Transformation System	Converts input into meaningful output	Question → Answer
Input Processing	Data Intake	Receives and prepares user input for analysis	Text prompt entered by a user
Encoding	Input Conversion	Transforms input into numerical representations	Words → token IDs
Context Building	Meaning Formation	Organizes input into a structured understanding	Sentence context tracking
Sequence Processing	Order Handling	Maintains the correct order of information	Word sequence in a sentence
Attention Mechanism	Focus System	Identifies important parts of input data	Highlighting key words
Representation Layer	Feature Mapping	Converts data into internal representations for processing	Embeddings
Decoding	Output Generation	Converts processed data back into human-readable form	Token IDs → words
Output Generation	Response Creation	Produces the final answer or result	AI-generated response
Multimodal Translation	Cross-Format Processing	Translates between different types of data	Image → text description
Feedback Loop	Improvement Cycle	Uses results to refine future outputs	Model learning over time

The AI Translator Architecture Family shows that artificial intelligence is not just about understanding information, but about transforming it into meaningful communication that humans can use and interact with.

AI Architecture Family Introduction

The AI Architecture Family represents the overall design and structure of an artificial intelligence system. While individual families such as Data, Parameters, and Neural Networks explain how AI learns and processes information, the AI Architecture Family shows how all these components are organized and work together as a complete system.

In artificial intelligence, architecture refers to the blueprint that defines how data flows through a system, how components interact, and how decisions are produced. It determines how input is received, how it is processed, and how output is generated. A well-designed architecture allows AI systems to operate efficiently, scale to large problems, and produce reliable results.

AI architectures can vary depending on the type of system being built. Some are designed for image recognition, others for language processing, and others for decision-making or automation. Despite these differences, most architectures share common elements such as input layers, processing layers, memory components, and output mechanisms.

The AI Architecture Family connects all foundational families. It integrates the Data Family for input, the Token Family for language processing, the Neural Network Family for computation, the Parameter Family for learning, and the Memory and Knowledge Families for storing and organizing information. It also works closely with the AI Translator Architecture Family to transform input into meaningful output.

Understanding the AI Architecture Family helps students see the "big picture" of artificial intelligence. Instead of viewing AI as separate parts, they begin to understand it as a coordinated system where each component plays a specific role.

In simple terms, if individual families are the parts of AI, the AI Architecture Family is the blueprint that brings everything together into one working system.

AI Architecture Family Breakdown Chart

Component	Role	Description	Example
AI Architecture	System Blueprint	The overall design that defines how an AI system is structured and operates	ChatGPT system design
Input Layer	Data Entry Point	Receives raw input from users or external sources	Text prompt, image upload
Preprocessing Layer	Data Preparation	Cleans and organizes input data before processing	Tokenization, normalization
Processing Core	Computation Engine	The main system where data is analyzed and transformed	Neural networks, transformers
Parameter System	Learning Core	Stores adjustable values that guide learning and predictions	Model weights and biases

Component	Role	Description	Example
Memory System	Context Storage	Maintains and retrieves information during processing	Context window, external memory
Knowledge System	Understanding Layer	Organizes relationships and meaning within the system	Knowledge graphs, learned patterns
Decision Layer	Output Logic	Determines the final output based on processed data	Selecting the best response
Output Layer	Result Delivery	Presents results to the user in a usable format	Text, image, or audio response
Feedback Loop	Improvement System	Uses outcomes to refine future performance	Model updates and retraining
Scalability System	Expansion Capability	Allows the system to handle increasing data and complexity	Cloud-based AI systems
Integration Layer	System Connection	Connects AI with external tools and platforms	APIs, databases, applications

The AI Architecture Family reveals that artificial intelligence is not a single technology, but a coordinated system of interconnected components working together to transform data into intelligent outcomes.

Chip Family Introduction

The Chip Family represents the physical hardware that powers artificial intelligence systems. While software components such as data, algorithms, and neural networks define how AI works, none of these systems can function without the computing chips that perform the actual calculations.

Chips are specialized electronic components designed to process information at extremely high speeds. In artificial intelligence, these chips handle the complex mathematical operations required for training models and generating outputs. Every prediction, calculation, and response produced by an AI system is executed by hardware within the Chip Family.

Different types of chips are used depending on the needs of the system. Central Processing Units (CPUs) handle general-purpose tasks, while Graphics Processing Units (GPUs) are optimized for parallel processing, making them ideal for training neural networks. More specialized chips, such as Tensor Processing Units (TPUs) and Neural Processing Units (NPUs), are designed specifically for AI workloads, enabling faster and more efficient computation.

The Chip Family works closely with the Neural Network Family, which defines the structure of computation, and the Parameter Family, which stores the values being processed. It also connects to the Infrastructure Family, where large-scale systems of chips are organized in data centers and cloud environments.

Understanding the Chip Family helps students recognize that artificial intelligence is not purely abstract. It depends on physical machines that require power, resources, and engineering to operate. These chips are the engines that bring AI models to life.

In simple terms, if AI is the intelligence, chips are the machines that make that intelligence possible.

Chip Family Breakdown Chart

Component	Role	Description	Example
Chip (Processor)	Computation Engine	Electronic hardware that performs calculations required for AI	CPU, GPU
CPU (Central Processing Unit)	General Processor	Handles a wide range of computing tasks	Running basic applications
GPU (Graphics Processing Unit)	Parallel Processor	Processes many calculations at once, ideal for AI training	Training neural networks
TPU (Tensor Processing Unit)	AI Accelerator	Specialized chip designed for machine learning tasks	Google TPU
NPU (Neural Processing Unit)	Edge AI Processor	Optimized for running AI on devices like phones	Smartphone AI features
AI Accelerator	Performance Booster	Hardware designed to speed up AI computations	Dedicated AI chips
Memory (Hardware)	Data Storage	Stores data and instructions for processing	RAM, VRAM
Parallel Processing	Speed Mechanism	Ability to perform multiple calculations simultaneously	GPUs processing thousands of operations
Throughput	Processing Capacity	Amount of data processed over time	High-performance computing systems
Latency	Response Time	Time it takes to process a request	Faster chips = lower latency
Power Consumption	Energy Usage	Amount of energy required to run the chip	High-performance GPUs use more power
Edge Devices	Local Processing	Devices that run AI locally without cloud support	Phones, smart cameras

The Chip Family reminds us that behind every intelligent system is powerful hardware performing millions or billions of calculations, turning abstract models into real-world functionality.

Watts Family Introduction

The Watts Family represents the measurement of power used by artificial intelligence systems. While the Chip Family provides the hardware that performs computations, the Watts Family explains how much energy those systems consume while operating.

A watt is a unit of power that measures the rate at which energy is used. In artificial intelligence, watts help us understand how much electricity is required to run processors, train models, and generate responses. Every time an AI system processes data, performs calculations, or produces output, it consumes power.

Different AI systems require different levels of power depending on their size and complexity. Small systems, such as those running on mobile devices, use relatively low amounts of power. In contrast, large-scale AI models operating in data centers can require significant amounts of electricity, especially during training, where billions of calculations are performed continuously.

The Watts Family works closely with the Chip Family, which determines how efficiently computations are performed, and the Infrastructure Family, where large networks of machines operate together. It also connects to the overall design of AI systems, as more efficient models can reduce power consumption while maintaining performance.

Understanding the Watts Family helps students recognize that artificial intelligence is not only about intelligence and computation, but also about energy use and resource management. As AI continues to grow, managing power efficiently becomes an important part of building responsible and sustainable systems.

In simple terms, if chips perform the work, watts measure how much power it takes to do that work.

Watts Family Breakdown Chart

Component	Role	Description	Example
Watt (W)	Power Measurement	Unit that measures the rate of energy use	A device using 100 watts
Power Consumption	Energy Usage Rate	Amount of power used during operation	AI model running on GPUs
Energy Efficiency	Performance Balance	How effectively a system uses power to perform tasks	More output with less power
High-Performance Computing	Intensive Power Use	Systems that require large amounts of power for complex tasks	AI training clusters

Component	Role	Description	Example
Idle Power	Standby Usage	Power consumed when systems are not actively processing	Servers waiting for requests
Peak Power	Maximum Usage	Highest level of power used during heavy workloads	Training large AI models
Thermal Output	Heat Generation	Heat produced as a result of power usage	Cooling systems in data centers
Cooling Systems	Temperature Control	Systems used to manage heat from high power usage	Air or liquid cooling
Power Supply	Energy Source	Provides electricity to AI systems	Electrical grid, batteries
Edge Power Usage	Local Energy Use	Power consumption on smaller devices	Smartphones, IoT devices
Data Center Power	Large-Scale Usage	Power required for large AI operations	Server farms running AI models
Sustainable Energy	Efficiency Goal	Use of renewable energy to reduce environmental impact	Solar-powered data centers

The Watts Family highlights that intelligence comes with a cost—every AI system requires power, and understanding that power is essential for building efficient and sustainable technologies.

Watts Family (AI Power Usage Scale)

Definition

The **Watts Family** represents the real-time power usage of artificial intelligence systems, measured in watts (W). It shows how much power AI systems consume at a given moment as they process data and perform computations.

Watts Scale

1 Watt
10 Watts
100 Watts
500 Watts
1,000 Watts (1 Kilowatt)
10,000 Watts (10 Kilowatts)
100,000 Watts (100 Kilowatts)
1,000,000 Watts (1 Megawatt)
10,000,000 Watts (10 Megawatts)
100,000,000+ Watts (100+ Megawatts)

Key Characteristics

Measured in real-world electrical power

Higher watt values indicate higher processing demand

Used to represent the scale of AI systems from small devices to large infrastructures

Closely connected to the Chip Family, Energy Family, and Infrastructure Family

Examples

Low watts → small devices and basic AI functions

Medium watts → computers and advanced applications

High watts → data centers and large AI systems

Summary

The **Watts Family** provides a numerical representation of how much power artificial intelligence systems use in real time, helping to illustrate the scale and intensity of AI operations.

Student Insight

Watts show how much power AI is using right now.

AI Energy Family Introduction

The AI Energy Family represents the total amount of energy consumed by artificial intelligence systems over time. While the Watts Family measures the rate at which power is used at any given moment, the Energy Family focuses on the accumulated energy required to perform tasks, run systems, and sustain operations.

In artificial intelligence, energy is used every time a model is trained, a system processes data, or a response is generated. Large-scale AI systems, especially those operating in data centers, can consume significant amounts of energy due to the continuous processing of massive datasets and complex computations.

Energy is typically measured over time using units such as kilowatt-hours (kWh), which reflect how much power has been used during a specific period. For example, running a high-performance AI system for several hours or days results in a total energy cost that goes beyond the moment-to-moment power usage measured in watts.

The AI Energy Family works closely with the Watts Family, which provides the rate of power consumption, and the Chip Family, which determines how efficiently computations are performed. It also connects to the Infrastructure Family, where large-scale systems operate continuously and require long-term energy management.

Understanding the AI Energy Family helps students recognize that artificial intelligence has real-world resource implications. It is not only about performance and speed, but also about sustainability, efficiency, and responsible use of technology.

In simple terms, if watts measure how fast energy is used, energy measures how much is used over time.

AI Energy Family Breakdown Chart

Component	Role	Description	Example
Energy	Total Consumption	The total amount of power used over a period of time	Running an AI system for hours or days
Kilowatt-hour (kWh)	Energy Measurement	Unit used to measure energy consumption over time	1 kWh = using 1,000 watts for 1 hour
Energy Usage	Consumption Tracking	Total energy required for AI operations	Training a large model
Training Energy	Learning Cost	Energy used during model training processes	Weeks of GPU usage
Inference Energy	Response Cost	Energy used when AI generates outputs	Answering a user prompt
Energy Efficiency	Optimization Goal	Reducing energy use while maintaining performance	Efficient AI models
Energy Scaling	Growth Impact	Increase in energy use as systems grow larger	Bigger models = more energy
Data Center Energy	Infrastructure Demand	Total energy used by large AI facilities	Server farms operating 24/7
Cooling Energy	Temperature Control	Energy required to cool systems and prevent overheating	Air conditioning in data centers
Renewable Energy	Sustainability Source	Use of clean energy to power AI systems	Solar, wind-powered data centers
Carbon Impact	Environmental Effect	Emissions associated with energy consumption	AI training carbon footprint
Energy Management	Resource Control	Strategies to monitor and reduce energy use	Efficient scheduling, hardware optimization

The AI Energy Family reminds us that artificial intelligence operates within the physical world, where every computation consumes energy and every system has an impact on resources and sustainability.

Energy Family (Total Power Consumption of Artificial Intelligence)

Definition

The **Energy Family** represents the total amount of electricity used by artificial intelligence systems over time. It is measured in watt-hours (Wh) or kilowatt-hours (kWh) and shows how much energy AI systems consume while running.

Energy Scale

1 Watt-hour (Wh)
10 Watt-hours (Wh)
100 Watt-hours (Wh)
500 Watt-hours (Wh)
1,000 Watt-hours (1 Kilowatt-hour, kWh)
10,000 Watt-hours (10 kWh)
100,000 Watt-hours (100 kWh)
1,000,000 Watt-hours (1 Megawatt-hour, MWh)
10,000,000 Watt-hours (10 MWh)
100,000,000+ Watt-hours (100+ MWh)

Key Characteristics

Measured over time (not instant like watts)

Represents total electricity consumption

Increases the longer AI systems run

Directly related to cost and energy usage

Closely connected to Watts Family, Chip Family, and Infrastructure Family

Examples

Low energy → short AI tasks or small devices

Medium energy → daily AI usage on computers

High energy → training AI models and running data centers

Summary

The **Energy Family** provides a numerical representation of the total electricity consumed by artificial intelligence systems over time, helping to illustrate the overall cost and impact of AI operations.

Student Insight

Energy shows how much total power AI has used over time.

AI Infrastructure Family Introduction

The AI Infrastructure Family represents the large-scale systems and environments that support, power, and connect artificial intelligence technologies. While individual components such as chips, data, and models explain how AI works, infrastructure explains where and how these systems operate in the real world.

AI infrastructure includes data centers, cloud platforms, networking systems, and storage environments that allow artificial intelligence to function at scale. These systems provide the computing power, data access, and connectivity needed to train models, process information, and deliver results to users around the world.

Modern AI systems rely heavily on cloud-based infrastructure, where thousands of machines work together to handle massive workloads. This allows AI to scale efficiently, making it possible to process large datasets, run complex models, and serve millions of users simultaneously. Infrastructure also ensures reliability, security, and continuous availability of AI services.

The AI Infrastructure Family works closely with the Chip Family, which provides the hardware, the Watts and Energy Families, which manage power consumption, and the Data Family, which supplies the information being processed. It also supports the AI Architecture Family by providing the environment where all system components are deployed and connected.

Understanding the AI Infrastructure Family helps students recognize that artificial intelligence is not contained within a single device. Instead, it operates across global systems that require coordination, resources, and engineering to function effectively.

In simple terms, if AI is the system and chips are the engines, infrastructure is the environment that allows everything to run at scale.

AI Infrastructure Family Breakdown Chart

Component	Role	Description	Example
AI Infrastructure	System Environment	The physical and digital systems that support AI operations	Global AI platforms
Data Center	Processing Hub	Facilities that house servers and computing equipment	Large server farms
Cloud Computing	Scalable Platform	Remote systems that provide computing resources over the internet	AWS, Azure, Google Cloud
Servers	Compute Units	Machines that process data and run AI models	Rack-mounted servers
Networking	Connectivity System	Systems that allow communication between machines	Internet, fiber networks
Storage Systems	Data Management	Systems that store large volumes of data	Databases, cloud storage
Distributed Computing	Workload Sharing	Splitting tasks across multiple machines for efficiency	Parallel processing across clusters
Edge Infrastructure	Local Processing	Running AI closer to the user or device	Smart devices, IoT systems
Load Balancing	Traffic Control	Distributes workloads to prevent overload	Managing user requests
Security Systems	Protection Layer	Safeguards data and systems from threats	Encryption, firewalls
Redundancy	Reliability System	Backup systems to ensure continuous operation	Failover servers
Scalability	Growth Capability	Ability to expand resources as demand increases	Adding more servers dynamically

The AI Infrastructure Family reveals that artificial intelligence operates on a global scale, relying on interconnected systems that provide the power, storage, and connectivity needed to support intelligent technologies.

AI Agent Family Introduction

The AI Agent Family represents systems that can take action, make decisions, and perform tasks on behalf of users or other systems. Unlike traditional AI models that only respond to input, AI agents are designed to operate with a level of autonomy, allowing them to plan, execute, and adapt to achieve specific goals.

An AI agent receives input from its environment, processes that information, and takes actions based on predefined objectives or learned behaviors. These actions can include answering questions, automating workflows, retrieving information, or interacting with other systems. Some agents operate in simple environments, while others function in complex systems that require continuous decision-making.

AI agents often combine multiple foundational families. They use the Data Family to gather information, the Memory and Knowledge Families to retain and understand context, and the Neural Network and Parameter Families to process and learn from interactions. They also rely on the AI Architecture and Infrastructure Families to operate reliably at scale.

Modern AI agents can work independently or as part of larger systems. For example, a customer support agent can respond to inquiries automatically, while a more advanced agent can complete multi-step tasks such as scheduling, research, or system management.

Understanding the AI Agent Family helps students see that artificial intelligence is not only about generating responses, but also about taking meaningful action in real-world scenarios.

In simple terms, if AI models think and respond, AI agents act and execute.

AI Agent Family Breakdown Chart

Component	Role	Description	Example
AI Agent	Action System	An AI system that can make decisions and perform tasks	Virtual assistant
Environment	Operating Context	The space where the agent interacts and gathers information	Web, apps, databases
Input Perception	Data Intake	Receives information from the environment	User query or sensor input
Decision Engine	Action Selection	Determines what action to take based on input	Choosing a response or task
Action Execution	Task Performance	Carries out decisions in the environment	Sending an email, retrieving data
Goal System	Objective Setting	Defines what the agent is trying to achieve	Complete a task or solve a problem
Planning Module	Strategy Builder	Breaks down tasks into steps	Multi-step problem solving
Feedback Loop	Learning Cycle	Improves performance based on outcomes	Adjusting actions over time
Autonomy Level	Independence Scale	Degree of independence in decision-making	Fully automated vs assisted

Component	Role	Description	Example
Multi-Agent System	Collaboration Network	Multiple agents working together	Coordinated AI systems

Ingredient Family Introduction

The Ingredient Family represents the essential components that come together to create an artificial intelligence system. Just as a recipe requires specific ingredients to produce a final dish, AI systems rely on a combination of foundational elements working together to function effectively.

Artificial intelligence is not built from a single component. It requires data to learn from, algorithms to guide processing, models to perform tasks, hardware to execute computations, and energy to power the entire system. Each of these elements plays a critical role, and the absence of any one component would prevent the system from operating properly.

The Ingredient Family provides a simplified way for students to understand AI as a system made up of interconnected parts. Instead of viewing AI as complex or mysterious, learners can begin to see it as something constructed from identifiable and understandable components.

This family connects directly with all other foundational families, including Data, Algorithm, Neural Network, Parameter, Chip, and Energy Families. It serves as an overview that brings these elements together into a unified perspective.

Understanding the Ingredient Family helps students recognize that artificial intelligence is built, not magical. It is the result of carefully combining the right components in the right way.

In simple terms, if AI is the final product, the Ingredient Family represents everything needed to build it.

Ingredient Family Breakdown Chart

Component	Role	Description	Example
Data	Learning Input	Provides the information AI uses to learn patterns	Text, images, audio
Algorithms	Instruction Set	Guides how data is processed and decisions are made	Sorting, classification
AI Models	Execution System	Performs tasks such as prediction or generation	Language models
Neural Networks	Processing Structure	Organizes how data is processed through layers	Deep learning models
Parameters	Learning Adjustments	Fine-tune how the model learns and makes predictions	Weights and biases

Component	Role	Description	Example
Tokens	Language Units	Breaks text into smaller pieces for processing	Words or subwords
Hardware (Chips)	Computation Engine	Executes calculations required by AI systems	GPUs, CPUs
Energy	Power Source	Supplies the energy needed to run systems	Electricity usage
Infrastructure	Support System	Provides the environment for AI to operate at scale	Cloud systems, data centers
Memory	Storage System	Stores and retrieves information for processing	Context memory
Knowledge	Understanding Layer	Represents meaning and relationships within data	Knowledge graphs

The Ingredient Family shows that artificial intelligence is built from a combination of essential components, each playing a vital role in creating intelligent systems.

The Frontend and Backend Family of Artificial Intelligence

How AI Systems Connect User Interaction to Intelligent Processing

Introduction

Every artificial intelligence system operates through two essential layers: the frontend and the backend. These layers work together to transform human interaction into intelligent responses, allowing AI systems to function smoothly and effectively.

The frontend is the part of the system that users see and interact with. It includes screens, input tools, and the display of results. Whether a user is typing a question, speaking a command, or uploading an image, all interaction begins at the frontend.

Behind the scenes, the backend serves as the processing engine of the system. It receives input from the frontend, manages data, connects to the AI model, and performs the computations needed to generate a response. The backend is where the intelligence of the system operates, using models, algorithms, and infrastructure to interpret and respond to user requests.

This visual illustrates how these two layers work together as a complete system. It shows the flow of information from user input to AI processing and back to the user as a result. By understanding this structure, students can see that AI is not a single tool, but a coordinated system of layers working together.

In simple terms, the frontend is where interaction happens, and the backend is where intelligence is created.

Every AI system has two sides: what you see and what actually does the thinking.

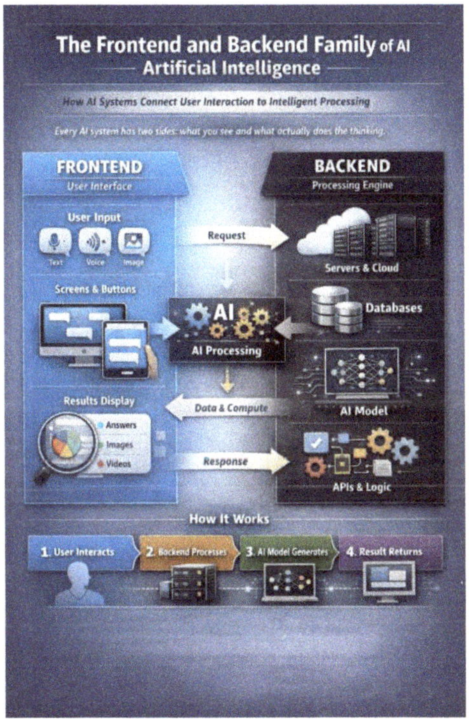

AI Qubit Family Introduction

The AI Qubit Family represents the foundation of quantum computing as it relates to artificial intelligence. While traditional computing relies on bits, which can exist as either 0 or 1, quantum computing uses qubits, which can exist in multiple states simultaneously.

A qubit is the basic unit of quantum information. Unlike classical bits, qubits can take advantage of properties such as superposition and entanglement, allowing quantum systems to process complex computations more efficiently in certain scenarios. This opens new possibilities for solving problems that are difficult or impossible for traditional computers.

In the context of artificial intelligence, qubits have the potential to accelerate learning processes, optimize large-scale systems, and improve complex simulations. Although quantum AI is still in development, it represents a future direction where computational power can expand beyond current limitations.

The AI Qubit Family connects with the Chip Family, as quantum processors are specialized hardware, and with the Algorithm Family, where new types of quantum algorithms are designed.

It also relates to the Parameter and Neural Network Families, as researchers explore quantum-enhanced learning models.

Understanding the AI Qubit Family helps students see that artificial intelligence is continuously evolving. It introduces the idea that the foundations of computing themselves can change, leading to new forms of intelligence and problem-solving.

In simple terms, if bits are the foundation of today's computing, qubits represent the foundation of tomorrow's possibilities.

AI Qubit Family Breakdown Chart

Component	Role	Description	Example
Qubit	Quantum Unit	Basic unit of quantum information	Quantum bit in a quantum computer
Superposition	Multi-State Ability	Ability to exist in multiple states at once	0 and 1 simultaneously
Entanglement	Connection Property	Linking qubits so they influence each other	Paired quantum states
Quantum Gate	Operation System	Performs operations on qubits	Quantum logic gates
Quantum Circuit	Processing Structure	Sequence of quantum operations	Quantum algorithms
Quantum Processor	Hardware Engine	Specialized chip for quantum computing	Quantum computer hardware
Quantum Algorithm	Computation Method	Algorithm designed for quantum systems	Optimization problems
Quantum Speedup	Performance Advantage	Faster processing for certain problems	Complex simulations
Quantum Noise	Stability Challenge	Errors caused by environmental interference	Qubit instability
Quantum Error Correction	Stability Solution	Techniques to reduce errors in quantum systems	Fault-tolerant computing

The AI Qubit Family introduces a new frontier in computing, where the limits of traditional systems are expanded, opening the door to more powerful and advanced forms of artificial intelligence.

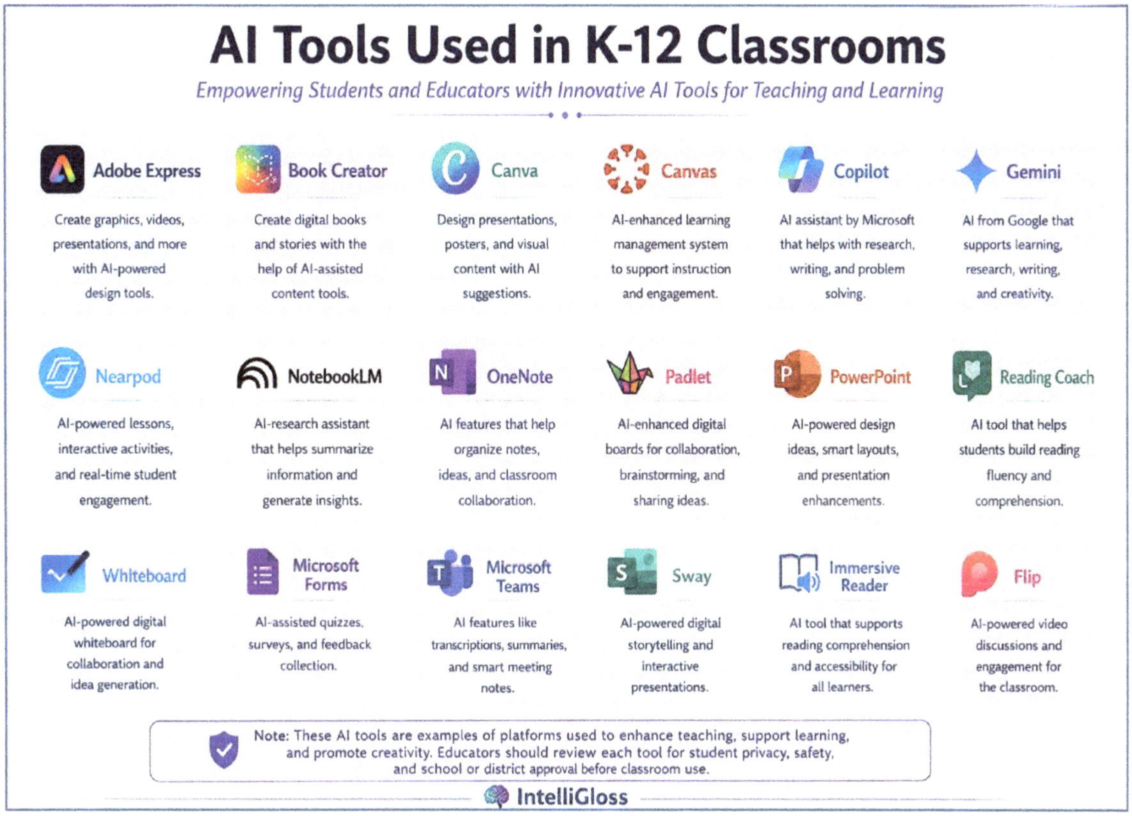

AI Tools Used in K-12 Classrooms
Empowering Students and Educators with Innovative AI Tools for Teaching and Learning
Adobe Express
Create graphics, videos, presentations, and more with AI-powered design tools.
Book Creator
Create digital books and stories with the help of AI-assisted content tools.
Canva
Design presentations, posters, and visual content with AI suggestions.
Canvas
AI-enhanced learning management system to support instruction and engagement.
Copilot
AI assistant by Microsoft that helps with research, writing, and problem solving.
Gemini
AI from Google that supports learning, research, writing, and creativity.
Nearpod
AI-powered lessons, interactive activities, and real-time student engagement.
NotebookLM
AI-research assistant that helps summarize information and generate insights.
OneNote
AI features that help organize notes, ideas, and classroom collaboration.
Padlet
AI-enhanced digital boards for collaboration, brainstorming, and sharing ideas.
PowerPoint
AI-powered design ideas, smart layouts, and presentation enhancements.
Reading Coach
AI tool that helps students build reading fluency and comprehension.
Whiteboard
AI-powered digital whiteboard for collaboration and idea generation.
Microsoft Forms
AI-assisted quizzes, surveys, and feedback collection.
Microsoft Teams
AI features like transcriptions, summaries, and smart meeting notes.
Sway
AI-powered digital storytelling and interactive presentations.
Immersive Reader
AI tool that supports reading comprehension and accessibility for all learners.
Flip
AI-powered video discussions and engagement for the classroom.
Note: These AI tools are examples of platforms used to enhance teaching, support learning, and promote creativity. Educators should review each tool for student privacy, safety, and school or district approval before classroom use.
IntelliGloss

TABLE OF CONTENTS

INTELLIGLOSS AI EDUCATION SERIES

MODULE 2: ARTIFICIAL GENERAL INTELLIGENCE (AGI)

AGI: REASONING INTELLIGENCE

How Intelligent Systems Think, Solve Problems, and Make Better Decisions

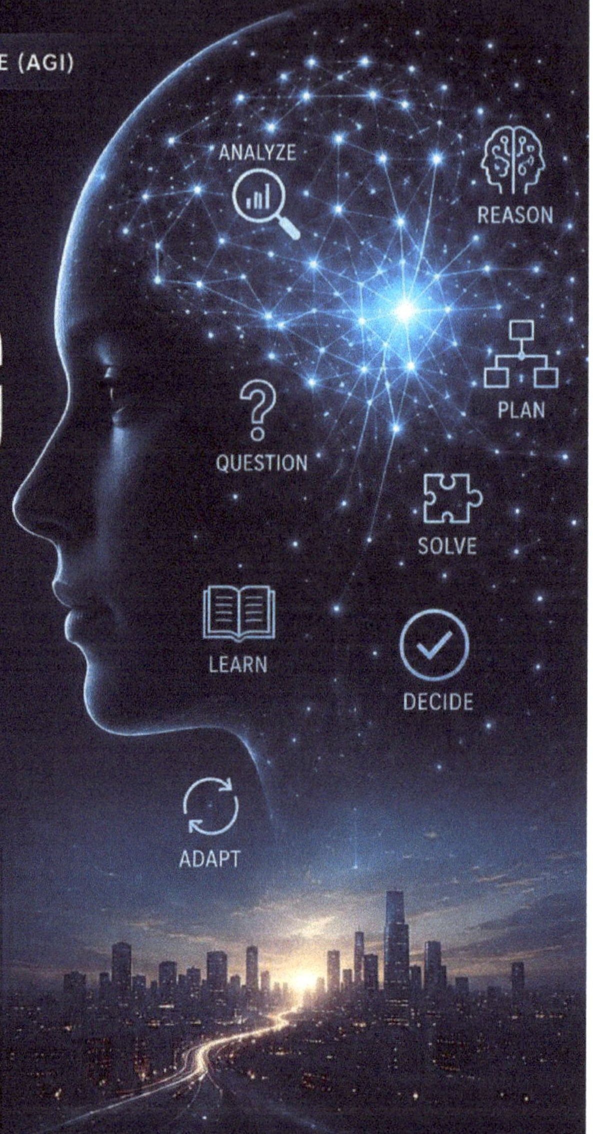

WELCOME TO THE AGE OF REASONING.

The world is changing faster than ever before. Information is everywhere. Data is unlimited. But true intelligence is not about how much you know—it's about how you think.

AGI: Reasoning Intelligence takes you inside the minds of tomorrow's most advanced intelligent systems. You will discover how AGI thinks through complex problems, connects ideas, learns from experience, and makes better decisions—even in uncertain situations.

This book is for students, educators, parents, and leaders who want to understand the power of reasoning and prepare for a future where human and artificial intelligence work together to build a better world.

> *"The greatest leap in intelligence is not in having more information, but in knowing how to reason with it."*

THINK DEEPLY

SOLVE COMPLEX PROBLEMS

MAKE BETTER DECISIONS

LEARN. ADAPT. IMPROVE.

BUILD A SMARTER, KINDER FUTURE.

REASONING IS THE BRIDGE BETWEEN KNOWING AND DOING.

THE FUTURE BELONGS TO THOSE WHO CAN THINK.

BY SUSIE HALA

Chapter 1

What Is Reasoning Intelligence?

Imagine meeting someone who has memorized thousands of facts but cannot explain why something happens, solve a new problem, or make a good decision when circumstances change. That person might possess a great deal of information, but information alone is not intelligence. Intelligence becomes meaningful when knowledge is used to understand situations, connect ideas, weigh evidence, and make thoughtful decisions. This ability is called reasoning. It is one of the most important characteristics that separates simple machines from truly intelligent systems. As the world moves closer to Artificial General Intelligence (AGI), reasoning is becoming the foundation upon which future intelligent systems will be built. Unlike today's Artificial Narrow Intelligence (ANI), which is designed to perform one task at a time, AGI is expected to understand unfamiliar situations, solve a wide variety of problems, learn continuously, and adapt to changing environments. None of these abilities can exist without reasoning. This chapter introduces the concept of reasoning intelligence and explains why it may become one of the defining characteristics of the next generation of artificial intelligence.

Reasoning intelligence is the ability to think through information instead of simply responding to it. It involves analyzing facts, comparing possibilities, recognizing relationships, identifying patterns, drawing conclusions, evaluating evidence, and making decisions based on logic rather than memorization alone. Human beings use reasoning every day, often without realizing it. A student deciding which study method works best for an upcoming exam is using reasoning. A doctor identifying the cause of an illness by comparing symptoms is using reasoning. An engineer selecting the safest design for a bridge is using reasoning. Even deciding what route to take home after noticing heavy traffic requires reasoning. In every case, individuals are doing more than recalling information—they are thinking about information. They examine what they know, consider new evidence, anticipate possible outcomes, and choose the best course of action. This process transforms knowledge into intelligent action.

Today's AI systems are impressive because they can recognize speech, identify faces, translate languages, generate images, answer questions, and even write essays. However, most of these systems rely heavily on recognizing statistical patterns learned from enormous amounts of data. They excel when facing situations similar to those they have encountered during training but often struggle when confronted with entirely new problems requiring deeper understanding. An image recognition system may correctly identify thousands of animals but fail to explain why one species behaves differently from another. A chatbot may generate fluent answers but occasionally produce incorrect conclusions because it lacks a complete understanding of the underlying concepts. These systems demonstrate extraordinary computational power, but computation alone does not equal reasoning. Reasoning requires understanding relationships, recognizing cause and effect, questioning assumptions, and adjusting conclusions when new information becomes available.

One useful way to understand reasoning intelligence is to compare it to building a puzzle. Imagine someone dumping one thousand puzzle pieces onto a table. A computer trained only to recognize patterns may identify the colors, shapes, and sizes of every piece almost instantly. It can group similar pieces together and even estimate where some pieces belong. However, reasoning begins when someone asks, "What picture are we trying to build?" or "Why does this piece belong here instead of somewhere else?" The reasoning process requires understanding the bigger picture rather than focusing only on individual pieces. AGI is expected to move beyond identifying puzzle pieces and instead understand the complete image they create together. This ability to see connections across different pieces of information allows intelligent systems to solve unfamiliar problems rather than simply repeating familiar solutions.

Reasoning also depends on asking questions. Human beings are naturally curious. Children constantly ask "why," "how," and "what if." These questions help build deeper understanding rather than simple memorization. Every scientific discovery, technological breakthrough, and important invention began with someone asking a question that had not yet been answered. AGI systems of the future will likely need similar abilities. Instead of simply responding to commands, they may need to investigate problems, gather evidence, test different possibilities, reject incorrect assumptions, and continue refining their understanding until they discover the best solution. This kind of curiosity-driven reasoning is one of the qualities researchers hope to develop as artificial intelligence becomes increasingly capable.

Another important feature of reasoning intelligence is flexibility. Human beings rarely encounter identical situations throughout life. Every challenge contains unique details that require adaptation. A firefighter responding to a wildfire cannot rely on exactly the same strategy used during a house fire. A teacher cannot instruct every student using the exact same method because each learner has different strengths, experiences, and learning styles. Similarly, future AGI systems must be able to adjust their thinking as situations change. Flexibility means recognizing when previous solutions no longer work and developing new approaches based on current circumstances. This ability separates adaptive intelligence from fixed programming. Instead of following rigid instructions, reasoning intelligence allows an intelligent system to modify its approach whenever necessary.

Reasoning intelligence also depends on understanding relationships between ideas. Information rarely exists in isolation. Everything in the world is connected in some way. Weather affects agriculture. Agriculture influences food supplies. Food supplies affect economies. Economies influence education, healthcare, technology, and national security. Human reasoning naturally recognizes these relationships, allowing people to understand complex systems rather than isolated facts. Future AGI systems will need to identify these interconnected relationships across countless fields of knowledge. Understanding one concept may require knowledge from mathematics, biology, economics, psychology, engineering, ethics, and many other disciplines working together. This ability to connect ideas across different domains is one reason AGI is expected to become far more capable than today's specialized AI systems.

Decision-making represents another essential component of reasoning intelligence. Every day, people make hundreds of decisions, ranging from simple choices to life-changing ones. Some decisions involve selecting the fastest route to work, while others involve choosing careers, making medical treatments, or designing public policies. Good decision-making requires gathering information, evaluating alternatives, considering possible risks, predicting future outcomes, and balancing competing priorities. These steps require much more than recalling stored information. They require reasoning. AGI systems designed to assist humans in medicine, engineering, education, disaster response, scientific research, or environmental protection must learn to evaluate multiple possibilities before recommending actions. Responsible reasoning will become far more valuable than simply producing fast answers.

One of the greatest strengths of human reasoning is learning from mistakes. Throughout history, people have advanced by recognizing errors, correcting assumptions, and improving future decisions. Scientists revise theories when new evidence appears. Engineers redesign products after failures. Teachers modify lessons when students struggle. Athletes adjust techniques after losing competitions. Every mistake becomes an opportunity for deeper understanding. Future AGI systems are expected to possess similar abilities. Instead of repeating unsuccessful strategies indefinitely, they may analyze failures, identify weaknesses, update internal knowledge, and develop more effective solutions over time. Continuous improvement through reflection is one of the characteristics that researchers believe will distinguish truly intelligent systems from today's static software applications.

Reasoning intelligence must also include ethical thinking. Intelligence without responsibility can create significant risks. History demonstrates that powerful technologies produce the greatest benefits when guided by ethical principles. As AGI systems become more capable of making decisions, they must consider fairness, safety, transparency, accountability, and respect for human values. For example, an AGI assisting doctors should recommend treatments based on medical evidence while respecting patient rights. An AGI supporting educators should promote learning without creating unfair advantages or discrimination. An AGI helping governments should balance efficiency with individual freedoms. Ethical reasoning requires considering not only whether something can be done, but whether it should be done. This balance between capability and responsibility will remain one of the most important challenges facing AGI development.

Reasoning intelligence is not limited to solving mathematical equations or scientific problems. It also includes understanding language, interpreting emotions, recognizing intentions, appreciating cultural differences, and communicating effectively with people from diverse backgrounds. Human conversations often contain humor, metaphors, emotions, and indirect meanings that require interpretation beyond literal words. Future AGI systems must learn to understand context rather than simply translating vocabulary. They must recognize when someone is confused, frustrated, uncertain, or seeking encouragement. Effective reasoning often depends on understanding both facts and human experiences. Combining logical thinking with emotional awareness may become one of the defining characteristics of advanced artificial intelligence.

As AGI develops, reasoning intelligence will likely transform nearly every profession. Doctors may receive assistance diagnosing complex diseases by analyzing millions of medical studies while reasoning through individual patient histories. Engineers may design safer buildings using systems capable of evaluating thousands of structural possibilities before recommending the most reliable solution. Scientists may accelerate discoveries by reasoning through enormous collections of experimental data. Teachers may personalize instruction by understanding each student's strengths, challenges, interests, and learning progress. Emergency responders may receive intelligent recommendations during natural disasters that consider weather patterns, transportation networks, available resources, and human safety simultaneously. Rather than replacing human expertise, reasoning intelligence has the potential to become a collaborative partner that helps professionals make more informed decisions.

Students entering today's classrooms are preparing for careers that will increasingly involve collaboration with intelligent systems. Memorizing facts will remain important, but future success will depend even more on developing reasoning skills. Employers already value individuals who can solve problems creatively, evaluate evidence objectively, think critically, communicate clearly, adapt to change, and make thoughtful decisions. These are precisely the abilities that reasoning intelligence seeks to model and support. As artificial intelligence continues evolving, human reasoning may become even more valuable because people will be responsible for guiding, supervising, questioning, and improving intelligent technologies. Understanding how reasoning works will allow future generations to use AGI responsibly rather than depending on it blindly.

Throughout this book, you will discover that reasoning intelligence is much more than a technical feature inside advanced computers. It represents a new way of thinking about intelligence itself. Intelligence is no longer measured only by how much information can be stored or how quickly calculations can be performed. Instead, true intelligence emerges from understanding, judgment, adaptability, learning, creativity, ethics, and thoughtful decision-making. These qualities allow both humans and future AGI systems to solve problems that have never been solved before.

The journey into reasoning intelligence is only beginning. Researchers around the world continue exploring how intelligent systems can analyze information more deeply, learn more efficiently, explain their decisions more clearly, and collaborate more naturally with people. Although many technical challenges remain, the future promises extraordinary advances that may reshape education, healthcare, science, business, engineering, environmental protection, and countless other fields. By understanding the principles introduced in this chapter, readers gain the foundation needed to explore the remarkable world of AGI reasoning. The chapters that follow will reveal how intelligent systems organize thoughts, analyze evidence, solve increasingly difficult problems, make better decisions, and ultimately become partners in building a smarter, safer, and more innovative future for humanity.

Learn AI. Understand AI. Shape the Future.
— Susie Hala, IntelliGloss Press

Chapter 1 Summary

What Is Reasoning Intelligence?

Reasoning intelligence is the ability to think through information, understand relationships, evaluate evidence, and make logical decisions. Unlike simply memorizing facts or recognizing patterns, reasoning requires understanding why something happens and determining the best course of action based on available information.

This chapter introduced one of the most important concepts behind Artificial General Intelligence (AGI). While today's Artificial Narrow Intelligence (ANI) performs specific tasks extremely well, AGI aims to reason across many different situations, solve unfamiliar problems, and continuously learn from experience.

Students learned that reasoning involves analyzing information, asking questions, comparing alternatives, recognizing cause-and-effect relationships, drawing conclusions, and adapting when circumstances change. These skills allow humans to solve problems in everyday life and will become essential capabilities for future AGI systems.

The chapter also explained that reasoning is closely connected to ethical decision-making, creativity, flexibility, and continuous learning. Future intelligent systems will need to combine knowledge with sound judgment, ensuring that technology supports humanity responsibly and safely.

Finally, the chapter emphasized that reasoning intelligence is not intended to replace human thinking. Instead, AGI has the potential to become a collaborative partner that helps people make better decisions in medicine, education, engineering, science, business, and many other fields. As AI continues to evolve, human reasoning will remain one of the most valuable skills for future generations.

Chapter 1 Reflection

Reasoning is one of the greatest abilities that humans possess. Every important decision we make—whether solving a math problem, choosing a career, helping a friend, or protecting our environment—depends on our ability to think carefully before acting. As artificial intelligence becomes more advanced, reasoning will become one of the defining features that separates simple automation from true intelligence.

This chapter reminds us that intelligence is not measured by how much information we can memorize. Real intelligence is demonstrated by how well we understand information, evaluate evidence, recognize connections, and make thoughtful decisions.

As students prepare for careers in a future filled with AI technologies, developing strong reasoning skills will become just as important as learning mathematics, science, reading, and writing. Future leaders will not simply use AI—they will guide it, question it, improve it, and ensure that it serves humanity responsibly.

Every question you ask strengthens your reasoning.

Every problem you solve builds your intelligence.

Every thoughtful decision prepares you to lead in the Age of AGI.

Chapter 1 Worksheet

Name: ____________________________

Date: ____________________________

Part A – Vocabulary

Write a definition for each term in your own words.

1. Reasoning Intelligence

____

2. Artificial General Intelligence (AGI)

____

3. Artificial Narrow Intelligence (ANI)

____

4. Critical Thinking

____

5. Decision-Making

____

____

Part B – Short Answer

1. What is reasoning intelligence?

____

____

2. How is reasoning different from memorizing information?

3. Why is reasoning important for AGI?

4. Give one example of reasoning that people use every day.

5. Why should future AI systems consider ethics when making decisions?

Part C – Critical Thinking

Imagine an AGI system is helping firefighters respond to a large wildfire.

What information should the AGI consider before recommending a plan?

How could reasoning help save lives during this emergency?

Part D – Personal Reflection

Describe a time when you had to carefully think through a difficult decision before making a choice.

What information did you consider?

How did reasoning help you?

Chapter 1 Quiz

Name: ________________________

Score: ________/20

Multiple Choice

1. What is reasoning intelligence?

A. Memorizing facts

B. Thinking logically to solve problems

C. Typing faster

D. Storing more information

2. Which type of AI is designed for one specific task?

A. AGI

B. ANI

C. Super Intelligence

D. Robotics

3. Why is reasoning important?

A. It helps make thoughtful decisions.

B. It stores more pictures.

C. It increases internet speed.

D. It replaces education.

4. Which skill is part of reasoning?

A. Guessing randomly

B. Evaluating evidence

C. Ignoring information

D. Avoiding questions

5. Future AGI systems are expected to

A. Only memorize data.

B. Solve unfamiliar problems.

C. Stop learning.

D. Never change.

True or False

6. Reasoning only involves remembering facts.

True / False

7. Human reasoning often considers cause and effect.

True / False

8. Ethical thinking is important in AGI.

True / False

9. Future AGI may work alongside humans.

Truc / Falsc

10. Asking questions is part of reasoning.

True / False

Short Answer

11. Explain the difference between ANI and AGI.

12. Give one real-world example of reasoning intelligence.

13. Why is learning from mistakes important?

14. How can reasoning improve decision-making?

15. What is one lesson you learned from this chapter?

Chapter 1 Answer Key

Multiple Choice

1. **B** – Thinking logically to solve problems
2. **B** – Artificial Narrow Intelligence (ANI)
3. **A** – It helps make thoughtful decisions.

4. **B** – Evaluating evidence
5. **B** – Solve unfamiliar problems

True or False

6. **False**
7. **True**
8. **True**
9. **True**
10. **True**

Short Answer (Sample Answers)

11. ANI performs specialized tasks, while AGI is designed to reason and solve many different types of problems.

12. Example: A doctor diagnosing a patient, a teacher adjusting a lesson, or a firefighter choosing the safest evacuation route.

13. Learning from mistakes helps improve future decisions, strengthens understanding, and leads to better solutions over time.

14. Reasoning allows people to analyze evidence, compare options, predict possible outcomes, and choose the most effective solution.

15. Answers will vary. Students should explain one important concept they learned about reasoning intelligence and AGI.

Chapter 2

From Pattern Recognition to Logical Thinking

If you ask a young child to point to a picture of a dog after showing hundreds of dog pictures, the child will probably succeed. However, if you ask why dogs bark, why wolves are related to dogs, or why some animals have evolved differently over thousands of years, the conversation changes completely. Identifying an object is very different from understanding it. This simple example helps explain one of the biggest differences between today's Artificial Narrow Intelligence (ANI) and the future vision of Artificial General Intelligence (AGI). Modern AI systems have become incredibly good at recognizing patterns. They can identify faces in photographs, detect tumors in medical images, recommend movies, predict traffic, translate languages, and generate realistic text. These accomplishments are remarkable, but recognizing patterns is only the first step toward intelligence. The next step is logical thinking—the ability to understand relationships, explain decisions, solve unfamiliar problems, and adapt knowledge to situations that have never been seen before. This chapter explores how intelligent systems move from recognizing patterns to developing reasoning abilities that resemble human thinking.

Pattern recognition is one of the most powerful tools in artificial intelligence. Every day, AI systems process enormous amounts of information and search for similarities within that data. A music streaming service notices the types of songs you enjoy and recommends new artists with similar styles. An email program learns to recognize spam by comparing millions of previous messages. A smartphone identifies a person's face by examining tiny details such as the distance between the eyes, the shape of the nose, and the outline of the jaw. None of these systems actually "understand" the information in the same way humans do. Instead, they recognize mathematical similarities between current data and information they have processed before. Pattern recognition allows computers to perform many tasks with impressive speed and accuracy, making it one of the greatest achievements in modern AI. However, recognizing patterns alone does not mean that a machine truly understands the world around it.

Human beings also recognize patterns, but they quickly move beyond them by asking questions and seeking explanations. Imagine walking outside and noticing dark clouds gathering overhead. Pattern recognition tells you that the sky looks similar to previous days when it rained. Logical thinking takes the next step by asking why storms form, how temperature and humidity influence weather, whether the forecast predicts heavy rain, and what actions should be taken to stay safe. Humans naturally combine observation with reasoning. We search for causes, predict consequences, evaluate possibilities, and make decisions based on understanding rather than appearance alone. This ability to build explanations instead of merely identifying similarities is one of the defining characteristics of human intelligence and one of the major goals of AGI research.

The difference between pattern recognition and logical thinking becomes even clearer when unexpected situations arise. Consider an autonomous delivery robot traveling through a city. If the streets look exactly like those in its training data, the robot can easily navigate using familiar patterns. But what happens if construction suddenly blocks the road? What if a bridge is closed because of flooding? What if emergency vehicles redirect traffic? A system that depends only on pattern recognition may become confused because the situation no longer matches what it has previously learned. A reasoning system, however, analyzes the new conditions, understands the purpose of reaching its destination, evaluates alternative routes, predicts possible delays, and selects the safest solution. Logical thinking allows intelligent systems to continue solving problems even when they encounter unfamiliar situations.

One important aspect of logical thinking is understanding relationships between facts. Information rarely exists by itself. Every event connects to countless other events. A drought affects crop production. Lower crop production influences food prices. Higher food prices impact family budgets, businesses, and governments. Logical reasoning allows people to connect these events into meaningful chains of cause and effect. Instead of seeing isolated pieces of information, reasoning reveals how those pieces influence one another. AGI will need this same ability if it is expected to solve complex problems involving healthcare, climate science, transportation, education, engineering, and public safety. Pattern recognition may identify individual events, but reasoning explains how they are connected.

Another major difference involves flexibility. Pattern recognition systems are often excellent at performing tasks they have practiced many times. However, human reasoning allows knowledge gained in one area to be applied in another. A student who learns about gravity in science class can later understand why engineers design stronger bridges or why astronauts experience different conditions in space. This ability to transfer knowledge from one subject to another is known as generalization. It is one of the greatest strengths of human intelligence. AGI researchers hope to create systems capable of similar flexible thinking. Instead of learning millions of unrelated tasks independently, future intelligent systems may develop broad understanding that allows knowledge to be shared across many different situations.

Logical thinking also requires asking whether information is reliable. Human beings naturally question evidence when something seems unusual. Imagine reading two different news articles that describe the same event but reach completely different conclusions. Rather than accepting the first article immediately, thoughtful readers compare sources, examine evidence, identify possible biases, and decide which explanation is more trustworthy. This evaluation process is reasoning in action. Pattern recognition systems may simply recognize familiar words or writing styles, while reasoning systems examine the quality, credibility, and consistency of the information itself. As AI becomes increasingly involved in education, journalism, science, and public policy, the ability to evaluate evidence carefully will become one of its most valuable skills.

Problem-solving provides another clear example of logical thinking. Imagine a doctor treating a patient who arrives with a high fever, fatigue, and difficulty breathing. Many illnesses share these symptoms. Pattern recognition may identify diseases with similar characteristics, but logical reasoning requires much more. The doctor reviews the patient's medical history, recent travel, medications, laboratory results, family health background, and possible environmental exposures. Each piece of evidence changes the doctor's understanding of the situation. New information may eliminate one diagnosis while strengthening another. This continuous process of collecting evidence, testing possibilities, eliminating unlikely explanations, and reaching a carefully supported conclusion demonstrates reasoning rather than simple recognition. Future AGI systems assisting physicians must learn to reason in similar ways if they are to become trusted partners in healthcare.

Education provides another powerful example of the transition from pattern recognition to logical thinking. Students often begin learning by memorizing multiplication tables, vocabulary words, historical dates, or scientific formulas. Memorization provides an important foundation, but true learning occurs when students understand why mathematical formulas work, how historical events influence one another, or why scientific principles explain natural phenomena. Teachers encourage students to explain their answers because explanation reveals understanding. A student who only memorizes information may struggle when faced with a new type of problem. A student who understands the underlying concepts can apply knowledge flexibly in unfamiliar situations. AGI seeks to develop similar understanding by moving beyond stored information toward deeper reasoning abilities.

Creativity also depends heavily on logical thinking. Many people assume creativity means producing something completely new without structure or rules. In reality, creativity often results from connecting existing ideas in original ways. Inventors combine technologies from different industries. Scientists apply mathematical concepts to biological research. Artists blend cultures, styles, and historical influences into unique works of art. These creative achievements require recognizing patterns, but they also depend on reasoning about how different ideas fit together. AGI systems capable of creativity must understand relationships between concepts rather than simply repeating patterns found in training data.

One challenge facing AI researchers is teaching machines to recognize when they do not know something. Human reasoning includes intellectual humility. People understand that their knowledge is incomplete and that additional information may change their conclusions. Scientists constantly revise theories as new evidence emerges. Engineers improve designs after discovering weaknesses. Teachers modify lessons after observing student performance. Logical thinking includes the willingness to question previous assumptions. Future AGI systems will likely need similar abilities. Instead of confidently producing incorrect answers, they may evaluate uncertainty, request additional information, explain limitations, and revise conclusions whenever new evidence becomes available. This capacity for self-correction represents an important step beyond simple pattern recognition.

Ethical reasoning also illustrates the limitations of pattern recognition. Imagine an AI system helping distribute limited medical resources after a natural disaster. Simply recognizing patterns from previous disasters may not produce fair decisions because every emergency contains unique circumstances. Ethical reasoning requires considering patient needs, available resources, long-term consequences, fairness, transparency, and human values. These decisions involve balancing competing priorities rather than following fixed patterns. As AGI becomes more capable, society will increasingly expect intelligent systems to explain not only what decision they recommend but also why that recommendation is ethically responsible.

Researchers developing AGI often describe logical thinking as building mental models of the world. A mental model is an internal understanding of how different parts of a system interact. Human beings constantly create mental models. We understand that planting seeds eventually produces crops, that exercise improves physical fitness over time, and that studying regularly leads to stronger academic performance. These models allow us to predict future outcomes and make informed decisions before events occur. AGI systems may develop similar internal representations that help them reason about situations instead of simply reacting to them. Rather than memorizing every possible scenario, reasoning systems could understand general principles that apply across many different circumstances.

Another important feature of logical thinking is explaining decisions. Human experts rarely answer important questions with only a single sentence. Doctors explain diagnoses. Engineers justify designs. Scientists describe experimental evidence. Teachers show students how problems are solved step by step. Explanations build trust because they allow others to understand the reasoning behind a conclusion. Future AGI systems will likely need to provide similar transparency. Instead of acting as mysterious "black boxes," they should explain how evidence was evaluated, why certain conclusions were reached, what uncertainties remain, and what alternative solutions were considered. Explainable reasoning will become essential as intelligent systems assume greater responsibility in society.

As artificial intelligence continues evolving, the transition from pattern recognition to logical thinking will shape nearly every field of human activity. Healthcare, education, transportation, environmental science, finance, engineering, law, and scientific research all depend upon understanding relationships rather than simply recognizing patterns. Intelligent systems capable of reasoning may help discover new medicines, design cleaner energy systems, improve disaster response, personalize education, and accelerate scientific discoveries. However, these achievements will require much more than faster computers or larger datasets. They will require machines capable of understanding why things happen, not merely recognizing that they have happened before.

The journey from pattern recognition to logical thinking represents one of the greatest scientific challenges of the twenty-first century. Pattern recognition has already transformed modern technology, making today's AI systems powerful assistants in countless industries. Yet the future of AGI depends upon something deeper: the ability to understand, explain, adapt, question, learn, and reason across an unlimited variety of situations. As researchers continue exploring these capabilities, humanity moves closer to intelligent systems that do far more than recognize information. They will think through problems, evaluate evidence, communicate their reasoning, and work alongside people to solve some of the world's most important challenges. Understanding this transition provides an essential foundation for everything that follows in the study of Artificial General Intelligence, because true intelligence begins not with seeing patterns, but with understanding what those patterns truly mean.

Learn AI. Understand AI. Shape the Future.
— Susie Hala, IntelliGloss Press

Chapter 2 Summary

From Pattern Recognition to Logical Thinking

This chapter explored one of the most important differences between today's Artificial Narrow Intelligence (ANI) and the future vision of Artificial General Intelligence (AGI): the difference between recognizing patterns and thinking logically.

Students learned that pattern recognition allows AI systems to identify similarities in large amounts of data. This ability powers many modern technologies such as facial recognition, language translation, recommendation systems, medical image analysis, and voice assistants. Although these systems perform specialized tasks with remarkable accuracy, they often depend on recognizing patterns they have previously learned.

Logical thinking goes much further than pattern recognition. It allows intelligent systems to understand relationships, explain why events happen, analyze cause and effect, evaluate evidence, solve unfamiliar problems, and make thoughtful decisions even when facing situations they have never encountered before.

The chapter also explained that reasoning requires flexibility. Human beings regularly apply knowledge learned in one situation to solve completely different problems. This ability, known as generalization, is one of the defining goals of AGI. Instead of memorizing millions of separate tasks, future intelligent systems are expected to build broad understanding that can be applied across many different fields.

Students also discovered that logical thinking involves evaluating evidence, questioning assumptions, learning from mistakes, explaining decisions, and considering ethical responsibilities. These abilities help transform information into knowledge and knowledge into wisdom.

Finally, the chapter emphasized that the future of AGI depends not simply on processing larger amounts of data but on developing intelligent systems capable of understanding the world, adapting to change, and working alongside humans to solve complex problems responsibly.

Chapter 2 Reflection

Every day we recognize patterns without even realizing it. We recognize familiar faces, remember favorite songs, notice weather changes, and identify common routines. While these abilities are important, true intelligence begins when we ask deeper questions.

Why did something happen?

How are these ideas connected?

What is the best solution?

What could happen next?

These questions require logical thinking.

As artificial intelligence continues to advance, society will increasingly depend on systems that do more than recognize information. We will need intelligent partners that can explain their thinking, evaluate evidence fairly, adapt to changing situations, and make responsible decisions.

For students, this chapter offers an important reminder that education is not about memorizing facts alone. Real learning happens when we understand concepts, connect ideas across different subjects, think critically, and apply knowledge to solve new challenges.

The future will belong to people who know how to think—not just what to remember. By strengthening your reasoning skills today, you are preparing yourself to work confidently with tomorrow's intelligent technologies and to become a thoughtful leader in the Age of AGI.

Chapter 2 Worksheet

Name: ________________________________

Date: ________________________________

Part A – Vocabulary

Write your own definition for each term.

1. Pattern Recognition

____

____

2. Logical Thinking

____

____

3. Generalization

____

____

4. Cause and Effect

____

____

5. Evidence

____

____

____

Part B – Short Answer

1. What is pattern recognition?

____

2. How is logical thinking different from pattern recognition?

3. Why is logical thinking important for AGI?

4. Explain what generalization means.

5. Why should intelligent systems explain how they reached a decision?

Part C – Critical Thinking

Imagine an AGI is helping emergency responders after a powerful hurricane.

List at least five types of information the AGI should analyze before recommending an evacuation plan.

1.
2.
3.
4.
5.

Now explain why logical thinking would be more useful than simple pattern recognition during this emergency.

Part D – Real-World Application

Think about a difficult decision you made recently.

Describe how you used logical thinking instead of simply relying on habit or previous experience.

____

____

____

____

____

____

Part E – Classroom Discussion

Discuss the following questions with a partner or small group.

• Can a machine truly understand information, or can it only recognize patterns?

• Should future AGI systems always explain their decisions? Why or why not?

• What careers will benefit most from reasoning-based AI?

Write one new idea you learned during your discussion.

____

____

____

Chapter 2 Answer Key

Part A – Vocabulary (Sample Answers)

1. **Pattern Recognition** – The ability to identify similarities, trends, or repeated features in data.
2. **Logical Thinking** – The process of analyzing information, evaluating evidence, and making reasoned decisions.
3. **Generalization** – Applying knowledge learned in one situation to solve different or unfamiliar problems.
4. **Cause and Effect** – Understanding how one event leads to another.
5. **Evidence** – Facts, observations, or information used to support a conclusion.

Part B – Short Answer (Sample Answers)

1. Pattern recognition allows AI systems to identify similarities within large amounts of information.

2. Pattern recognition identifies familiar examples, while logical thinking explains relationships, evaluates evidence, and solves new problems.

3. AGI needs logical thinking so it can understand unfamiliar situations, adapt to change, and make thoughtful decisions.

4. Generalization is the ability to use knowledge learned in one area to solve problems in another area.

5. Explaining decisions builds trust, improves transparency, helps people verify conclusions, and allows humans to understand the reasoning process.

Part C – Critical Thinking (Sample Answers)

Possible information includes:

- Weather forecasts
- Flood levels
- Road conditions
- Population density
- Hospital locations
- Emergency shelter capacity
- Traffic patterns
- Power outages
- Communication availability
- Rescue resources

Reasoning should explain that logical thinking evaluates changing conditions, compares alternatives, predicts outcomes, and selects the safest evacuation strategy rather than simply repeating previous responses.

Part D – Real-World Application

Answers will vary.

Students should demonstrate that they considered evidence, compared options, predicted possible outcomes, and made a thoughtful decision.

Part E – Classroom Discussion

Answers will vary.

Students should demonstrate thoughtful participation by explaining how reasoning differs from pattern recognition and why explainable AI is valuable in real-world situations.

Chapter 3

The Building Blocks of Intelligent Reasoning

Imagine trying to build a house without bricks, wood, concrete, or steel. No matter how talented the builder might be, the house could never stand without the materials that form its foundation. The same idea applies to intelligence. Reasoning does not appear magically inside a human mind or an intelligent machine. It is built from many smaller parts working together. Every thoughtful decision, scientific discovery, engineering breakthrough, or everyday solution depends on combining these building blocks into a logical process. Just as letters form words and words form sentences, individual pieces of information combine to create understanding. In Artificial General Intelligence (AGI), these building blocks will allow intelligent systems to move beyond simply recognizing patterns toward understanding problems, evaluating evidence, and making sound decisions. This chapter explores the essential components that make intelligent reasoning possible and explains why each building block is necessary for creating machines that can think more like humans.

One of the most important building blocks of reasoning is **facts**. Facts are pieces of information that can be verified through observation, measurement, or reliable evidence. For example, water freezes at approximately 0 degrees Celsius under normal atmospheric pressure. Earth revolves around the Sun. The human heart pumps blood throughout the body. These statements are supported by scientific evidence and remain true regardless of personal opinions. Human reasoning depends on accurate facts because every conclusion begins with information that can be trusted. If the facts are incorrect, the reasoning built upon them may also become incorrect. Future AGI systems will require reliable sources of factual knowledge to make informed decisions. They must constantly distinguish verified information from rumors, misinformation, or unsupported claims. Building trustworthy intelligence begins with building trustworthy knowledge.

Facts alone, however, do not produce reasoning. They must be connected through **relationships**. Relationships explain how one fact connects to another. A doctor knows that bacteria can cause infections, but the relationship between bacteria, the immune system, medications, and patient symptoms creates a complete understanding of illness. An engineer knows that steel is strong, but understanding how steel behaves under pressure, temperature, and weight allows safe bridges to be designed. Relationships transform isolated facts into meaningful knowledge. Without relationships, information remains disconnected, much like individual puzzle pieces scattered across a table. Reasoning begins when those pieces are assembled into a complete picture.

Another critical building block is **observation**. Every intelligent decision begins with careful observation of the environment. Human beings constantly gather information through their senses. We observe movement, sounds, colors, temperatures, facial expressions, written information, and countless other details. Scientists make discoveries because they observe natural events carefully before drawing conclusions. Detectives solve mysteries by observing evidence that others overlook. Teachers recognize when students need additional help by observing classroom behavior. Future AGI systems must also become skilled observers. Through cameras, sensors, microphones, scientific instruments, and digital data, intelligent systems gather information about the world before reasoning about what it means. Accurate observations provide the raw material from which intelligent thinking grows.

Once observations have been collected, reasoning requires identifying **patterns**. Patterns reveal repeated similarities that help predict future events. Farmers recognize seasonal weather patterns that influence planting schedules. Financial analysts study economic patterns to understand market behavior. Meteorologists analyze atmospheric patterns to forecast storms. Physicians recognize symptom patterns associated with particular diseases. Pattern recognition helps intelligent systems organize information efficiently. However, as discussed in the previous chapter, recognizing patterns alone does not produce understanding. Patterns simply identify regularities. Reasoning asks why those patterns exist and whether they will continue under changing conditions.

Reasoning also depends heavily on **rules**. Rules describe how information behaves under specific conditions. Mathematical formulas, scientific laws, grammar rules, traffic regulations, and engineering standards all provide structured guidance for decision-making. For example, the law of gravity explains how objects behave when released near Earth's surface. Traffic rules help drivers navigate roads safely. Medical treatment guidelines assist physicians in selecting appropriate therapies. Rules create consistency by allowing similar situations to be handled in predictable ways. Future AGI systems will use many different kinds of rules while also recognizing that some situations require flexibility rather than rigid obedience. Understanding when to apply rules and when exceptions exist is itself a sophisticated reasoning skill.

Another essential building block is the **assumption**. Assumptions are ideas accepted temporarily until better evidence becomes available. Human beings use assumptions constantly because complete information is rarely available. Imagine hearing a smoke alarm in your home. You may initially assume that something is burning. However, after investigation, you might discover that burnt toast triggered the alarm rather than a dangerous fire. Good reasoning recognizes that assumptions are useful starting points but should always remain open to revision. Poor reasoning occurs when assumptions are treated as permanent facts without sufficient evidence. Future AGI systems must learn to identify assumptions clearly, distinguish them from verified facts, and update them whenever new information becomes available.

Closely connected to assumptions are **hypotheses**. A hypothesis is a possible explanation that can be tested. Scientists develop hypotheses whenever they investigate new questions. Rather than immediately accepting the first explanation, they collect evidence, perform experiments, compare results, and revise ideas until stronger conclusions emerge. For example, a scientist studying declining fish populations may propose several hypotheses involving pollution, water temperature, habitat destruction, or invasive species. Each possibility must be tested before reaching a reliable conclusion. This careful process protects science from jumping to unsupported conclusions. Future AGI systems performing scientific research may use similar methods by generating multiple hypotheses, evaluating evidence for each one, eliminating weaker explanations, and identifying the most likely solution.

Evidence serves as another foundation of intelligent reasoning. Evidence consists of observations, measurements, documents, experiments, or reliable information that supports or challenges an idea. In a courtroom, evidence helps determine whether someone is guilty or innocent. In medicine, laboratory results provide evidence supporting diagnoses. In engineering, stress tests supply evidence about material strength. Intelligent reasoning requires evaluating both supporting and conflicting evidence before reaching conclusions. One of the greatest dangers in reasoning occurs when individuals ignore evidence that contradicts their beliefs. Effective reasoning welcomes new evidence because stronger information leads to better decisions. AGI systems will need sophisticated methods for collecting, organizing, verifying, and weighing evidence from multiple sources before recommending actions.

Once evidence has been examined, intelligent reasoning moves toward **conclusions**. Conclusions are judgments reached after carefully analyzing available information. A good conclusion follows logically from the evidence rather than personal opinions or emotions alone. For example, after examining weather forecasts, soil moisture levels, and crop conditions, a farmer may conclude that irrigation should begin immediately. After reviewing engineering calculations and safety inspections, an engineer may conclude that a bridge is ready for public use. Strong conclusions remain connected to evidence and can be revised whenever better information appears. Future AGI systems must learn that intelligent conclusions are not guesses but carefully supported judgments based on reasoning.

Reasoning rarely occurs in a single step. Instead, intelligent systems build **reasoning chains**, sometimes called chains of thought. Each conclusion becomes a new fact supporting the next stage of analysis. Imagine planning a family vacation. First, you determine the available budget. Next, you compare transportation options. Then you evaluate hotel locations, weather forecasts, activities, and travel times. Each decision influences the next until a complete travel plan emerges. Engineers designing spacecraft, physicians diagnosing illnesses, and scientists conducting research all rely on similar reasoning chains. AGI systems capable of solving complex problems must construct these multi-step reasoning processes while keeping track of intermediate conclusions, assumptions, uncertainties, and changing information.

Memory also plays a central role in intelligent reasoning. Human memory stores experiences, facts, skills, and lessons learned from previous situations. When solving new problems, people draw upon earlier experiences to guide future decisions. A firefighter remembers previous emergencies. A teacher recalls instructional strategies that helped struggling students. A pilot relies upon years of flight training during unexpected situations. Memory allows intelligence to accumulate over time rather than starting from the beginning each day. Future AGI systems will require advanced memory structures capable of storing not only information but also experiences, successful strategies, failed attempts, and explanations that improve future reasoning.

Reasoning becomes even more powerful through **context**. Context refers to the surrounding circumstances that give information its meaning. Consider the simple word "bank." Without context, it could refer to a financial institution or the side of a river. Human beings naturally use surrounding information to determine the correct meaning. Similarly, a doctor's recommendation depends upon a patient's age, medical history, medications, allergies, and current symptoms. Context allows reasoning to become accurate rather than mechanical. AGI systems must understand context if they are expected to communicate naturally with humans, interpret language correctly, and make appropriate decisions across different situations.

Another important building block is recognizing **uncertainty**. Human reasoning often operates with incomplete information. Weather forecasts predict probabilities rather than guarantees. Medical diagnoses sometimes remain uncertain until additional tests become available. Financial markets constantly change due to unpredictable events. Intelligent reasoning acknowledges uncertainty instead of pretending absolute certainty exists. Future AGI systems should estimate confidence levels, explain remaining uncertainties, request additional information when necessary, and avoid presenting unsupported conclusions as established facts. Recognizing uncertainty demonstrates maturity in reasoning because it reflects intellectual honesty rather than false confidence.

One of the most remarkable building blocks of reasoning is **learning**. Every experience provides opportunities to improve future decisions. Children learn language through practice. Athletes improve through repetition. Scientists refine theories through experimentation. Businesses improve products based on customer feedback. Learning transforms mistakes into valuable knowledge. Future AGI systems are expected to improve continuously by analyzing successes and failures, updating knowledge, refining strategies, and adapting to changing environments. Learning ensures that reasoning becomes stronger over time instead of remaining fixed.

Ethics also forms an essential component of intelligent reasoning. Intelligence without ethical guidance can produce harmful outcomes even when logical calculations appear correct. Imagine an AGI helping distribute food after a natural disaster. The system must consider fairness, urgency, accessibility, and human dignity rather than simply maximizing efficiency. Ethical reasoning balances competing priorities while respecting human values. As intelligent systems become increasingly capable, ethical building blocks will become just as important as technical ones. Responsible intelligence requires both logical accuracy and moral responsibility.

Perhaps the greatest strength of intelligent reasoning comes from combining all these building blocks into one unified process. Facts provide reliable information. Observations gather new data. Relationships connect ideas. Patterns reveal regularities. Rules guide decisions. Assumptions create starting points. Hypotheses generate possible explanations. Evidence supports conclusions. Memory recalls previous experiences. Context provides meaning. Uncertainty encourages caution. Learning improves future performance. Ethics ensures responsible decision-making. Together, these building blocks create reasoning that is flexible, reliable, explainable, and continuously improving. Removing any one component weakens the entire reasoning process.

As researchers continue developing Artificial General Intelligence, understanding these building blocks becomes increasingly important. Building reasoning intelligence is not simply about creating faster computers or larger databases. It requires constructing systems that organize information thoughtfully, question assumptions, evaluate evidence fairly, explain conclusions clearly, adapt to changing conditions, and continuously improve through experience. Every major achievement in science, medicine, engineering, education, and technology has depended upon these same reasoning principles. The future of AGI will depend on how successfully these building blocks are combined into intelligent systems capable of thinking responsibly alongside humanity.

The journey toward reasoning intelligence begins with understanding its foundation. Just as every magnificent building starts with carefully placed materials, every intelligent decision begins with the building blocks explored in this chapter. As you continue reading this book, you will discover how these individual components work together to create increasingly sophisticated reasoning abilities. By understanding these foundations, you are not only learning how future AGI systems may think—you are also strengthening your own ability to reason more carefully, solve problems more effectively, and make wiser decisions throughout your own life.

Learn AI. Understand AI. Shape the Future.
— Susie Hala, IntelliGloss Press

Chapter 3 Summary

The Building Blocks of Intelligent Reasoning

This chapter introduced the essential components that work together to create intelligent reasoning. Just as a building requires a strong foundation, reasoning depends on many individual building blocks that allow both humans and future AGI systems to think carefully, solve problems, and make informed decisions.

Students learned that facts provide reliable information, while relationships connect those facts into meaningful knowledge. Observation allows intelligent systems to gather information from the world, and pattern recognition helps organize that information by identifying similarities. However, reasoning goes further by asking why those patterns exist and how they influence future events.

The chapter also explained the importance of rules, assumptions, hypotheses, evidence, and conclusions. These elements help organize thinking into logical steps that can be tested and improved. Students discovered that assumptions should always remain open to change when better evidence becomes available and that conclusions should always be supported by reliable information rather than personal opinions alone.

Other important building blocks discussed included memory, context, uncertainty, learning, and ethics. Memory allows intelligent systems to benefit from previous experiences. Context helps determine the meaning of information based on surrounding circumstances. Recognizing uncertainty encourages careful decision-making instead of false confidence. Learning enables continuous improvement, while ethics ensures that intelligence is used responsibly and fairly.

The chapter concluded by showing that intelligent reasoning is not based on one ability but on many interconnected skills working together. These building blocks form the foundation upon which future Artificial General Intelligence will be developed and will also strengthen the reasoning abilities of every student who learns to use them.

Chapter 3 Reflection

Strong reasoning is built one step at a time.

Just as a beautiful building depends on a solid foundation, intelligent thinking depends on reliable facts, careful observation, thoughtful analysis, and ethical decision-making. Every time we ask questions, gather evidence, evaluate different possibilities, and explain our conclusions, we strengthen our ability to reason.

Artificial General Intelligence will not become intelligent because it stores enormous amounts of information. It will become more intelligent only if it can organize knowledge, understand relationships, learn from experience, recognize uncertainty, and make responsible decisions.

This chapter also reminds us that reasoning is a lifelong skill. Scientists, engineers, teachers, doctors, business leaders, and inventors all rely on these same building blocks every day. They understand that good decisions come from careful thinking rather than quick assumptions.

As future leaders living in the Age of AGI, students should continue developing these reasoning skills. The ability to analyze evidence, solve unfamiliar problems, communicate clearly, and think ethically will remain valuable no matter how technology evolves.

The stronger your reasoning foundation becomes today, the greater your opportunities will be tomorrow.

Chapter 3 Worksheet

Name: ______________________________________

Date: ________________________________

Part A – Vocabulary

Write your own definition for each term.

1. Fact

____

____

2. Observation

____

____

3. Hypothesis

____

____

4. Evidence

____

____

5. Context

____

____

6. Uncertainty

____

____

____

Part B – Short Answer

1. Why are facts important in reasoning?

____

____

2. How do relationships connect information?

3. What is the difference between an assumption and a fact?

4. Why should conclusions always be supported by evidence?

5. How does learning improve reasoning over time?

Part C – Building a Reasoning Chain

A school notices that student attendance has suddenly decreased.

Using the reasoning building blocks from this chapter, complete the investigation.

Observation:

Possible Assumptions:

Evidence to Collect:

Possible Hypothesis:

Conclusion:

Part D – Critical Thinking

Imagine an AGI system is helping scientists study ocean pollution.

Explain how each of the following building blocks would help the AGI make better decisions.

Facts:

Relationships:

Evidence:

Learning:

Ethics:

Part E – Personal Reflection

Describe a situation where you changed your opinion after learning new information.

What evidence caused you to change your thinking?

Chapter 3 Quiz

Name: ______________________________

Score: _________ /20

Multiple Choice

1. Which building block provides information that can be verified?

A. Assumption

B. Fact

C. Guess

D. Opinion

2. A hypothesis is

A. A final answer.

B. A possible explanation that can be tested.

C. A random prediction.

D. A computer program.

3. Why is context important?

A. It increases computer speed.

B. It helps determine the meaning of information.

C. It stores more data.

D. It replaces evidence.

4. Which building block allows intelligent systems to improve over time?

A. Memory only

B. Learning

C. Guessing

D. Memorization

5. Ethics helps intelligent systems

A. Ignore people.

B. Make responsible and fair decisions.

C. Memorize faster.

D. Eliminate all uncertainty.

True or False

6. Facts should be supported by reliable evidence.

True / False

7. Assumptions should never be questioned.

True / False

8. Good reasoning welcomes new evidence.

True / False

9. Context can change the meaning of information.

True / False

10. Learning allows reasoning to improve over time.

True / False

Short Answer

11. Explain why evidence is important.

12. What is the difference between an observation and a conclusion?

13. Why should AGI recognize uncertainty?

14. Give one example of ethical reasoning.

15. Name three building blocks of intelligent reasoning and explain why they are important.

Chapter 3 Answer Key

Multiple Choice

1. **B** – Fact
2. **B** – A possible explanation that can be tested.
3. **B** – It helps determine the meaning of information.
4. **B** – Learning
5. **B** – Make responsible and fair decisions.

True or False

6. **True**
7. **False**
8. **True**
9. **True**
10. **True**

Short Answer (Sample Answers)

11. Evidence supports conclusions by providing reliable facts, observations, measurements, or experimental results that help determine whether an idea is correct.

12. An observation is information that is noticed or measured. A conclusion is a judgment reached after analyzing observations and evidence.

13. AGI should recognize uncertainty because complete information is not always available. Acknowledging uncertainty encourages careful reasoning, additional investigation, and more trustworthy decisions.

14. Example: An AGI helping hospitals distribute limited medical supplies fairly based on patient needs rather than personal preferences or bias.

15. Sample answers may include:

- **Facts** provide trustworthy information.
- **Evidence** supports conclusions.
- **Learning** improves future decisions.
- **Context** helps determine meaning.
- **Memory** recalls previous experiences.
- **Ethics** guides responsible decision-making.

Students should explain how each selected building block contributes to effective reasoning.

Extension Activity (Optional)

Choose a real-world profession such as a doctor, engineer, scientist, teacher, architect, firefighter, or pilot. Write one paragraph explaining how that professional uses at least five building blocks of intelligent reasoning every day to make informed and responsible decisions.

Chapter 4

Deductive, Inductive, and Abductive Reasoning

Imagine standing at the entrance of three different roads, each leading toward the same destination but taking a different path. One road follows carefully marked signs and predictable rules. Another road is built from observations gathered over time, allowing travelers to estimate where it might lead. The third road begins with only a few clues, requiring thoughtful judgment to determine the most likely direction. Although the roads are different, they all help people reach answers and solve problems. Human reasoning works in much the same way. We do not rely on a single method of thinking. Instead, our minds use several approaches depending on the type of problem we face and the information available. Among the most important are deductive reasoning, inductive reasoning, and abductive reasoning. These three forms of reasoning serve as the foundation for science, engineering, medicine, education, law, business, and everyday decision-making. Future Artificial General Intelligence (AGI) systems will also need to master these reasoning methods if they are to think flexibly, solve unfamiliar problems, and make responsible decisions across many different situations.

Reasoning is often compared to building a bridge between information and understanding. Facts alone are valuable, but they do not automatically produce intelligent decisions. A person must know how to organize those facts, connect them logically, evaluate their reliability, and reach conclusions supported by evidence. Different reasoning methods provide different ways of crossing that bridge. Sometimes the evidence is complete and the answer follows naturally. Other times only partial information is available, requiring educated predictions. In many situations, people must choose the explanation that best fits the available evidence while remaining willing to revise their thinking if new information appears. Understanding these three reasoning methods helps explain why human intelligence is so adaptable and why AGI researchers consider them essential for building truly intelligent systems.

The first method is **deductive reasoning**. Deductive reasoning begins with general rules or established facts and applies them to reach specific conclusions. If the starting information is true and the reasoning process is correct, the conclusion will also be true. Because of this reliability, deductive reasoning is often considered the strongest form of logical reasoning. It follows a structured path where each conclusion naturally grows from previously accepted information. Mathematicians, engineers, scientists, and computer programmers frequently rely on deductive reasoning because it produces predictable and verifiable results.

Consider a simple example. All mammals breathe air. Dolphins are mammals. Therefore, dolphins breathe air. The conclusion is not based on guessing or probability. It follows directly from the two established facts. The same process appears in many everyday situations. If school begins at 8:00 a.m. and you know it takes thirty minutes to travel to school, deductive reasoning tells you what time you must leave home. A mechanic may know that a particular engine problem always causes a specific warning light to appear. When the warning light is present, the mechanic applies deductive reasoning to identify the likely mechanical issue. In each example, general knowledge guides specific decisions.

Deductive reasoning is especially valuable because it reduces uncertainty. Engineers designing airplanes cannot rely on guesses when calculating structural strength. Architects constructing skyscrapers depend upon mathematical laws that consistently produce safe results. Pharmacists calculate medication dosages using carefully tested formulas. In these professions, reliable conclusions are essential because human safety depends upon accurate reasoning. Future AGI systems working alongside professionals in these fields must also learn to apply deductive reasoning carefully and consistently.

However, not every situation provides complete information. Many decisions require people to examine observations and discover broader patterns. This brings us to the second reasoning method: **inductive reasoning**. Inductive reasoning begins with specific observations and gradually develops general conclusions. Instead of starting with rules, it builds new rules by studying repeated experiences. Unlike deductive reasoning, inductive conclusions are not guaranteed to be true. They are based on probability because future observations may reveal exceptions. Nevertheless, inductive reasoning remains one of humanity's most valuable learning tools because it allows knowledge to grow through experience.

Imagine a student notices that every time dark clouds gather, rain usually follows. After observing this pattern repeatedly, the student concludes that dark clouds often indicate approaching rain. This conclusion is reasonable because it is based on repeated observations. However, there may still be occasions when dark clouds appear without rainfall. The conclusion remains useful even though it is not absolutely certain. Scientists rely heavily on inductive reasoning when conducting research. They observe natural events, collect data, identify recurring patterns, and gradually develop scientific theories that explain what they have discovered.

Medical research provides an excellent example of inductive reasoning. Researchers studying thousands of patients may observe that individuals who exercise regularly often experience lower rates of heart disease. After analyzing many observations, scientists conclude that regular physical activity contributes to better cardiovascular health. This conclusion becomes stronger as additional evidence accumulates. Future studies may refine or expand the understanding, but the reasoning process begins with careful observation rather than fixed rules. AGI systems assisting scientific discovery will likely use inductive reasoning to recognize emerging patterns hidden within enormous collections of data.

Education also demonstrates the value of inductive reasoning. Teachers constantly observe how students respond to different instructional methods. They may discover that visual demonstrations improve understanding of certain scientific concepts or that collaborative discussions strengthen reading comprehension. These observations gradually shape better teaching strategies. Rather than relying on assumptions alone, educators use evidence gathered through experience to improve learning outcomes. AGI systems designed to personalize education may someday analyze student progress in similar ways, identifying learning patterns and recommending instructional approaches tailored to each learner's needs.

The third reasoning method is **abductive reasoning**, sometimes called reasoning to the best explanation. Abductive reasoning begins with incomplete information and attempts to identify the most likely explanation based on the available evidence. Unlike deductive reasoning, which guarantees conclusions, or inductive reasoning, which builds generalizations from repeated observations, abductive reasoning focuses on finding the explanation that currently makes the most sense. As new evidence appears, the explanation may change. This flexibility makes abductive reasoning especially valuable in situations where quick decisions must be made despite uncertainty.

Imagine arriving home and finding the front lawn wet. Several explanations are possible. It may have rained while you were away. The sprinkler system may have activated automatically. A neighbor may have watered the grass. A water pipe could have burst underground. Abductive reasoning evaluates the available clues. If nearby sidewalks are dry but the sprinkler timer indicates recent activity, the sprinkler explanation becomes the most likely conclusion. Additional evidence may later confirm or disprove that conclusion. This process illustrates how people reason effectively even when complete information is unavailable.

Doctors use abductive reasoning every day. A patient arrives with a fever, headache, fatigue, and muscle aches. These symptoms could indicate influenza, COVID-19, pneumonia, or several other illnesses. The physician considers medical history, recent travel, laboratory tests, and physical examination findings before selecting the diagnosis that best explains the available evidence. As additional test results become available, the diagnosis may be confirmed or revised. Future AGI systems assisting healthcare professionals must master abductive reasoning because medicine often involves uncertainty, incomplete information, and rapidly changing circumstances.

Detectives solving criminal investigations also depend heavily on abductive reasoning. They gather fingerprints, witness statements, surveillance footage, physical evidence, and timelines. Rarely does one piece of evidence immediately reveal the complete solution. Instead, investigators develop possible explanations, compare them with available facts, eliminate unlikely possibilities, and refine their understanding as new information emerges. The goal is not simply to identify any explanation but to identify the explanation that best fits all available evidence. This reasoning process mirrors the type of flexible thinking AGI researchers hope intelligent systems will eventually perform.

Although these three reasoning methods differ, they rarely operate independently. Human intelligence often combines them within the same problem-solving process. Imagine engineers designing a new electric vehicle. Deductive reasoning ensures that physical laws governing electricity, mechanics, and safety are correctly applied. Inductive reasoning analyzes thousands of test results to identify performance trends and improve efficiency. Abductive reasoning helps engineers investigate unexpected equipment failures by identifying the most likely causes before conducting additional experiments. Together, these reasoning methods create stronger decisions than any one approach could achieve alone.

Artificial General Intelligence will likely depend upon this same combination of reasoning methods. A reasoning system limited to deduction might struggle when encountering unfamiliar situations lacking established rules. A system relying only on induction might recognize patterns but fail to apply universal principles accurately. A system using only abduction might generate plausible explanations without sufficient verification. True intelligence requires selecting the appropriate reasoning strategy for each situation while combining multiple methods whenever necessary. This flexibility allows humans to solve problems across countless professions, environments, and cultures.

One challenge facing AGI researchers involves teaching intelligent systems when to trust each reasoning method. Deductive reasoning works best when reliable rules already exist. Inductive reasoning excels when large amounts of observational data are available. Abductive reasoning becomes valuable when evidence is incomplete but decisions cannot wait. An intelligent physician, engineer, teacher, scientist, or emergency responder naturally shifts between these approaches depending on the circumstances. Future AGI systems must develop similar adaptability if they are to function effectively in the real world.

Reasoning methods also influence creativity. Many people mistakenly believe creativity occurs without structure, yet creative breakthroughs often emerge from combining different reasoning styles. Scientists may observe unexpected experimental results through induction, explain those observations through abduction, and verify discoveries using deduction. Inventors often imagine possible solutions before testing them scientifically. Artists observe the world, interpret experiences, and create original expressions that communicate deeper understanding. Reasoning provides the invisible framework supporting innovation across every field of human achievement.

Ethics also depends upon reasoning. Decisions involving fairness, privacy, safety, environmental responsibility, or human well-being rarely have simple answers. Leaders must evaluate evidence, consider consequences, balance competing priorities, and remain open to revising decisions when circumstances change. Deductive reasoning applies established ethical principles. Inductive reasoning learns from historical outcomes. Abductive reasoning identifies the most responsible course of action when uncertainty remains. Together, these approaches help create thoughtful and compassionate decision-making. As AGI becomes more capable, combining logical accuracy with ethical reasoning will become increasingly important.

Students preparing for the future should recognize that mastering these reasoning methods strengthens every area of learning. Mathematics develops deductive thinking. Science encourages inductive investigation. Literature often explores abductive reasoning as readers interpret characters' motives and predict future events. History asks students to evaluate evidence and explain why civilizations succeeded or declined. Even sports require reasoning as athletes analyze opponents, predict strategies, and adjust tactics during competition. Reasoning is not confined to one classroom subject; it is the foundation of lifelong learning.

As Artificial General Intelligence continues developing, the ability to reason in multiple ways will distinguish advanced intelligent systems from today's specialized AI applications. Rather than simply recognizing patterns, future AGI may apply established rules, discover new principles, generate thoughtful explanations, revise conclusions when evidence changes, and explain its decisions clearly to human partners. These capabilities will allow intelligent systems to contribute meaningfully across medicine, education, engineering, science, business, environmental protection, and many other fields.

Understanding deductive, inductive, and abductive reasoning provides an essential step toward understanding intelligence itself. These reasoning methods demonstrate that thinking is not a single process but a collection of complementary strategies working together. They remind us that true intelligence is flexible, evidence-based, adaptable, and always willing to learn. As you continue exploring the remarkable world of AGI, remember that every intelligent decision begins with choosing the right way to think. By strengthening your own reasoning skills today, you are preparing to thrive alongside the intelligent technologies that will shape tomorrow's world.

Learn AI. Understand AI. Shape the Future.
— Susie Hala, IntelliGloss Press

Chapter 4 Summary

Deductive, Inductive, and Abductive Reasoning

This chapter introduced three of the most important methods of reasoning used by both humans and future Artificial General Intelligence (AGI): deductive reasoning, inductive reasoning, and abductive reasoning. Each method approaches problem-solving differently, yet together they form the foundation of intelligent thinking.

Deductive reasoning begins with general facts or established rules and applies them to reach specific conclusions. When the starting facts are true and the reasoning is correct, the conclusion is also true. This type of reasoning is widely used in mathematics, engineering, computer programming, and other fields where accuracy and consistency are essential.

Inductive reasoning works in the opposite direction. It begins with specific observations and identifies patterns that lead to broader conclusions. Although inductive conclusions are based on probability rather than certainty, they play an important role in scientific research, education, medicine, and many areas where knowledge grows through experience and observation.

Abductive reasoning focuses on finding the most likely explanation when information is incomplete. Doctors diagnosing illnesses, detectives solving investigations, and emergency responders making quick decisions often rely on abductive reasoning because they must evaluate evidence and make informed judgments before every fact is known.

Students also learned that these reasoning methods are not isolated from one another. Most real-world decisions combine all three approaches. Scientists, engineers, educators, business leaders, and future AGI systems regularly shift between deductive, inductive, and abductive reasoning depending on the problem they are trying to solve.

The chapter concluded by emphasizing that strong reasoning is flexible, evidence-based, and open to new information. Mastering these three reasoning methods prepares students to think critically, solve complex problems, and collaborate effectively with future intelligent technologies.

Chapter 4 Reflection

One of the greatest strengths of the human mind is its ability to approach problems from different directions. Sometimes we apply established rules. Sometimes we learn from repeated experiences. Other times we carefully examine limited evidence and choose the explanation that seems most reasonable.

These three approaches—deductive, inductive, and abductive reasoning—allow us to solve problems that no single method could solve alone.

Artificial General Intelligence will likely depend on the same flexibility. Instead of simply memorizing information or recognizing patterns, future intelligent systems must learn when to apply rules, when to search for patterns, and when to evaluate competing explanations under uncertainty.

This chapter also reminds us that good reasoning requires humility. Intelligent people are willing to change their conclusions when better evidence becomes available. They understand that learning never ends and that every new discovery improves our understanding of the world.

As students prepare for careers in the Age of AGI, developing multiple reasoning skills will become increasingly valuable. Whether solving scientific problems, making business decisions, teaching students, designing technology, or improving healthcare, thoughtful reasoning will remain one of humanity's greatest strengths.

The future belongs to those who can think carefully, question wisely, and continue learning throughout their lives.

Chapter 4 Worksheet

Name: ____

Date: ____

Part A – Vocabulary

Write a definition for each term in your own words.

1. Deductive Reasoning

____

____

2. Inductive Reasoning

____

____

3. Abductive Reasoning

4. Observation

5. Conclusion

Part B – Short Answer

1. How does deductive reasoning work?

2. How is inductive reasoning different from deductive reasoning?

3. Why is abductive reasoning useful when information is incomplete?

4. Give one profession that regularly uses deductive reasoning.

5. Why will AGI need all three reasoning methods?

Part C – Identify the Type of Reasoning

Write **Deductive**, **Inductive**, or **Abductive** next to each example.

1. A scientist studies hundreds of experiments before developing a new scientific theory.

2. A doctor reviews symptoms and selects the illness that best explains the evidence.

3. A math teacher applies a proven formula to solve an equation.

4. A detective analyzes clues to determine the most likely suspect.

5. An engineer applies the laws of physics while designing a bridge.

Part D – Critical Thinking

Imagine an AGI system is helping a city prepare for a hurricane.

Explain how the AGI could use each reasoning method.

Deductive Reasoning

Inductive Reasoning

Abductive Reasoning

Which reasoning method do you think would be most important during the emergency? Explain your answer.

Part E – Personal Reflection

Describe a situation where you changed your mind after receiving new information.

Which reasoning method did you use?

Chapter 4 Quiz

Name: ______________________________

Score: _________ /20

Multiple Choice

1. Deductive reasoning begins with

A. A guess

B. General rules or facts

C. Random observations

D. Opinions

2. Inductive reasoning develops conclusions by

A. Starting with general laws

B. Ignoring evidence

C. Studying specific observations

D. Memorizing information

3. Abductive reasoning is used when

A. Every fact is already known.

B. Information is incomplete and the best explanation is needed.

C. Only mathematics is involved.

D. No evidence exists.

4. Which profession frequently uses abductive reasoning?

A. Detective

B. Musician

C. Painter

D. Athlete

5. Why are all three reasoning methods important for AGI?

A. They increase computer memory.

B. They allow intelligent systems to solve many different types of problems.

C. They eliminate uncertainty.

D. They replace human intelligence.

True or False

6. Deductive reasoning always begins with observations.

True / False

7. Inductive reasoning looks for patterns in experience.

True / False

8. Abductive reasoning often works with incomplete information.

True / False

9. Scientists frequently use inductive reasoning.

True / False

10. Future AGI will likely combine multiple reasoning methods.

True / False

Short Answer

11. Explain deductive reasoning in your own words.

12. Why are inductive conclusions not always certain?

13. Give one example of abductive reasoning from everyday life.

14. How do these three reasoning methods work together?

15. What is the most important lesson you learned from this chapter?

Chapter 4 Answer Key

Multiple Choice

1. **B** – General rules or facts
2. **C** – Studying specific observations
3. **B** – Information is incomplete and the best explanation is needed
4. **A** – Detective
5. **B** – They allow intelligent systems to solve many different types of problems.

True or False

6. **False**
7. **True**
8. **True**
9. **True**
10. **True**

Short Answer (Sample Answers)

11. Deductive reasoning begins with accepted facts or rules and applies them to reach a specific conclusion. If the facts and logic are correct, the conclusion will also be correct.

12. Inductive conclusions are based on observations and patterns rather than absolute proof. New evidence may reveal exceptions or require conclusions to be revised.

13. Example: A doctor diagnosing a patient, a detective investigating a crime, or noticing wet streets and concluding that it probably rained.

14. Deductive reasoning applies known rules, inductive reasoning discovers patterns from observations, and abductive reasoning selects the most likely explanation when information is incomplete. Together, they help solve complex problems more effectively.

15. Answers will vary. Students should explain one important concept they learned about the three reasoning methods and how these methods can improve decision-making.

Extension Activity (Optional)

Choose a current event from science, technology, healthcare, or environmental studies. Write one page explaining how deductive, inductive, and abductive reasoning could each be used to analyze the situation and make responsible decisions. Include specific examples of how each reasoning method contributes to a better understanding of the problem.

Chapter 5

Solving Problems Step by Step

Every day, people solve problems without realizing how much thinking is involved. A student figures out how to finish homework before soccer practice. A parent decides the fastest route to work after hearing about heavy traffic. A doctor determines the best treatment for a patient. An engineer designs a bridge that must safely carry thousands of vehicles every day. A scientist searches for a cure to a disease that has challenged researchers for decades. Although these problems are very different, they all share one important characteristic: they are solved step by step. Rarely does a person wake up with the perfect answer to a difficult problem. Instead, successful problem-solvers gather information, understand the situation, divide the challenge into smaller parts, explore different possibilities, test solutions, learn from mistakes, and continue improving until they reach the best possible outcome. This structured process is one of the most important abilities that future Artificial General Intelligence (AGI) systems must develop. Solving problems is not simply about finding answers—it is about thinking through each stage of the journey.

When people first encounter a difficult problem, it often appears overwhelming because they see the entire challenge at once. Imagine being asked to build a new hospital for a growing community. At first glance, the task seems almost impossible. However, experienced planners immediately begin dividing the project into manageable pieces. They identify the location, estimate the budget, design the building, secure permits, hire construction teams, install medical equipment, recruit healthcare professionals, and prepare for patient care. Each step builds upon the one before it. By breaking a large challenge into smaller tasks, the impossible becomes achievable. This strategy is known as **problem decomposition**, and it is one of the most valuable skills in both human reasoning and artificial intelligence.

Problem decomposition is used in nearly every profession. Software developers divide complex computer programs into smaller modules that can be tested independently. Teachers organize an entire school year into individual lessons that gradually build student understanding. Scientists break complicated research projects into carefully designed experiments. Emergency responders divide disaster relief into search and rescue, medical treatment, transportation, communication, and recovery efforts. Future AGI systems will also rely on decomposition because solving large problems directly is often inefficient or impossible. By organizing challenges into logical stages, intelligent systems become more accurate, more adaptable, and easier for humans to understand.

Once a problem has been divided into smaller parts, the next step is defining the actual goal. Surprisingly, many people begin solving problems before clearly identifying what they are trying to achieve. Consider a student struggling in mathematics. One person might assume the goal is simply to improve test scores. Another might discover that the real challenge is understanding fractions, building confidence, or developing better study habits. Solving the wrong problem rarely produces meaningful success. Intelligent reasoning begins by asking an important question: **What is the real objective?** Future AGI systems must learn to identify goals accurately before selecting solutions. Understanding the destination makes it much easier to choose the correct path.

Gathering information is another essential stage of problem-solving. Decisions made without sufficient information often lead to unnecessary mistakes. Imagine a city planning to build a new bridge across a river. Engineers cannot begin construction immediately. They first collect information about soil conditions, river depth, weather patterns, traffic volume, environmental regulations, construction materials, and long-term maintenance requirements. Every piece of information contributes to a better understanding of the challenge. Similarly, future AGI systems must gather reliable information from many different sources before recommending solutions. The quality of a decision depends heavily on the quality of the information supporting it.

After information has been collected, successful problem-solvers begin generating possible solutions. Rarely is there only one correct answer. A teacher helping a struggling student may consider tutoring, different learning materials, small-group instruction, technology-assisted learning, or peer mentoring. A business owner facing declining sales may improve customer service, redesign products, reduce prices, expand advertising, or enter new markets. Creative problem-solving involves exploring multiple possibilities before choosing one. This stage requires imagination as well as logic. AGI systems of the future will need to generate numerous potential solutions, compare their strengths and weaknesses, and recommend the option that best matches the established goals.

Evaluating alternatives is one of the most important parts of intelligent reasoning. Every solution has advantages, disadvantages, costs, risks, and possible consequences. For example, suppose a city wants to reduce traffic congestion. Building additional highways may improve transportation but require significant financial investment and environmental impact. Expanding public transportation may reduce pollution but require years of planning and construction. Encouraging remote work may decrease traffic immediately but may not be suitable for every profession. Intelligent decision-making requires carefully comparing these alternatives before taking action. Future AGI systems must evaluate not only whether a solution works but also how it affects people, resources, safety, fairness, and long-term sustainability.

Prediction plays an equally important role in solving problems. Good decision-makers constantly ask, **What is likely to happen next?** Farmers predict weather conditions before planting crops. Investors estimate future market trends before making financial decisions. Emergency managers forecast hurricane paths before ordering evacuations. Teachers anticipate which concepts students may find difficult before introducing new lessons. Prediction does not guarantee perfect accuracy, but it helps people prepare for possible outcomes. AGI systems are expected to improve predictive reasoning by analyzing enormous amounts of information while continuously updating predictions as new evidence becomes available.

One of the greatest strengths of human intelligence is the willingness to test ideas before fully committing to them. Engineers build prototypes before manufacturing products. Scientists perform experiments before announcing discoveries. Software developers release trial versions before launching complete applications. Teachers introduce new instructional strategies and observe student responses before expanding their use. Testing allows mistakes to be discovered early when they are easier and less expensive to correct. Future AGI systems must adopt similar strategies by simulating possible outcomes, evaluating different scenarios, and identifying weaknesses before implementing recommendations in the real world.

Mistakes are often misunderstood as failures, but in reality they are powerful learning opportunities. Throughout history, many important discoveries resulted from experiments that did not produce the expected results. Scientists learned valuable information from unsuccessful research. Inventors improved designs after identifying weaknesses. Athletes refined techniques after losing competitions. Students strengthened understanding after correcting errors on assignments. Intelligent reasoning treats mistakes as valuable feedback rather than permanent defeat. Future AGI systems must learn from unsuccessful decisions by updating knowledge, improving strategies, and avoiding repeated errors. Continuous improvement transforms experience into wisdom.

Flexibility is another essential characteristic of effective problem-solving. Real-world situations rarely remain unchanged. A business strategy that succeeds today may become outdated next year. Medical recommendations evolve as new research becomes available. Emergency conditions change rapidly during natural disasters. Successful leaders adjust their decisions as circumstances change rather than stubbornly following outdated plans. AGI systems must demonstrate similar flexibility by monitoring changing conditions, recognizing when previous solutions no longer work, and adapting accordingly. Intelligent systems that cannot adjust to new information quickly become less useful.

Collaboration greatly strengthens problem-solving. Few major achievements result from one individual working alone. Building spacecraft, developing life-saving medicines, constructing transportation systems, improving schools, and responding to emergencies all require teams of people contributing different skills and perspectives. Collaboration allows individuals to examine problems from multiple viewpoints, identify overlooked risks, and generate more creative solutions. Future AGI systems are expected to become collaborative partners rather than independent decision-makers. Instead of replacing human expertise, AGI may assist doctors, teachers, engineers, scientists, and business leaders by providing additional analysis while leaving final decisions under human supervision.

Communication is closely connected to successful problem-solving. A brilliant solution provides little value if it cannot be clearly explained. Doctors must communicate treatment plans to patients. Engineers explain safety recommendations to construction teams. Teachers describe difficult concepts in ways students understand. Scientists publish research so others can verify discoveries and build upon them. Future AGI systems should communicate reasoning transparently by explaining how conclusions were reached, what evidence was considered, what uncertainties remain, and why certain recommendations were selected over others. Explainable reasoning builds trust between humans and intelligent systems.

Ethical thinking must also remain part of every problem-solving process. Sometimes a solution that appears efficient may not be fair or responsible. Imagine an AGI helping distribute emergency supplies after a major earthquake. Delivering resources only to easily accessible areas might maximize speed but neglect communities with the greatest need. Ethical reasoning requires balancing efficiency with compassion, fairness, and human dignity. Future AGI systems must evaluate not only whether a solution is technically effective but also whether it respects human values and promotes the well-being of society.

Complex problems often require long-term thinking rather than immediate solutions. Climate change, public health, education reform, scientific research, and economic development involve decisions whose effects may not become visible for years or even decades. Intelligent problem-solvers consider both short-term benefits and long-term consequences. Planting a tree today may provide shade decades later. Investing in education strengthens future generations. Scientific research conducted today may produce medical breakthroughs many years from now. AGI systems designed to support governments, researchers, educators, and business leaders must learn to balance immediate needs with future opportunities.

One of the greatest challenges facing future AGI involves solving problems that have never been encountered before. Human history demonstrates remarkable creativity when confronting unfamiliar situations. New diseases, environmental changes, technological revolutions, and scientific mysteries require original thinking rather than repeating previous solutions. This ability to adapt knowledge creatively is one of the defining characteristics of general intelligence. AGI researchers hope to develop systems capable of transferring knowledge from one field to another, allowing intelligent machines to solve entirely new classes of problems rather than depending solely on prior experience.

Students preparing for careers in the future should recognize that problem-solving is one of the most valuable skills they can develop. Memorizing information remains useful, but employers increasingly seek individuals who can analyze situations, identify challenges, organize information, evaluate alternatives, communicate effectively, collaborate with others, and continue learning throughout their careers. These abilities apply equally to medicine, education, engineering, science, business, law, agriculture, technology, and countless other professions. As intelligent technologies become more capable, human problem-solving skills will become even more valuable because people will guide, supervise, question, and improve the work of advanced AI systems.

Artificial General Intelligence represents far more than faster computers or larger collections of information. At its heart, AGI seeks to create systems capable of solving problems thoughtfully, responsibly, and collaboratively. Every successful solution begins by understanding the challenge, dividing it into manageable parts, gathering reliable information, exploring alternatives, testing ideas, learning from experience, adapting to change, communicating clearly, and considering ethical responsibilities. These steps transform confusion into clarity and uncertainty into informed action.

As you continue your journey through this book, remember that every great achievement in human history began as a difficult problem waiting to be solved. From curing diseases to exploring space, from building civilizations to advancing scientific knowledge, progress has always depended on people willing to think carefully, ask meaningful questions, and work patiently through each step of the problem-solving process. The same principles will guide the future development of AGI. By strengthening your own ability to solve problems step by step, you are not only preparing to understand intelligent machines—you are preparing to become a thoughtful problem-solver who can help shape a better future for humanity.

Learn AI. Understand AI. Shape the Future.
— Susie Hala, IntelliGloss Press

Chapter 5 Summary

Solving Problems Step by Step

This chapter explained that successful problem-solving is not about finding quick answers—it is about following a thoughtful process that leads to the best possible solution. Whether solving a simple classroom assignment or addressing a global challenge, intelligent reasoning works one step at a time.

Students learned that the first step in solving any problem is understanding the challenge and clearly defining the goal. Large problems become much easier to solve when they are divided into smaller, manageable parts through a process called **problem decomposition**.

The chapter also introduced several important stages of effective problem-solving, including gathering reliable information, generating multiple possible solutions, comparing alternatives, predicting outcomes, testing ideas, learning from mistakes, and adapting when new information becomes available.

Students discovered that mistakes are not failures but opportunities to improve future decisions. Human intelligence grows through experience, reflection, and continuous learning, and future AGI systems are expected to improve in similar ways.

Another important lesson was that communication and collaboration strengthen problem-solving. People working together often discover better solutions than individuals working alone because they contribute different perspectives, knowledge, and experiences.

Finally, the chapter emphasized that ethical thinking must always remain part of intelligent decision-making. The best solution is not simply the fastest or easiest one—it is the solution that is responsible, fair, safe, and beneficial to society.

By understanding each stage of the problem-solving process, students are building skills that will help them succeed in school, future careers, and the rapidly evolving world of Artificial General Intelligence.

Chapter 5 Reflection

Every important achievement in history began as a problem waiting to be solved.

People built bridges because rivers separated communities.

Scientists developed medicines because diseases threatened lives.

Engineers created airplanes because people dreamed of flying.

Teachers developed new ways of learning because every student deserves the opportunity to succeed.

None of these accomplishments happened overnight. They required patience, careful planning, teamwork, creativity, and a willingness to learn from mistakes.

This chapter reminds us that intelligent problem-solving is a process. It begins by asking the right questions, collecting reliable information, considering different possibilities, and making thoughtful decisions based on evidence rather than emotion or guesswork.

Artificial General Intelligence will one day assist people in solving some of humanity's most difficult challenges. However, the responsibility for guiding these intelligent systems will remain with people who know how to reason carefully and ethically.

Every problem you solve strengthens your mind.

Every mistake teaches a valuable lesson.

Every thoughtful decision prepares you to become a leader in the Age of AGI.

Chapter 5 Worksheet

Name: ______________________________

Date: ______________________________

Part A – Vocabulary

Write a definition for each term in your own words.

1. Problem Decomposition

____

____

2. Goal

____

____

3. Alternative Solution

____

____

4. Prediction

____

____

5. Collaboration

____

____

6. Ethical Decision-Making

____

____

____

Part B – Short Answer

1. Why is it important to define the real problem before trying to solve it?

____

____

2. Explain what problem decomposition means.

3. Why should intelligent systems consider more than one possible solution?

4. How can mistakes improve future decision-making?

5. Why is collaboration valuable during problem-solving?

Part C – Problem-Solving Activity

Your school wants to reduce food waste in the cafeteria.

Complete the following problem-solving steps.

Step 1 – Define the Problem

Step 2 – Gather Information

List at least four types of information you would collect.

1.
2.
3.
4.

Step 3 – Brainstorm Solutions

List three possible solutions.

1.
2.
3.

Step 4 – Choose the Best Solution

Explain why you selected this solution.

Step 5 – Evaluate Results

How would you know if your solution worked?

Part D – Critical Thinking

Imagine an AGI system is helping a hospital prepare for a future disease outbreak.

Describe how the AGI should use each of these steps.

- Understand the problem

- Gather information

- Compare possible solutions

- Predict future outcomes

- Learn from mistakes

- Consider ethical responsibilities

Part E – Personal Reflection

Think about a difficult challenge you recently solved.

Describe each step you used to solve the problem.

____

____

____

____

____

Chapter 5 Quiz

Name: ___________________________________

Score: _________ /20

Multiple Choice

1. What is the first step in solving a problem?

A. Guess the answer

B. Clearly define the problem

C. Ignore the information

D. Choose the easiest solution

2. Problem decomposition means

A. Making a problem more difficult

B. Breaking a large problem into smaller parts

C. Memorizing information

D. Avoiding difficult work

3. Why should we compare different solutions?

A. To waste time

B. To find the best possible option

C. Because every solution is identical

D. To avoid making decisions

4. Why are mistakes valuable?

A. They should always be avoided.

B. They help us learn and improve.

C. They prove failure.

D. They stop progress.

5. Ethical decision-making focuses on

A. Speed only

B. Fairness, responsibility, and human well-being

C. Saving money only

D. Avoiding teamwork

True or False

6. Every large problem should be solved all at once.

True / False

7. Gathering reliable information improves decision-making.

True / False

8. Good problem-solvers consider multiple solutions.

True / False

9. Collaboration often produces stronger solutions.

True / False

10. AGI will likely use structured problem-solving processes.

True / False

Short Answer

11. Why is defining the problem important?

---

12. Explain problem decomposition.

---

13. Why should intelligent systems predict future outcomes?

---

14. How can communication improve problem-solving?

---

15. Name one important lesson you learned from this chapter.

Chapter 5 Answer Key

Multiple Choice

1. **B** – Clearly define the problem.

2. **B** – Breaking a large problem into smaller parts.
3. **B** – To find the best possible option.
4. **B** – They help us learn and improve.
5. **B** – Fairness, responsibility, and human well-being.

True or False

6. **False**
7. **True**
8. **True**
9. **True**
10. **True**

Short Answer (Sample Answers)

11. Clearly defining the problem ensures that time and effort are focused on solving the correct challenge instead of addressing the wrong issue.

12. Problem decomposition is the process of breaking a large or complex problem into smaller, easier-to-manage tasks that can be solved step by step.

13. Predicting future outcomes helps intelligent systems evaluate risks, prepare for possible consequences, and choose solutions that provide the greatest long-term benefit.

14. Communication allows people to share ideas, explain reasoning, coordinate teamwork, clarify goals, and build trust among everyone working on the problem.

15. Answers will vary. Students should describe one key concept from the chapter, such as defining problems clearly, learning from mistakes, collaborating with others, or making ethical decisions.

Extension Activity (Optional)

Choose a real-world problem facing your school or community, such as reducing litter, improving attendance, increasing recycling, conserving water, or enhancing school safety. Create a step-by-step problem-solving plan using the process introduced in this chapter. Explain how both humans and a future AGI system could work together to solve the problem responsibly and effectively.

Chapter 6

Understanding Cause and Effect

Every event that happens in our world has a story behind it. A tree grows because it receives sunlight, water, nutrients, and time. A bridge stands because engineers carefully designed it using strong materials and sound scientific principles. A student earns higher grades because of consistent study, practice, and determination. Even the most advanced technology exists because thousands of discoveries were made over many years. Nothing simply happens without a reason. Understanding why events occur is one of the most valuable thinking skills humans possess. This ability is known as understanding **cause and effect**, and it plays a central role in reasoning intelligence. If Artificial General Intelligence (AGI) is expected to think, solve problems, and make responsible decisions, it must move beyond recognizing patterns and begin understanding why events happen, how actions create consequences, and what effects today's decisions may have on tomorrow's world.

Human beings begin learning cause and effect early in life. A child touches a hot stove and learns that heat can cause pain. A student studies regularly and notices improved grades. An athlete practices every day and develops greater strength and skill. These experiences teach that actions produce results. Over time, people build an internal understanding of how the world works. This understanding helps them predict future events, avoid unnecessary risks, and make better decisions. Cause-and-effect reasoning allows people not only to explain the past but also to prepare for the future. Researchers developing AGI hope to create systems that develop similar understanding by connecting actions with outcomes rather than simply storing information.

It is important to recognize that cause and effect is different from simple pattern recognition. Imagine noticing that many people carry umbrellas on rainy days. Pattern recognition identifies the repeated association between rain and umbrellas. However, reasoning asks a deeper question: **Why are people carrying umbrellas?** The answer is that rain causes people to seek protection from getting wet. Understanding this causal relationship is far more useful than simply observing that umbrellas often appear when it rains. If an intelligent system understands cause and effect, it can apply this knowledge even in unfamiliar situations. It can recommend raincoats, suggest delaying outdoor activities, or predict increased traffic because it understands the underlying relationships rather than only recognizing repeated patterns.

One of the greatest challenges in reasoning is distinguishing between **correlation** and **causation**. These two concepts are often confused, yet they are very different. Correlation means that two events happen together or appear related. Causation means that one event directly produces another. For example, ice cream sales and swimming pool attendance often increase during the summer. These events are correlated because they occur during the same season. However, buying ice cream does not cause people to go swimming, nor does swimming cause people to purchase ice cream. Both activities increase because warm weather encourages outdoor recreation. Understanding this distinction prevents incorrect conclusions and improves decision-making. Future AGI systems must carefully analyze whether observed relationships truly represent cause and effect or merely happen at the same time.

Scientists spend much of their careers searching for causal relationships. Medical researchers investigate whether certain viruses cause diseases. Environmental scientists study how pollution affects ecosystems. Agricultural researchers examine how different fertilizers influence crop growth. Physicists explore how forces interact to produce motion. Every scientific experiment seeks to answer the same basic question: **What causes this outcome?** Controlled experiments allow researchers to isolate individual factors while keeping other conditions constant. By changing one variable at a time, scientists can identify genuine cause-and-effect relationships instead of relying on assumptions. Future AGI systems supporting scientific research will likely assist in analyzing enormous amounts of experimental data while helping researchers identify previously unknown causal connections.

Healthcare provides one of the clearest examples of why understanding cause and effect matters. A patient visits a doctor complaining of headaches, fatigue, and dizziness. These symptoms may result from dehydration, illness, stress, medication side effects, nutritional deficiencies, or many other causes. Simply recognizing symptom patterns is helpful, but effective treatment depends upon identifying the actual cause. Treating symptoms without understanding their origin may provide temporary relief while allowing the underlying condition to worsen. Physicians therefore gather medical histories, perform physical examinations, order laboratory tests, and analyze evidence before recommending treatment. AGI systems assisting healthcare professionals must reason about causes rather than merely matching symptoms to diseases if they are to become trusted partners in medicine.

Education also depends heavily on cause-and-effect reasoning. Suppose a teacher notices declining student performance in mathematics. Several possible causes exist. Students may need additional practice. The lessons may move too quickly. Attendance may have declined. Classroom distractions may interfere with concentration. Some students may lack prerequisite knowledge from earlier grades. Rather than assuming one explanation, thoughtful educators investigate multiple possibilities before deciding how to help students improve. By identifying the true causes of learning difficulties, teachers can develop targeted solutions that address the root of the problem instead of treating only its visible effects. Future AGI tutoring systems may assist educators by identifying learning patterns and suggesting instructional strategies based on evidence rather than assumptions.

Business leaders also rely on understanding cause and effect. A company notices declining sales over several months. The decrease could result from changing customer preferences, stronger competition, economic conditions, pricing decisions, product quality, advertising effectiveness, or many other factors. Successful business leaders investigate these possibilities before making major decisions. Reducing prices may increase sales if cost is the primary concern, but if customers are dissatisfied with product quality, lower prices alone may not solve the problem. Identifying the true cause allows businesses to allocate resources more effectively and improve long-term success. AGI systems supporting business decisions will need similar reasoning abilities to analyze multiple factors influencing organizational performance.

Environmental science demonstrates how countless causes interact simultaneously. Climate change, for example, involves relationships among greenhouse gas emissions, energy production, transportation, agriculture, forests, oceans, weather patterns, and human behavior. No single cause explains every environmental change. Instead, many interconnected factors influence one another over long periods. Understanding these complex systems requires analyzing vast amounts of information while recognizing how small changes in one area may produce significant effects elsewhere. Future AGI systems may help scientists model these interactions more accurately, allowing governments and communities to make better environmental decisions.

One important concept in reasoning intelligence is recognizing that **one cause can produce many effects**, and **one effect can result from many different causes**. Consider heavy rainfall. Rain may replenish water supplies, improve agricultural production, increase river levels, reduce wildfire risk, and create flooding if excessive. One event produces multiple outcomes depending on local conditions. Similarly, a student arriving late to school may have experienced traffic delays, transportation problems, illness, family emergencies, or oversleeping. Intelligent reasoning requires examining several possible causes before reaching conclusions. This flexibility prevents oversimplified thinking and encourages careful investigation.

Feedback loops add another layer of complexity to cause-and-effect reasoning. A feedback loop occurs when the effects of an action influence future actions. Imagine a student who studies consistently and earns higher grades. Improved grades increase confidence, leading the student to study even more effectively. This positive cycle strengthens learning over time. Negative feedback loops also exist. A person experiencing chronic stress may sleep poorly, reducing concentration and increasing additional stress the following day. Understanding these cycles allows people to intervene before small problems become larger ones. Future AGI systems designed to improve healthcare, education, transportation, or environmental management will need to recognize these ongoing feedback relationships.

Prediction depends directly on understanding cause and effect. Weather forecasting combines knowledge of atmospheric pressure, temperature, humidity, wind patterns, and historical observations to predict future conditions. Engineers predict how buildings will respond to earthquakes by understanding physical forces. Financial analysts estimate economic trends by examining employment, production, inflation, and consumer behavior. Parents predict how consistent encouragement influences children's confidence. Prediction is never perfect because many factors remain uncertain, but understanding causal relationships significantly improves the quality of forecasts. AGI systems may eventually analyze far more information than humans alone, allowing more accurate predictions across many different fields.

Another valuable reasoning skill involves identifying **root causes** rather than treating symptoms. Imagine a manufacturing company experiencing frequent equipment failures. Replacing broken parts each week solves the immediate problem but does not prevent future breakdowns. Engineers investigate deeper and discover inadequate maintenance procedures causing excessive wear. By correcting the maintenance process, they eliminate the underlying cause rather than repeatedly addressing the visible symptoms. The same principle applies to education, healthcare, cybersecurity, transportation, and environmental protection. Solving root causes creates lasting improvement. Future AGI systems must learn to distinguish between symptoms and underlying causes if they are to provide meaningful assistance.

Ethical decision-making also depends upon understanding consequences. Every action creates effects extending beyond the immediate moment. Introducing new technology may improve productivity while affecting employment opportunities. Expanding transportation networks may improve mobility while influencing environmental conditions. Medical treatments may provide tremendous benefits while producing possible side effects. Responsible reasoning considers both intended and unintended consequences before taking action. Future AGI systems should evaluate how recommendations affect individuals, families, communities, businesses, and future generations. Ethical intelligence requires thinking beyond immediate results to consider the broader impact of every decision.

History offers countless lessons about cause and effect. Economic changes influence political decisions. Scientific discoveries transform industries. Educational improvements strengthen societies. Public health measures increase life expectancy. Wars reshape national boundaries. Every historical event grows from chains of causes stretching across years or even centuries. Studying history teaches students that important events rarely have single explanations. Instead, multiple social, economic, cultural, scientific, and political factors combine to create change. AGI systems analyzing historical information may help researchers identify long-term patterns and improve understanding of how complex societies evolve.

Artificial General Intelligence will require much deeper understanding than today's AI systems because real-world problems rarely have simple causes. Medical conditions involve genetics, lifestyle, environment, and biology. Educational success depends upon teaching methods, family support, motivation, resources, and individual learning styles. Transportation systems involve engineering, economics, weather, human behavior, and government policy. AGI must reason across these interconnected systems while recognizing uncertainty, adapting to new evidence, and explaining its conclusions clearly. Understanding cause and effect provides the foundation for this advanced reasoning ability.

Students entering the future workforce will increasingly collaborate with intelligent technologies capable of analyzing enormous amounts of information. However, technology alone cannot replace thoughtful human judgment. People must continue asking meaningful questions, evaluating evidence carefully, considering long-term consequences, and making ethical decisions. Understanding cause and effect strengthens critical thinking, improves problem-solving, and prepares students to lead responsibly in a rapidly changing world.

As you continue learning about reasoning intelligence, remember that every discovery begins by asking one simple question: **Why?** Why do things happen? Why do people make certain decisions? Why do systems succeed or fail? Why do small changes sometimes produce enormous consequences? The search for these answers has driven every major scientific breakthrough, medical advancement, engineering achievement, and technological innovation throughout history. Artificial General Intelligence will continue that journey by helping humanity understand not only what happens, but why it happens. The better we understand cause and effect, the better prepared we become to solve today's challenges and create a brighter future for generations to come.

Chapter 6 Summary

Understanding Cause and Effect

This chapter explored one of the most important abilities of reasoning intelligence: understanding cause and effect. Students learned that intelligent thinking goes beyond recognizing patterns by asking why events happen and how one action leads to another.

The chapter explained that cause and effect help humans and future Artificial General Intelligence (AGI) systems understand relationships between actions and outcomes. This ability allows intelligent systems to predict future events, solve problems more effectively, and make responsible decisions based on evidence rather than assumptions.

Students also learned the important difference between **correlation** and **causation**. Correlation means that two events happen together, while causation means that one event directly causes another. Understanding this distinction prevents incorrect conclusions and leads to better reasoning.

The chapter demonstrated how cause-and-effect reasoning is used in medicine, education, engineering, business, environmental science, and many other fields. Professionals must identify root causes rather than simply treating symptoms if they want to create lasting solutions.

Another major concept introduced was the idea that one cause can produce many effects, and one effect can have many possible causes. This complexity requires careful investigation, thoughtful analysis, and the willingness to consider multiple explanations before making decisions.

Students also explored feedback loops, prediction, root-cause analysis, and ethical decision-making. These concepts help both humans and future AGI systems evaluate long-term consequences and improve future outcomes.

The chapter concluded by emphasizing that understanding cause and effect is one of the foundations of reasoning intelligence. It allows people and intelligent systems to explain the past, improve the present, and prepare wisely for the future.

Chapter 6 Reflection

One simple question has driven human progress throughout history:

Why?

Why do storms form?

Why do diseases spread?

Why do bridges stand?

Why do students succeed?

Every scientific discovery, medical breakthrough, engineering achievement, and technological innovation began because someone wanted to understand the causes behind what they observed.

This chapter reminds us that intelligence is not measured by how many facts we know but by how well we understand the relationships between those facts. People who understand cause and effect make better decisions because they look beyond the surface of a problem and search for its true source.

Artificial General Intelligence will also need this ability. Future intelligent systems must understand not only what is happening but also why it is happening and what consequences may result from every decision.

As future leaders, students should develop the habit of asking thoughtful questions, gathering evidence, and thinking carefully before reaching conclusions. These habits strengthen reasoning, improve decision-making, and prepare us to work responsibly with advanced AI technologies.

When we understand causes, we gain the power to create better effects—for ourselves, our communities, and future generations.

Chapter 6 Worksheet

Name: ______________________________

Date: ______________________________

Part A – Vocabulary

Write your own definition for each term.

1. Cause

____

____

2. Effect

____

3. Correlation

4. Causation

5. Root Cause

6. Feedback Loop

Part B – Short Answer

1. What is the difference between cause and effect?

2. Explain the difference between correlation and causation.

3. Why is identifying the root cause important?

4. How does understanding cause and effect improve decision-making?

5. Why will AGI need to understand cause-and-effect relationships?

Part C – Cause and Effect Activity

Read each situation and identify one possible cause and one possible effect.

Situation 1: A student's grades improve after attending tutoring sessions.

Cause:

Effect:

Situation 2: A city plants thousands of new trees.

Cause:

Effect:

Situation 3: A hospital introduces a new safety procedure.

Cause:

Effect:

Part D – Critical Thinking

Imagine an AGI system is helping scientists reduce air pollution.

Describe how understanding cause and effect could help the AGI:

• Identify pollution sources

• Predict future environmental changes

• Recommend effective solutions

• Evaluate long-term consequences

• Improve future decisions

Part E – Personal Reflection

Think about a goal you achieved.

What actions helped you succeed?

What cause-and-effect relationships can you identify?

Chapter 6 Quiz

Name: ________________________________

Score: _________ /20

Multiple Choice

1. Cause and effect help us understand

A. Random events only

B. Why events happen and what results they produce

C. Computer speed

D. Internet connections

2. Correlation means

A. One event directly causes another

B. Two events occur together but may not have a direct causal relationship

C. Every observation is correct

D. Two events are always unrelated

3. Root-cause analysis helps people

A. Ignore problems

B. Find the underlying reason for a problem

C. Memorize facts

D. Eliminate evidence

4. Which profession regularly uses cause-and-effect reasoning?

A. Doctor

B. Engineer

C. Scientist

D. All of the above

5. Why is understanding cause and effect important for AGI?

A. It helps intelligent systems reason, predict outcomes, and make better decisions.

B. It increases computer memory.

C. It replaces human judgment.

D. It eliminates uncertainty.

True or False

6. Every correlation is also a causation.

True / False

7. Cause-and-effect reasoning helps identify root causes.

True / False

8. One cause can produce several different effects.

True / False

9. Future AGI systems will need to evaluate consequences before making recommendations.

True / False

10. Ethical reasoning includes considering the long-term effects of decisions.

True / False

Short Answer

11. Explain the difference between correlation and causation.

---

12. Why is root-cause analysis valuable?

13. Give one example of a feedback loop.

14. How does prediction depend on understanding cause and effect?

15. What is the most important lesson you learned from this chapter?

Chapter 6 Answer Key

Multiple Choice

1. **B** – Why events happen and what results they produce.
2. **B** – Two events occur together but may not have a direct causal relationship.
3. **B** – Find the underlying reason for a problem.
4. **D** – All of the above.
5. **A** – It helps intelligent systems reason, predict outcomes, and make better decisions.

True or False

6. **False**
7. **True**
8. **True**
9. **True**
10. **True**

Short Answer (Sample Answers)

11. Correlation means two events happen together, while causation means one event directly produces another. Correlated events are not always cause-and-effect relationships.

12. Root-cause analysis helps solve the actual source of a problem instead of only treating its symptoms. This leads to more effective and long-lasting solutions.

13. Example: A student studies more, earns higher grades, gains confidence, and becomes even more motivated to study. Another example is exercise improving fitness, which encourages continued exercise.

14. Prediction depends on understanding how present actions influence future outcomes. By recognizing cause-and-effect relationships, intelligent systems can estimate likely consequences and recommend better decisions.

15. Answers will vary. Students should explain one key concept they learned, such as distinguishing correlation from causation, identifying root causes, understanding feedback loops, or recognizing how cause-and-effect reasoning improves intelligent decision-making.

Extension Activity (Optional)

Choose a real-world issue such as traffic congestion, water conservation, school attendance, public health, or recycling. Create a cause-and-effect diagram that identifies at least five possible causes, five possible effects, and three practical solutions. Explain how a future AGI system could analyze these relationships to help people make better decisions while considering ethical responsibilities and long-term outcomes.

Chapter 7

Learning Through Experience

Imagine trying to learn how to ride a bicycle by reading only a book. You could study every diagram, memorize every instruction, and understand every scientific explanation about balance and motion. Yet the first time you climb onto the bicycle, you quickly discover that reading alone is not enough. Real learning begins when you pedal, wobble, lose your balance, adjust your movements, and try again. Every attempt teaches your brain something new. Eventually, balancing becomes almost automatic because your mind has learned from experience. This simple example illustrates one of the most remarkable abilities of human intelligence. We do not simply collect information—we improve through experience. Every success teaches us what works, and every mistake teaches us what needs to change. This ability to learn continuously is one of the defining characteristics of intelligence and one of the greatest goals of Artificial

General Intelligence (AGI). For future intelligent systems to think, reason, and adapt like humans, they must do more than store information. They must learn from experience.

Human learning begins long before formal education starts. Babies learn to recognize familiar faces, understand language, crawl, walk, and communicate by interacting with the world around them. None of these skills develop perfectly on the first attempt. Instead, the brain constantly observes outcomes, compares them with expectations, makes adjustments, and improves future performance. This cycle continues throughout life. Students become better readers by reading regularly. Musicians improve through daily practice. Athletes strengthen their abilities through repetition and coaching. Scientists refine theories through experimentation. Business leaders improve by learning from successes and setbacks. Experience transforms knowledge into wisdom because it connects information with real-world results.

Artificial intelligence has already demonstrated impressive learning abilities in specialized areas. Modern AI systems improve their performance by analyzing enormous amounts of data during training. Image recognition systems become more accurate after studying millions of photographs. Language models improve by processing large collections of books, articles, and conversations. Recommendation systems learn user preferences by analyzing previous choices. Although these achievements are remarkable, most current AI systems complete their learning during the training process and perform relatively fixed tasks afterward. Artificial General Intelligence seeks something much broader. Researchers envision intelligent systems that continue learning throughout their operational lives, constantly improving as they encounter new experiences, just as humans do.

One of the most powerful ways humans learn is through **feedback**. Feedback provides information about the results of an action. Imagine a student solving a mathematics problem incorrectly. A teacher explains the mistake and demonstrates the correct method. The student then applies this feedback to future problems, gradually improving understanding. Feedback appears in every area of life. Coaches review athletic performance. Music instructors correct finger placement. Driving instructors explain safer techniques. Managers evaluate employee performance. Friends offer advice during difficult situations. Constructive feedback allows people to identify weaknesses while building stronger skills over time. Future AGI systems will also require feedback mechanisms that help them evaluate decisions, recognize errors, and improve future reasoning.

Not all feedback comes from other people. Individuals constantly generate **self-feedback** through reflection. After completing an important project, a person may ask, "What worked well? What mistakes did I make? What should I do differently next time?" Reflection transforms ordinary experiences into valuable lessons. Without reflection, people often repeat the same mistakes because they fail to examine why previous decisions succeeded or failed. Reflection encourages thoughtful learning by connecting actions with outcomes. Researchers developing AGI believe that intelligent systems may also require internal evaluation processes that review previous decisions, identify strengths and weaknesses, and adjust future reasoning accordingly.

One of the greatest teachers is **trial and error**. Although mistakes often feel discouraging, they provide valuable information about what does not work. Thomas Edison reportedly tested thousands of materials before developing a practical electric light bulb. Each unsuccessful attempt eliminated one possibility while bringing him closer to success. Scientific research follows the same principle. Experiments rarely produce perfect results immediately. Instead, researchers revise methods, improve equipment, collect additional evidence, and continue testing until stronger conclusions emerge. Future AGI systems must learn that unsuccessful outcomes are not simply failures but opportunities to improve future performance.

Learning through experience also requires recognizing **patterns across time**. A single experience may not provide enough information to support meaningful conclusions. Suppose a student studies one evening before an examination and earns a high score. Was the success caused by studying that evening, prior preparation over several weeks, previous classroom participation, or perhaps the difficulty level of the test itself? One experience rarely answers every question. However, repeated experiences gradually reveal reliable patterns. Students who consistently practice reading often improve comprehension. Athletes who maintain regular training usually perform better during competitions. Healthy eating and regular exercise generally improve physical well-being over time. Experience becomes increasingly valuable as repeated observations strengthen understanding.

Adaptation represents another essential part of learning. Imagine a soccer player competing against a stronger opponent. During the first half of the game, certain strategies prove ineffective. Instead of repeating unsuccessful tactics, the player adjusts positioning, passing techniques, or defensive strategies during the second half. Adaptation means changing behavior in response to experience. Successful learners remain flexible because they recognize that different situations require different solutions. Future AGI systems must demonstrate similar adaptability by modifying reasoning strategies whenever new evidence indicates that previous approaches no longer produce the best results.

Experience also teaches the importance of **context**. A solution that works well in one environment may fail completely in another. Consider a teacher who develops an engaging science lesson for one classroom. Another classroom with different student backgrounds, learning styles, or available resources may require significant modifications. Skilled educators recognize these differences and adapt instruction accordingly. Human intelligence continuously adjusts knowledge based on context. Future AGI systems must avoid applying identical solutions blindly across every situation. Instead, they should evaluate surrounding conditions before determining how previous experiences apply to current challenges.

Learning often accelerates through **collaboration**. Human beings rarely develop knowledge entirely alone. Students learn from teachers, classmates, parents, mentors, books, and shared experiences. Scientists publish discoveries so researchers worldwide can build upon previous work. Engineers improve designs by exchanging ideas with colleagues. Medical professionals discuss difficult cases to gain new perspectives. Collaboration allows individuals to benefit from experiences they have never personally encountered. AGI systems may eventually collaborate with humans and with other intelligent systems, sharing knowledge to solve increasingly complex problems more efficiently.

One fascinating aspect of human learning is the ability to transfer knowledge across different situations. This process is called **transfer learning**. A person who learns to play the piano often develops stronger hand coordination useful in other activities. A student who understands mathematical logic may apply similar reasoning to computer programming. A scientist trained in biology may contribute valuable ideas to environmental research. Transfer learning allows knowledge gained in one field to support progress in another. Current AI systems can perform limited forms of transfer learning, but future AGI aims to expand this ability dramatically. Intelligent systems capable of applying previous experiences across many different domains will become much more flexible and useful than today's specialized AI.

Emotions also influence human learning. Excitement often increases curiosity and motivation. Fear may encourage caution during dangerous situations. Frustration sometimes signals the need for a different strategy. Confidence grows as experience confirms successful performance. Although AGI may not experience emotions exactly as humans do, future intelligent systems may benefit from computational equivalents that prioritize learning, identify uncertainty, evaluate confidence levels, and adjust behavior accordingly. Understanding how emotional factors influence decision-making may help AGI collaborate more naturally with human users.

Memory plays an essential role in learning through experience. Every experience leaves traces that influence future behavior. When children learn that touching fire causes burns, they remember the experience and avoid repeating it. When doctors successfully treat rare diseases, they remember effective procedures for future patients. Pilots remember emergency training during unexpected situations. Experience becomes valuable because memory preserves previous lessons. Future AGI systems will require advanced memory structures capable of storing not only facts but also successful strategies, unsuccessful attempts, explanations, confidence levels, and contextual details. This rich memory allows intelligent reasoning to improve over time.

Learning also depends upon recognizing **uncertainty**. Human beings rarely know everything about a situation. Instead of pretending certainty exists, effective learners remain open to new information. Scientists revise theories when better evidence appears. Businesses adjust strategies as markets change. Teachers modify instruction after observing student progress. This willingness to change reflects intellectual maturity. AGI systems must demonstrate similar openness by updating knowledge whenever additional evidence becomes available. Intelligent learning requires continuous revision rather than rigid certainty.

One of the greatest challenges facing AGI research is creating systems capable of **lifelong learning**. Humans continue learning from infancy through old age. Every conversation, book, observation, experiment, and experience adds new understanding. Lifelong learning allows people to adapt to changing careers, technologies, cultures, and environments. Future AGI systems should similarly continue learning after deployment rather than remaining limited to their original training. This ongoing development may allow intelligent systems to improve continuously while responding effectively to new challenges that did not exist during their initial creation.

Ethics must also guide learning. Intelligence becomes more valuable when experience strengthens fairness, responsibility, honesty, and respect for others. Imagine an AGI system assisting teachers in recommending learning materials. If the system learns from biased information without careful oversight, it may unintentionally reinforce unfair educational opportunities. Responsible learning requires evaluating not only whether conclusions improve performance but also whether they promote ethical outcomes benefiting society. Human guidance will remain essential to ensure that AGI learns values alongside knowledge.

History demonstrates that humanity's greatest achievements emerged through generations of accumulated experience. Medical discoveries built upon previous research. Space exploration advanced through countless successful and unsuccessful missions. Modern transportation evolved from centuries of engineering improvements. Educational systems continue improving as teachers learn more about effective instruction. Progress occurs because knowledge grows through shared experience rather than remaining fixed. AGI represents another step in this long tradition of continuous learning. Its success will depend not only on computational power but also on the ability to learn responsibly from experience.

Students preparing for the future should recognize that learning does not end when school assignments are completed or diplomas are earned. Every new experience provides opportunities for growth. Every challenge teaches resilience. Every mistake offers valuable information. Every success demonstrates what is possible through persistence and thoughtful reflection. The world will continue changing rapidly as artificial intelligence advances, creating careers, technologies, and opportunities that may not yet exist today. Those who remain curious, adaptable, and committed to lifelong learning will be best prepared to thrive alongside intelligent technologies.

Learning through experience is one of the greatest gifts of intelligence. It transforms information into understanding, understanding into skill, and skill into wisdom. Future Artificial General Intelligence will strive to develop similar capabilities by continuously evaluating outcomes, learning from feedback, adapting to new situations, and improving over time. Yet even as intelligent systems become more capable, the human ability to reflect upon experiences, learn ethically, collaborate with others, and apply wisdom compassionately will remain one of our greatest strengths. As you continue exploring reasoning intelligence, remember that every experience—whether successful or challenging—is building the knowledge and character that will shape both your future and the future of intelligent technology.

Learn AI. Understand AI. Shape the Future.
— Susie Hala, IntelliGloss Press

Chapter 7 Summary

Learning Through Experience

This chapter explained that one of the greatest strengths of both human intelligence and future Artificial General Intelligence (AGI) is the ability to learn from experience. Intelligence is not simply about collecting information—it is about improving over time by observing results, making adjustments, and applying lessons learned to future situations.

Students learned that human learning begins through experience long before formal education starts. Every success, mistake, observation, and challenge teaches valuable lessons that strengthen reasoning and decision-making. This process continues throughout life and is known as lifelong learning.

The chapter introduced several important concepts that support learning through experience, including **feedback**, **self-reflection**, **trial and error**, **adaptation**, **transfer learning**, **memory**, and **collaboration**. These building blocks allow people and future AGI systems to improve continuously rather than repeating the same actions.

Students also discovered that mistakes should not be viewed as failures. Instead, mistakes provide important information that helps people recognize weaknesses, improve strategies, and achieve better outcomes in the future.

Another important lesson was that learning depends on context. A solution that works well in one situation may need to be adjusted when circumstances change. Intelligent systems must therefore remain flexible and willing to update their understanding whenever new information becomes available.

The chapter also emphasized the importance of ethical learning. Future AGI systems should learn not only how to become more effective but also how to make decisions that are fair, responsible, transparent, and beneficial to society.

Finally, students learned that lifelong learning is essential in a world where technology continues to evolve. Curiosity, adaptability, and continuous improvement will remain valuable skills for everyone living and working alongside advanced AI systems.

Chapter 7 Reflection

Every experience teaches us something.

Sometimes the lesson comes from success.

Sometimes it comes from failure.

Sometimes it comes from simply asking one more question than we asked yesterday.

Learning through experience is one of the most remarkable abilities humans possess. Every challenge we face, every mistake we correct, and every achievement we celebrate adds another piece to our understanding of the world.

Artificial General Intelligence will also depend on this ability. Instead of remaining fixed after training, future intelligent systems must continue learning, adapting, improving, and refining their decisions throughout their operational lives.

This chapter reminds us that intelligence is never complete. There is always something new to discover, another perspective to consider, or another skill to develop.

Students who embrace lifelong learning will be well prepared for a future where technology changes rapidly. Curiosity, resilience, critical thinking, and ethical decision-making will become some of the most valuable abilities anyone can possess.

Every experience becomes a lesson when we choose to learn from it.

That commitment to continuous improvement is one of the greatest strengths of both human intelligence and the future of AGI.

Chapter 7 Worksheet

Name: ______________________________

Date: ______________________________

Part A – Vocabulary

Write a definition for each term.

1. Feedback

____

____

2. Trial and Error

____

____

3. Adaptation

____

____

4. Transfer Learning

____

____

5. Lifelong Learning

6. Reflection

Part B – Short Answer

1. Why is learning through experience important?

2. How does feedback improve future performance?

3. Why should mistakes be viewed as learning opportunities?

4. What is transfer learning?

5. Why will future AGI systems need lifelong learning?

Part C – Learning Cycle Activity

Think about learning to ride a bicycle, play a musical instrument, participate in a sport, or develop another new skill.

Complete the learning cycle.

Goal

First Attempt

Feedback Received

Changes Made

Improved Result

Part D – Critical Thinking

Imagine an AGI system is helping teachers improve student learning.

Explain how the AGI could use each of the following.

Feedback

Reflection

Memory

Transfer Learning

Ethical Learning

Part E – Personal Reflection

Describe something you once found difficult but can now do well.

What experiences helped you improve?

Chapter 7 Worksheet

Name: ____

Date: ____

Part A – Vocabulary

Write a definition for each term.

1. Feedback

2. Trial and Error

3. Adaptation

4. Transfer Learning

5. Lifelong Learning

6. Reflection

Part B – Short Answer

1. Why is learning through experience important?

2. How does feedback improve future performance?

3. Why should mistakes be viewed as learning opportunities?

4. What is transfer learning?

5. Why will future AGI systems need lifelong learning?

Part C – Learning Cycle Activity

Think about learning to ride a bicycle, play a musical instrument, participate in a sport, or develop another new skill.

Complete the learning cycle.

Goal

First Attempt

Feedback Received

Changes Made

Improved Result

Part D – Critical Thinking

Imagine an AGI system is helping teachers improve student learning.

Explain how the AGI could use each of the following.

Feedback

Reflection

Memory

Transfer Learning

Ethical Learning

Part E – Personal Reflection

Describe something you once found difficult but can now do well.

What experiences helped you improve?

Chapter 7 Quiz

Name: ________________________________

Score: _________ /20

Multiple Choice

1. Learning through experience allows people to

A. Stop making decisions.

B. Improve over time.

C. Memorize everything instantly.

D. Avoid challenges.

2. Feedback helps us

A. Ignore mistakes.

B. Improve future performance.

C. Eliminate learning.

D. Replace reasoning.

3. Trial and error teaches us by

A. Avoiding practice.

B. Learning from successes and mistakes.

C. Ignoring evidence.

D. Repeating incorrect actions forever.

4. Transfer learning means

A. Moving to another school.

B. Applying knowledge from one situation to another.

C. Forgetting previous experiences.

D. Starting over every time.

5. Lifelong learning means

A. Learning ends after graduation.

B. Continuing to learn throughout life.

C. Memorizing facts only.

D. Avoiding change.

True or False

6. Mistakes can help improve future decisions.

True / False

7. Reflection allows people to evaluate their own experiences.

True / False

8. Future AGI systems will likely need to adapt as they gain new experiences.

True / False

9. Context can influence how previous experiences should be applied.

True / False

10. Ethical learning is an important part of responsible AGI development.

True / False

Short Answer

11. Explain why feedback is valuable.

12. What is adaptation?

13. Why is lifelong learning important?

14. Give one example of transfer learning.

15. What is the most important lesson you learned from this chapter?

Chapter 7 Answer Key

Multiple Choice

1. **B** – Improve over time.
2. **B** – Improve future performance.
3. **B** – Learning from successes and mistakes.
4. **B** – Applying knowledge from one situation to another.
5. **B** – Continuing to learn throughout life.

True or False

6. **True**
7. **True**
8. **True**
9. **True**
10. **True**

Short Answer (Sample Answers)

11. Feedback helps identify strengths and weaknesses, allowing people and intelligent systems to improve future performance by making informed adjustments.

12. Adaptation is the ability to change behavior, strategies, or decisions based on new experiences or changing circumstances.

13. Lifelong learning allows individuals to continue developing new knowledge and skills throughout life, helping them adapt to new technologies, careers, and challenges.

14. Example: A student who learns logical thinking in mathematics applies those reasoning skills to computer programming, science, or engineering.

15. Answers will vary. Students should describe one key concept they learned, such as the importance of feedback, learning from mistakes, adaptation, transfer learning, or lifelong learning.

Extension Activity (Optional)

Interview a family member, teacher, coach, business owner, healthcare professional, or community leader. Ask them to describe an experience that taught them an important life lesson. Write a one-page summary explaining how feedback, reflection, adaptation, and continuous learning helped that person grow. Then explain how a future AGI system might use a similar learning process while maintaining ethical decision-making and human oversight.

Chapter 8

Common Sense Reasoning

Imagine walking into your kitchen and seeing a glass of milk sitting on the edge of the counter. Most people immediately think, "Someone should move that before it falls." You probably do not perform a complicated calculation or search through thousands of previous experiences before reaching that conclusion. Instead, you rely on something that feels natural and almost effortless—common sense. You understand that glasses can tip over, spilled milk creates a mess, broken glass can cause injuries, and moving the glass a few inches toward the center of the counter is the safest choice. This simple decision takes only a moment, yet it demonstrates one of the most remarkable abilities of human intelligence. We constantly make reasonable decisions based on everyday knowledge that we rarely stop to think about. Developing this kind of practical understanding has become one of the greatest challenges in Artificial General Intelligence (AGI). While today's artificial intelligence systems can process enormous amounts of information and recognize complex patterns, they often struggle with the everyday reasoning that people perform almost automatically. This chapter explores what common sense reasoning is, why it matters, and why it represents one of the most important frontiers in the development of intelligent machines.

Common sense reasoning is the ability to apply practical knowledge to everyday situations. It combines experience, observation, logic, context, and judgment to make decisions that most people consider reasonable. Common sense is rarely learned from a single lesson or textbook. Instead, it develops gradually through countless daily experiences. Children learn that ice melts when left in the sun, that people become tired after working hard, that plants need water to grow, and that kindness usually builds stronger friendships than selfishness. These lessons become part of an internal understanding of how the world works. Rather than memorizing isolated facts, people organize these experiences into a flexible system that helps them respond effectively to new situations. Future AGI systems must develop similar practical understanding if they are to function naturally alongside humans.

One reason common sense is difficult to define is that much of it remains unspoken. People rarely explain obvious facts because everyone assumes others already know them. For example, if someone says, "Please close the window; it's getting cold," most people understand that the speaker hopes to make the room warmer. They recognize that open windows allow cold air to enter and that closing the window may improve comfort. Very little of this reasoning is spoken aloud. Human conversations often depend on shared background knowledge that remains invisible. For intelligent machines, however, this hidden knowledge creates enormous challenges. If information is never explicitly stated, how can a machine learn it? Researchers developing AGI must teach systems not only what people say but also what people assume without saying.

Language provides many examples of common sense reasoning. Imagine hearing someone say, "The baby is sleeping." Most people automatically lower their voices, close doors quietly, or avoid making unnecessary noise. The sentence itself never instructs anyone to become quieter, yet common sense fills in the missing information. Similarly, if someone says, "The roads are covered with ice," drivers understand they should slow down even though the sentence does not explicitly mention reducing speed. Human beings constantly interpret language using practical understanding rather than relying only on literal definitions. Future AGI systems capable of natural conversation must recognize these implied meanings to communicate successfully.

Everyday problem-solving depends heavily on common sense. Suppose you enter a classroom and notice water spreading across the floor from a leaking sink. Most people immediately recognize several concerns. Someone could slip and fall. Books or electronic equipment might be damaged. The leak should be reported before it becomes worse. Towels or warning signs may reduce immediate danger. None of these actions require detailed scientific calculations. Instead, they arise from practical understanding developed through experience. Common sense allows people to identify priorities quickly while responding appropriately to changing situations. AGI systems designed to assist schools, hospitals, transportation systems, or emergency responders must develop similar abilities if they are to provide meaningful support.

One of the greatest strengths of common sense reasoning is understanding **context**. Consider the simple statement, "It's cold in here." Depending on the situation, the speaker may simply be making an observation. Alternatively, the speaker may be requesting that someone close a window, adjust the thermostat, or provide a blanket. Human listeners naturally interpret these possibilities based on context. They consider where the conversation is taking place, who is speaking, recent events, and the relationship between the individuals involved. Current AI systems sometimes struggle because they interpret words literally while overlooking contextual clues. AGI researchers recognize that context is essential for building machines capable of truly understanding human communication.

Another important feature of common sense reasoning is recognizing **physical reality**. Humans understand that heavy objects require more effort to lift than light ones, that liquids flow downhill, that fragile objects break when dropped, and that people cannot be in two places simultaneously. These ideas seem obvious because they are learned naturally through everyday experiences. Yet encoding this knowledge into intelligent machines has proven surprisingly difficult. A computer may recognize photographs of cups, tables, and books, but understanding that a cup placed upside down cannot hold water requires deeper reasoning about physical properties. AGI systems will need rich internal models of the physical world if they are to interact safely with people and their environments.

Time also plays an important role in common sense reasoning. Human beings understand that actions occur in sequences. Before eating dinner, food must be prepared. Before planting a garden, the soil must be prepared. Before taking a vacation, travel arrangements must be made. Everyday activities involve predictable steps that most people learn through experience. This understanding helps individuals anticipate future events and plan effectively. Future AGI systems must develop similar temporal reasoning, recognizing not only what happens but also when actions should occur and how earlier events influence later outcomes.

Social interactions depend heavily on common sense. People recognize facial expressions, tone of voice, body language, and emotional cues that provide information beyond spoken words. A friend smiling while saying, "I'm fine," may genuinely feel happy. However, crossed arms, a quiet voice, and tearful eyes may suggest sadness despite the same words. Human beings naturally combine verbal and nonverbal information to understand one another. AGI systems designed to assist in education, healthcare, customer service, or caregiving must learn to interpret these subtle signals respectfully and responsibly. Understanding people requires more than processing language—it requires appreciating human emotions, relationships, and social expectations.

One challenge facing AGI researchers is that common sense often changes depending on culture, location, and individual experience. Greeting customs differ across countries. Family traditions vary widely. Social expectations evolve over time. A behavior considered polite in one culture may be interpreted differently elsewhere. Intelligent systems must therefore avoid assuming that one set of experiences applies universally. Instead, they must learn to recognize cultural diversity while adapting respectfully to different communities. Building globally useful AGI requires flexibility rather than rigid assumptions.

Children provide fascinating examples of how common sense develops. Young children frequently ask questions adults rarely consider. Why does the moon appear to follow the car? Why can't fish live outside water? Why do people sleep? These questions reveal that common sense is not inherited automatically. It grows through observation, curiosity, experimentation, and explanation. Every answered question strengthens a child's understanding of the world. AGI systems may require similar developmental learning, gradually building practical knowledge through countless interactions rather than receiving every answer in advance.

One useful way to understand common sense is to imagine solving unfamiliar problems using existing knowledge. Suppose a power outage suddenly occurs during a winter storm. Most people immediately think about finding flashlights, checking on family members, preserving food, avoiding unnecessary travel, and staying warm. These actions result from combining previous experiences with practical reasoning. Very few individuals have memorized a formal list covering every possible emergency, yet common sense allows them to respond effectively. Future AGI systems supporting disaster response will require similar flexibility, applying practical understanding to situations that differ from previous experiences.

Memory plays a central role in common sense reasoning. People constantly recall previous experiences when making decisions. Someone who has accidentally touched a hot pan remembers being burned and uses oven mitts next time. A driver who encountered icy roads becomes more cautious during winter weather. Teachers adjust lessons based on previous classroom experiences. These memories become part of practical wisdom that guides future actions. AGI systems must develop memory systems capable of storing not only facts but also meaningful experiences and their outcomes. Experience transforms information into practical judgment.

Common sense also includes recognizing what is **reasonable**. Imagine someone carrying groceries while struggling to open a door. Most people instinctively offer assistance without requiring detailed instructions. They recognize another person's difficulty and understand that helping is appropriate. This type of practical social reasoning depends on empathy, observation, and shared human values. Although AGI may not experience emotions exactly as humans do, future intelligent systems should recognize situations where assistance is appropriate while respecting human preferences, privacy, and independence.

Mistakes often reveal gaps in common sense reasoning. Current AI systems occasionally produce responses that appear logical on the surface but ignore obvious real-world facts. For example, suggesting impossible travel routes, misunderstanding everyday objects, or interpreting humorous expressions literally demonstrates the difference between processing information and understanding practical reality. These limitations remind researchers that intelligence involves much more than statistical prediction. True reasoning requires connecting knowledge with everyday experience, physical understanding, and social awareness.

Ethics is deeply connected to common sense. Most people recognize that honesty builds trust, fairness strengthens communities, and kindness improves relationships. These principles are reinforced through families, schools, cultures, and personal experiences. Future AGI systems must learn not only practical reasoning but also responsible reasoning. Recommending efficient solutions without considering fairness or human well-being could create harmful consequences. Common sense should therefore include ethical judgment alongside logical thinking.

The future of AGI depends heavily on solving the challenge of common sense reasoning. Intelligent systems may become extraordinarily skilled at mathematics, language, scientific analysis, and data processing, yet still struggle with everyday decisions if they lack practical understanding of the world. Researchers continue developing methods that combine reasoning, memory, experience, physical understanding, language comprehension, and ethical decision-making into unified systems capable of behaving naturally in human environments. Achieving this goal represents one of the greatest scientific challenges of modern artificial intelligence.

Students entering the future workforce will increasingly collaborate with intelligent technologies capable of performing tasks once considered impossible. Yet one uniquely human strength will remain valuable: the ability to apply practical wisdom in unpredictable situations. Common sense helps people recognize danger, cooperate with others, adapt to changing conditions, understand emotions, and make thoughtful decisions using limited information. As AGI develops, people who strengthen their own common sense reasoning will become better prepared to guide intelligent systems responsibly rather than depending upon them blindly.

As you continue your journey through reasoning intelligence, remember that intelligence is not measured only by solving difficult mathematical equations or processing enormous amounts of information. Sometimes intelligence is demonstrated by recognizing that a child needs encouragement, that a slippery floor requires attention, that a quiet conversation deserves respect, or that helping another person makes a community stronger. Common sense transforms knowledge into practical wisdom. It allows people to navigate everyday life safely, responsibly, and compassionately. Building this same capability into future AGI may become one of the most important achievements in the history of artificial intelligence, creating systems that not only calculate correctly but also understand the ordinary experiences that make us human.

Learn AI. Understand AI. Shape the Future.
— Susie Hala, IntelliGloss Press

Chapter 8 Summary

Common Sense Reasoning

This chapter introduced one of the greatest challenges in the development of Artificial General Intelligence (AGI): common sense reasoning. Students learned that common sense is the ability to use practical knowledge, experience, observation, and judgment to make reasonable decisions in everyday situations.

Unlike memorizing facts or recognizing patterns, common sense reasoning helps people understand situations that are not always explained directly. Humans naturally use background knowledge to interpret conversations, recognize potential dangers, understand social situations, and solve everyday problems.

The chapter explained that common sense develops gradually through experience. Children learn about the world by observing, asking questions, making mistakes, and interacting with people and their environment. These experiences build an internal understanding that helps guide future decisions.

Students also explored how common sense depends on understanding context, physical reality, time, memory, and social interactions. These abilities allow people to interpret implied meanings, predict likely outcomes, and respond appropriately even when information is incomplete.

Another important lesson was that common sense is influenced by culture, personal experience, and ethical values. What seems obvious in one community may differ in another, making flexibility and respect essential for future intelligent systems.

The chapter concluded by explaining that common sense remains one of the most difficult abilities to develop in AI. While today's AI systems excel at processing information, future AGI must also understand everyday life, human behavior, practical reasoning, and ethical decision-making in order to become truly intelligent partners for society.

Chapter 8 Reflection

Many of the smartest decisions people make every day are based on common sense rather than advanced mathematics or scientific formulas.

We know not to touch a hot stove.

We help someone carrying a heavy box.

We slow down when roads become slippery.

We lower our voices when someone is sleeping.

These actions may seem simple, but they represent years of learning through observation, experience, relationships, and practical understanding.

This chapter reminds us that intelligence is not measured only by how much information someone knows. True intelligence also involves understanding people, recognizing context, making thoughtful judgments, and acting responsibly.

Artificial General Intelligence will eventually need this same practical understanding if it is to work safely alongside humans. Future intelligent systems must recognize not only facts but also everyday situations that require empathy, flexibility, and good judgment.

As students prepare for careers in an AI-driven world, strengthening common sense reasoning will become increasingly valuable. Technology may provide information, but people will continue to provide wisdom, compassion, and responsible leadership.

Common sense is where knowledge meets everyday life—and where intelligence becomes truly useful.

Chapter 8 Worksheet

Name: ______________________________________

Date: ______________________________________

Part A – Vocabulary

Write your own definition for each term.

1. Common Sense Reasoning

____

____

2. Context

____

____

3. Practical Knowledge

4. Physical Reality

5. Social Awareness

6. Ethical Judgment

Part B – Short Answer

1. What is common sense reasoning?

2. Why is common sense difficult for today's AI systems?

3. How does context influence understanding?

4. Why is memory important for common sense reasoning?

5. Why should future AGI systems understand social situations?

Part C – Everyday Reasoning Activity

For each situation, describe the common sense action you would take and explain why.

Situation 1

You notice a puddle of water on the classroom floor.

Action:

Reason:

Situation 2

A classmate drops several books in the hallway.

Action:

Reason:

Situation 3

You hear a fire alarm while inside a school building.

Action:

Reason:

Part D – Critical Thinking

Imagine an AGI system is helping elderly people live independently.

Explain why the AGI should understand each of the following.

Context

Memory

Common Sense

Safety

Ethical Responsibility

Part E – Personal Reflection

Describe a time when your common sense helped you avoid a problem or make a better decision.

Chapter 8 Quiz

Name: ________________________________

Score: _________ /20

Multiple Choice

1. Common sense reasoning is the ability to

A. Memorize every fact.

B. Usc practical knowledge and experience to make reasonable decisions.

C. Solve math problems only.

D. Store large amounts of data.

2. Common sense develops mainly through

A. Memorization alone.

B. Experience and observation.

C. Guessing.

D. Luck.

3. Why is context important?

A. It helps determine the meaning of a situation.

B. It increases computer speed.

C. It replaces reasoning.

D. It eliminates uncertainty.

4. Which is an example of common sense reasoning?

A. Touching a hot stove to see if it is hot.

B. Helping someone pick up dropped books.

C. Ignoring a fire alarm.

D. Walking across a flooded street without caution.

5. Why is common sense important for AGI?

A. It allows intelligent systems to understand everyday situations and make practical decisions.

B. It improves internet speed.

C. It eliminates the need for humans.

D. It replaces scientific knowledge.

True or False

6. Common sense is based only on memorizing information.

True / False

7. Human conversations often include information that is implied rather than directly stated.

True / False

8. Context helps people understand meaning.

True / False

9. Future AGI systems should understand both physical and social environments.

True / False

10. Ethical reasoning is part of common sense.

True / False

Short Answer

11. Explain common sense reasoning in your own words.

12. Why is common sense difficult to teach AI?

13. Give one example of using common sense in everyday life.

14. How does memory improve common sense reasoning?

15. What is one important lesson you learned from this chapter?

Chapter 8 Answer Key

Multiple Choice

1. **B** – Use practical knowledge and experience to make reasonable decisions.
2. **B** – Experience and observation.
3. **A** – It helps determine the meaning of a situation.
4. **B** – Helping someone pick up dropped books.
5. **A** – It allows intelligent systems to understand everyday situations and make practical decisions.

True or False

6. **False**
7. **True**
8. **True**
9. **True**
10. **True**

Short Answer (Sample Answers)

11. Common sense reasoning is the ability to use everyday knowledge, experience, observation, and good judgment to make practical decisions in daily life.

12. Common sense is difficult to teach AI because much of it is learned through experience and includes unstated knowledge, context, physical understanding, social awareness, and cultural differences.

13. Examples include moving a glass away from the edge of a table, helping someone who drops books, slowing down on icy roads, or lowering your voice when someone is sleeping.

14. Memory stores previous experiences and lessons learned, allowing people and future AGI systems to apply past knowledge when facing similar situations.

15. Answers will vary. Students should explain one key lesson from the chapter, such as the importance of context, practical reasoning, ethical judgment, or understanding everyday situations.

Extension Activity (Optional)

Spend one day observing situations where people use common sense. Record at least ten examples, such as helping others, avoiding hazards, solving everyday problems, or making thoughtful decisions. For each example, explain what background knowledge was used and describe how a future AGI system could learn to respond appropriately while respecting human safety, values, and social expectations.

Chapter 9

Analogies and Creative Reasoning

Imagine trying to explain electricity to someone who has never seen a power line, a light bulb, or a battery. Instead of beginning with complicated scientific formulas, you might say, "Electricity moves through wires much like water flows through pipes." Instantly, the listener has a picture in their mind. They understand that something moves from one place to another, that flow can be controlled, and that blockages can prevent movement. Although electricity and water are very different, the comparison helps make a difficult idea easier to understand. This simple example demonstrates the power of analogies. Human beings constantly use analogies to explain unfamiliar ideas, solve new problems, discover creative solutions, and connect knowledge from different fields. Analogies are much more than figures of speech. They are one of the most powerful reasoning tools ever developed by the human mind. As researchers continue building

Artificial General Intelligence (AGI), teaching machines to understand and create analogies has become one of the most important challenges in developing reasoning intelligence.

Reasoning is often described as the process of moving from what we already know to what we do not yet understand. Analogies make this journey possible by connecting familiar experiences with unfamiliar ideas. Instead of learning every new concept from the beginning, people use previous knowledge as a bridge. A teacher explaining the human circulatory system may compare blood vessels to highways carrying traffic throughout a city. A computer engineer may describe computer memory as a digital filing cabinet where information is stored and retrieved. Parents often explain difficult concepts to children by comparing them to everyday experiences. These comparisons simplify learning while helping people organize new information within existing knowledge. Future AGI systems capable of creating useful analogies may communicate far more naturally with people while solving problems more creatively.

One reason analogies are so valuable is that they reveal **relationships** rather than isolated facts. Consider the relationship between the Sun and the planets in our solar system. A teacher might compare this system to a family gathered around a campfire. The campfire represents the Sun because it provides warmth and light. The family members represent the planets because they remain nearby while moving around the fire. Although the comparison is not perfect, it highlights important relationships that help students understand astronomical concepts. Good analogies focus on the similarities that matter most while recognizing that every comparison has limitations. Intelligent reasoning requires identifying meaningful relationships rather than assuming two situations are identical.

Human creativity depends heavily on this ability to connect ideas across different fields. Many important inventions began because someone recognized similarities between completely different situations. Engineers studying birds developed new aircraft designs after observing the principles of flight. Medical researchers learned from nature when designing new medicines. Architects borrowed ideas from tree structures to create stronger buildings. Scientists studying spider silk developed stronger synthetic materials. These breakthroughs occurred because creative thinkers asked an important question: **What can one field teach another?** Analogical reasoning allows knowledge to travel across disciplines, leading to discoveries that might never have occurred if each subject remained isolated.

Children naturally demonstrate analogical reasoning during learning. A young student who understands that adding numbers combines quantities may later recognize that combining ingredients follows a similar idea. Reading stories helps children understand human emotions because they compare fictional experiences with real life. Building blocks teach structural concepts that later support engineering and architecture. Every new experience expands the number of comparisons available for future reasoning. Researchers developing AGI hope intelligent systems will gradually build similar networks of connected knowledge, allowing previous experiences to support new learning across many different situations.

Analogies also strengthen **problem-solving**. Imagine a city struggling with traffic congestion. Rather than studying only transportation systems, engineers may examine how blood flows through the human circulatory system. They discover that the body automatically redirects blood around blockages through smaller vessels. Inspired by this biological analogy, engineers design alternate traffic routes that reduce congestion by distributing vehicles across multiple streets instead of relying on one crowded highway. This example illustrates how analogies help people solve difficult problems by transferring successful ideas from one domain to another. Future AGI systems may become valuable partners by discovering useful analogies hidden across enormous collections of knowledge that humans alone might overlook.

Scientific research provides countless examples of analogical reasoning. The structure of the atom has often been compared to a miniature solar system because electrons move around a central nucleus much like planets orbit the Sun. Although modern physics recognizes important differences between these systems, the analogy helped generations of students visualize atomic structure. In biology, DNA is frequently compared to a blueprint because it contains instructions for building living organisms. In computer science, computer viruses are compared to biological viruses because both spread by replicating themselves within larger systems. These comparisons allow complex ideas to become understandable without sacrificing important scientific principles. AGI systems capable of generating accurate analogies could become powerful educational tools that explain difficult concepts in ways appropriate for learners of different ages.

Creative reasoning involves much more than making comparisons. It also requires imagining possibilities that do not yet exist. Creativity begins by asking questions such as, **What if?**, **Could this idea work somewhere else?**, or **Is there another way to solve this problem?** Human progress depends on these questions. The invention of the airplane required imagining transportation beyond roads and railways. Space exploration required imagining travel beyond Earth's atmosphere. Renewable energy required imagining alternatives to traditional fuels. Every major innovation began with someone willing to think differently about familiar ideas. AGI researchers hope future intelligent systems will contribute to innovation by generating original possibilities while evaluating them logically and responsibly.

One important difference exists between creativity and randomness. Creative reasoning is not simply producing unusual ideas without purpose. Instead, creativity combines originality with usefulness. A bridge designed to resemble a giant balloon might appear creative, but if it cannot safely support vehicles, it fails as engineering. Likewise, an AGI system generating imaginative ideas must also evaluate whether those ideas satisfy practical requirements. Successful creativity balances innovation with logic, imagination with evidence, and originality with responsibility.

Pattern recognition supports analogical reasoning, but it is only the beginning. Pattern recognition notices similarities between situations. Analogical reasoning explains why those similarities matter. Imagine recognizing that both rivers and electrical circuits involve movement. Pattern recognition identifies this similarity. Analogical reasoning examines how water pressure resembles electrical voltage, how water flow resembles electrical current, and how restrictions in pipes resemble electrical resistance. This deeper analysis transforms observation into understanding. Future AGI systems capable of analogical reasoning will move beyond identifying patterns to discovering meaningful structural relationships across different fields of knowledge.

Memory plays an essential role in creative reasoning because every new analogy depends upon previous experiences. A writer creates memorable stories by connecting historical events, personal experiences, and imaginative ideas. A scientist develops new theories by combining knowledge from many different experiments. An inventor improves products by remembering previous designs while imagining better alternatives. The richer a person's experiences become, the more opportunities exist for creating valuable analogies. AGI systems will require advanced memory structures capable of organizing knowledge in flexible ways so that information from one area can support reasoning in another.

Education benefits tremendously from analogical reasoning because students often learn best when new concepts connect to familiar experiences. A mathematics teacher comparing fractions to slices of pizza makes abstract numbers easier to understand. A geography teacher comparing river systems to tree branches helps students visualize water movement across landscapes. A history teacher comparing the growth of civilizations to the growth of living organisms illustrates how societies develop, mature, and sometimes decline. Effective educators constantly search for analogies that make learning more meaningful. Future AGI tutoring systems may personalize analogies based on each student's interests, experiences, and learning style, making education more engaging and effective.

Analogies also strengthen communication between people. Professionals often simplify technical information by relating it to everyday experiences. Doctors explain clogged arteries by comparing them to blocked plumbing. Financial advisors compare investment diversification to not placing all eggs in one basket. Weather forecasters describe approaching storm systems using examples familiar to local communities. These analogies build understanding by reducing unnecessary complexity while preserving essential ideas. Future AGI systems communicating with people must learn to create clear, accurate, and culturally appropriate analogies that improve understanding rather than causing confusion.

Another important feature of creative reasoning is recognizing the limitations of analogies. Every comparison eventually reaches a point where differences become important. For example, comparing the brain to a computer helps explain information processing, but human brains continuously grow, adapt, experience emotions, and develop consciousness in ways computers currently do not. Good reasoning recognizes both similarities and differences. AGI systems must avoid assuming that two situations are identical simply because they share certain characteristics. Responsible reasoning requires identifying where analogies remain useful and where they should no longer be applied.

Ethics also influences creative reasoning. Throughout history, technological innovations have produced both tremendous benefits and unexpected challenges. Creative ideas should therefore be evaluated not only for originality but also for fairness, safety, environmental responsibility, and respect for human dignity. Imagine an AGI developing new educational technologies. The system should consider whether every student can benefit equally, whether privacy is protected, and whether technology strengthens rather than replaces meaningful human relationships. Responsible creativity balances innovation with ethical reflection.

One fascinating goal of AGI research involves creating systems capable of discovering entirely new analogies beyond current human knowledge. Such systems might identify unexpected connections between biology and engineering, astronomy and climate science, neuroscience and education, or economics and environmental sustainability. These discoveries could accelerate scientific research, improve medical treatments, strengthen educational methods, and inspire technological breakthroughs benefiting society. However, these advances will require intelligent systems capable of flexible reasoning rather than simply retrieving existing information.

Students preparing for the future should recognize that creativity is not limited to artists, musicians, or writers. Scientists create new theories. Engineers invent new technologies. Teachers design engaging lessons. Entrepreneurs develop innovative businesses. Healthcare professionals discover improved treatments. Every profession benefits from individuals capable of connecting ideas in new ways while solving meaningful problems. Developing analogical reasoning strengthens creativity because it encourages students to see relationships others may overlook.

As Artificial General Intelligence continues evolving, the ability to reason creatively through analogies may become one of its defining characteristics. Rather than merely repeating existing knowledge, future AGI systems may help humanity understand difficult concepts, communicate more effectively, solve complex global challenges, and generate innovative ideas that improve lives around the world. Yet the most valuable creativity will always combine intelligence with responsibility, imagination with ethics, and innovation with compassion.

As you continue exploring reasoning intelligence, remember that every great discovery began when someone noticed a connection that others had not seen before. Every invention, every scientific breakthrough, every artistic masterpiece, and every educational innovation emerged because someone asked, **What if these two ideas belong together?** Analogies help us answer that question. They transform unfamiliar ideas into understandable ones, inspire creative thinking, and reveal hidden relationships throughout the world. By strengthening your ability to think creatively and reason through analogies, you are developing one of the most powerful skills needed to succeed in the Age of Artificial General Intelligence.

Learn AI. Understand AI. Shape the Future.
— Susie Hala, IntelliGloss Press

Chapter 9 Summary

Analogies and Creative Reasoning

This chapter explored how analogies and creative reasoning help humans and future Artificial General Intelligence (AGI) understand new ideas, solve unfamiliar problems, and develop innovative solutions. Students learned that analogies connect what we already know with what we are trying to understand.

An analogy compares two different ideas by focusing on important similarities. Teachers, scientists, engineers, doctors, and business leaders frequently use analogies to explain complex concepts in simple ways. For example, electricity can be compared to water flowing through pipes, helping students understand how electrical current moves.

The chapter explained that analogical reasoning goes beyond simple pattern recognition. Instead of only noticing similarities, it helps people understand relationships, transfer knowledge from one field to another, and discover creative solutions to difficult problems.

Students also learned that creativity is not random thinking. True creativity combines imagination with logical reasoning, evidence, and practical usefulness. Many important inventions and scientific discoveries were made because someone recognized connections between different fields of knowledge.

The chapter introduced the idea that memory, experience, communication, and education all contribute to creative reasoning. The more experiences people have, the more connections they can make when solving new challenges.

Finally, the chapter emphasized that future AGI systems will likely use analogical reasoning to communicate more naturally, explain difficult concepts, discover innovative solutions, and collaborate with humans across many professions. However, creativity must always be guided by ethics, responsibility, and careful reasoning.

Chapter 9 Reflection

Some of the greatest discoveries in history began with one simple thought:

"This reminds me of something else."

That single comparison has inspired inventions, scientific breakthroughs, works of art, and technological innovations that changed the world.

Analogies help us connect ideas that seem unrelated. They make difficult concepts easier to understand and encourage us to look beyond traditional ways of thinking. Creative reasoning allows people to ask new questions, imagine better solutions, and see opportunities where others see only problems.

Artificial General Intelligence will also need this ability. Future intelligent systems must do more than memorize information—they must recognize meaningful relationships, transfer knowledge across different fields, and generate ideas that are both creative and practical.

This chapter reminds us that creativity belongs to everyone. Scientists, engineers, teachers, healthcare professionals, entrepreneurs, and students all use creative reasoning to solve problems every day.

As technology continues to evolve, one of the greatest strengths people can develop is the ability to think creatively while remaining thoughtful, ethical, and responsible.

Innovation begins with curiosity.

Discovery begins with comparison.

Progress begins with imagination guided by reason.

Chapter 9 Worksheet

Name: ____

Date: ____

Part A – Vocabulary

Write a definition for each term.

1. Analogy

____

____

2. Creative Reasoning

____

____

3. Pattern Recognition

____

____

4. Transfer of Knowledge

____

____

5. Innovation

6. Relationship

Part B – Short Answer

1. What is an analogy?

2. Why are analogies useful when learning something new?

3. How does creative reasoning differ from random guessing?

4. Why is transferring knowledge from one field to another valuable?

5. Why will future AGI systems need analogical reasoning?

Part C – Create Your Own Analogies

Complete each analogy.

1. **The human brain is like ________________________________ because**

2. **Learning is like ____ because**

3. **Artificial General Intelligence is like ____________________________ because**

Part D – Critical Thinking

Imagine an AGI system is helping engineers design a new bridge.

Explain how analogical reasoning could help.

Using ideas from nature

Using previous engineering projects

Creating new design ideas

Evaluating safety

Considering ethical responsibilities

Part E – Personal Reflection

Describe a time when comparing one idea to another helped you understand something difficult.

Chapter 9 Quiz

Name: ______________________________

Score: _________ /20

Multiple Choice

1. An analogy helps people

A. Memorize random facts.

B. Compare familiar ideas to unfamiliar ones.

C. Ignore relationships.

D. Avoid learning.

2. Creative reasoning allows people to

A. Repeat information exactly.

B. Develop new ideas and solve problems.

C. Eliminate imagination.

D. Avoid evidence.

3. Which profession regularly uses analogies?

A. Teacher

B. Scientist

C. Engineer

D. All of the above

4. Creative ideas should always be

A. Random.

B. Practical, logical, and responsible.

C. Impossible.

D. Unrelated to evidence.

5. Why is analogical reasoning important for AGI?

A. It helps intelligent systems connect ideas and solve unfamiliar problems.

B. It increases computer memory only.

C. It replaces learning.

D. It removes the need for human thinking.

True or False

6. Analogies compare relationships between different ideas.

True / False

7. Pattern recognition and analogical reasoning are exactly the same.

True / False

8. Creativity often involves connecting knowledge from different fields.

True / False

9. Ethical thinking should guide innovation.

True / False

10. Future AGI may use analogies to explain difficult concepts.

True / False

Short Answer

11. Explain analogical reasoning in your own words.

____

____

12. Give one example of an analogy.

____

____

13. Why is creativity important in problem-solving?

____

____

14. How can analogies improve education?

____

____

15. What is the most important lesson you learned from this chapter?

____

____

Chapter 9 Answer Key

Multiple Choice

1. **B** – Compare familiar ideas to unfamiliar ones.
2. **B** – Develop new ideas and solve problems.
3. **D** – All of the above.
4. **B** – Practical, logical, and responsible.
5. **A** – It helps intelligent systems connect ideas and solve unfamiliar problems.

True or False

6. **True**
7. **False**
8. **True**
9. **True**
10. **True**

Short Answer (Sample Answers)

11. Analogical reasoning is the ability to understand a new idea by comparing it to something already familiar while focusing on meaningful relationships between the two.

12. Examples include:

- Electricity is like water flowing through pipes.
- The brain is like an orchestra where different sections work together.
- DNA is like a blueprint because it contains instructions for building living organisms.

13. Creativity helps people develop original ideas, discover new solutions, improve existing designs, and solve problems that have never been solved before.

14. Analogies make difficult concepts easier to understand by connecting new information to familiar experiences, helping students build stronger understanding and remember concepts more effectively.

15. Answers will vary. Students should explain one key lesson from the chapter, such as the value of analogies, the importance of creativity, transferring knowledge across different fields, or using innovation responsibly.

Extension Activity (Optional)

Choose one complex topic from science, mathematics, technology, healthcare, or engineering. Create three different analogies that explain the concept to an elementary school student, a middle school student, and a high school student. Then explain why each analogy is appropriate for its audience and how a future AGI tutoring system could personalize analogies to improve learning while remaining accurate and responsible.

Chapter 10

Decision-Making Under Uncertainty

Imagine standing at the edge of a hiking trail deep in the mountains. Dark clouds are beginning to gather overhead, your map shows two possible routes, and your phone has lost its signal. One path is shorter but crosses a narrow river that could quickly flood if heavy rain begins. The other path is longer but follows higher ground and offers several emergency shelters along the way. No one can tell you exactly what will happen during the next few hours. You must make a decision without having complete information. Situations like this occur every day, although they may not always seem as dramatic. Doctors make medical decisions before every laboratory result is available. Teachers adjust lessons before knowing exactly how every student will respond. Business leaders invest in new ideas without knowing future market conditions. Emergency managers prepare for storms before they know the exact path of the weather system. Every one of these situations requires decision-making under uncertainty. The future of Artificial General Intelligence (AGI) depends heavily on developing this ability because the real world rarely provides perfect information. Intelligent systems must learn to make thoughtful decisions even when uncertainty cannot be completely eliminated.

Many people believe that intelligence means always knowing the correct answer. In reality, one of the greatest signs of intelligence is recognizing when complete certainty does not exist. Human beings constantly make decisions using incomplete information. We estimate, predict, compare possibilities, evaluate evidence, and choose the option that appears most reasonable at the time. Good decision-makers understand that waiting for perfect certainty is often impossible. Instead, they learn how to manage uncertainty responsibly while remaining prepared to adjust their decisions if new information becomes available. This balance between confidence and flexibility is one of the defining characteristics of mature reasoning and one of the most important goals for future AGI systems.

Uncertainty appears in many different forms. Sometimes important information is simply unavailable. A doctor may still be waiting for laboratory test results before confirming a diagnosis. A firefighter responding to a wildfire may not yet know how quickly wind conditions will change. A teacher introducing a new instructional method cannot predict exactly how every student will respond. In other situations, uncertainty results from the complexity of the environment itself. Financial markets respond to countless interacting factors. Weather systems change continuously. Human behavior often surprises even experienced psychologists. These examples remind us that uncertainty is a natural part of life rather than a sign of poor planning. Intelligent reasoning requires learning how to work with uncertainty instead of pretending it does not exist.

One of the first steps in making decisions under uncertainty is gathering as much reliable information as possible. Although perfect knowledge may be impossible, better information usually leads to better decisions. Imagine a family planning a camping trip. Before leaving home, they check weather forecasts, trail conditions, emergency contacts, available water sources, and park regulations. Even though unexpected events may still occur, collecting information reduces unnecessary risks. Similarly, future AGI systems will analyze enormous amounts of data from sensors, scientific research, historical records, and real-time observations before recommending actions. The goal is not to eliminate uncertainty completely but to understand it more clearly.

Another important skill is evaluating the **quality** of information. Not every source provides equally reliable evidence. During emergencies, rumors often spread quickly through social media while official agencies continue gathering verified information. Responsible decision-makers compare multiple sources before reaching conclusions. Scientists examine peer-reviewed research rather than relying on isolated opinions. Physicians evaluate medical evidence from trusted clinical studies. Journalists confirm facts before publishing important stories. Future AGI systems must learn to distinguish reliable information from misinformation, incomplete evidence, or unsupported claims. Trustworthy reasoning depends not only on having information but also on understanding which information deserves confidence.

Probability plays an essential role in decision-making under uncertainty. Probability estimates how likely different outcomes are to occur. Meteorologists may predict a seventy percent chance of rain. Doctors estimate the effectiveness of medical treatments based on clinical studies. Engineers calculate the probability of equipment failure while designing safety systems. Insurance companies estimate risks before providing coverage. Probability does not guarantee future events, but it provides valuable guidance when certainty is impossible. Future AGI systems will likely use sophisticated probability models to evaluate multiple possible outcomes while explaining the confidence associated with each recommendation.

Imagine a city preparing for a possible hurricane. Meteorologists cannot predict the exact path of the storm several days in advance, but they can identify several likely scenarios. Emergency managers must decide whether to prepare shelters, organize evacuation plans, distribute supplies, or mobilize rescue teams before the final forecast becomes available. Waiting until absolute certainty exists may leave insufficient time to protect lives. Acting too early may create unnecessary expense and disruption. Good decision-making balances available evidence with responsible preparation. AGI systems assisting emergency management must learn to evaluate uncertain forecasts while recommending actions that protect public safety.

One useful strategy for managing uncertainty is considering **multiple possible futures** instead of assuming only one outcome. Business leaders often prepare best-case, worst-case, and most-likely scenarios before launching new products. Farmers prepare for both wet and dry growing seasons. Hospitals develop emergency plans for different types of disasters. Students preparing for college consider several educational pathways before making final decisions. Thinking across multiple scenarios allows people to remain flexible while reducing the impact of unexpected events. Future AGI systems may rapidly simulate thousands of possible futures before recommending the most resilient course of action.

Risk assessment is another essential part of intelligent decision-making. Risk combines two important questions: **How likely is something to happen?** and **What would happen if it does?** Consider crossing a quiet neighborhood street compared to crossing a busy highway. Although accidents remain possible in both situations, the likelihood and potential consequences differ greatly. Responsible reasoning evaluates both factors before acting. Engineers assess risks when designing buildings. Doctors evaluate treatment risks before recommending surgery.

Environmental scientists assess risks associated with pollution or climate change. Future AGI systems must learn to estimate risks carefully while explaining the reasoning behind their recommendations.

Decision-making also involves weighing **trade-offs**. Very few decisions provide only benefits without any costs. Installing solar panels reduces fossil fuel use but requires financial investment. Expanding public transportation improves mobility but demands years of planning and construction. Increasing cybersecurity protects information but may require additional resources and training. Intelligent decision-makers recognize that choosing one option often means giving up another. Rather than searching for perfect solutions, they seek the option that provides the greatest overall benefit while minimizing negative consequences. AGI systems must evaluate these trade-offs transparently so that human decision-makers understand both advantages and limitations.

Experience strengthens decision-making under uncertainty. Imagine an experienced airline pilot encountering unexpected turbulence. Years of training and previous flights help the pilot remain calm while evaluating available information. Similarly, experienced teachers adjust classroom instruction when lessons do not proceed as expected. Physicians recognize subtle symptoms because they have treated many patients over time. Human expertise grows through repeated exposure to uncertain situations. Future AGI systems may also improve through experience by analyzing previous decisions, evaluating outcomes, identifying successful strategies, and continuously refining future recommendations.

Another important skill is recognizing when **not** to make immediate decisions. Some situations require patience while additional evidence becomes available. Scientists often delay conclusions until experiments have been repeated. Engineers postpone construction until safety inspections are complete. Doctors order additional diagnostic tests before recommending complex treatments. Knowing when to wait demonstrates wisdom rather than weakness. Future AGI systems must recognize situations where additional information significantly improves decision quality while distinguishing them from emergencies requiring immediate action.

Communication becomes especially important during uncertain situations. Leaders who explain uncertainty honestly build greater trust than those who pretend certainty exists when it does not. During public health emergencies, weather events, or scientific discoveries, responsible communication includes explaining what is known, what remains uncertain, and how recommendations may change as new evidence appears. Future AGI systems should communicate uncertainty clearly by providing confidence levels, explaining assumptions, describing possible alternatives, and identifying information still needed for stronger conclusions. Transparent reasoning encourages informed human decision-making.

Ethics becomes even more important when uncertainty increases. Imagine an AGI system assisting hospitals during a public health emergency where medical resources are limited. Decisions involving patient care require fairness, compassion, transparency, and respect for human dignity. Even when uncertainty prevents perfect solutions, ethical principles provide guidance. Responsible reasoning asks not only what decision appears effective but also whether it respects human rights and promotes the greatest overall well-being. Future AGI systems must integrate ethical reasoning into every stage of uncertain decision-making.

Scientific progress itself depends upon uncertainty. Every important discovery begins with unanswered questions. Researchers investigating new diseases, exploring distant planets, studying climate systems, or developing advanced technologies rarely know the final answers in advance. Instead, they gather evidence, test hypotheses, revise theories, and gradually reduce uncertainty through careful investigation. Curiosity thrives because uncertainty exists. AGI systems designed to support scientific discovery may help researchers explore countless possibilities while accelerating the search for reliable knowledge.

Education also prepares students to make thoughtful decisions under uncertainty. Classroom discussions encourage students to evaluate evidence, compare viewpoints, defend conclusions, and revise opinions when presented with stronger arguments. Rather than memorizing answers, students develop reasoning skills that help them navigate uncertain situations throughout life. As technology continues advancing, these reasoning abilities will become increasingly valuable because future careers will involve solving new problems that have no simple answers.

One remarkable feature of human intelligence is resilience. People rarely stop making decisions simply because uncertainty exists. Families continue planning for the future. Entrepreneurs launch new businesses. Scientists pursue ambitious research. Students apply to colleges. Communities rebuild after disasters. Every important step forward requires courage to act despite incomplete information. Responsible decision-making balances careful analysis with thoughtful action rather than allowing uncertainty to create paralysis.

Artificial General Intelligence will eventually operate in environments filled with changing information, unexpected events, incomplete evidence, and competing priorities. Success will require much more than rapid calculations. Intelligent systems must evaluate probabilities, compare alternatives, estimate risks, communicate uncertainty honestly, adapt to new evidence, and support ethical human decision-making. These abilities will distinguish truly reasoning systems from machines that merely process information.

As you continue your journey through reasoning intelligence, remember that uncertainty is not an obstacle to intelligence—it is an opportunity to demonstrate it. Every thoughtful decision made with limited information reflects careful reasoning, responsible judgment, and the willingness to continue learning. The future will always contain unknowns, but those who gather reliable information, evaluate evidence carefully, consider multiple possibilities, and remain open to improvement will be best prepared to navigate whatever challenges lie ahead. By understanding how to make wise decisions under uncertainty, you are developing one of the most valuable skills needed for both human leadership and the responsible development of Artificial General Intelligence.

Learn AI. Understand AI. Shape the Future.
— Susie Hala, IntelliGloss Press

Chapter 10 Summary

Decision-Making Under Uncertainty

This chapter explored how humans and future Artificial General Intelligence (AGI) make thoughtful decisions when complete information is unavailable. Students learned that uncertainty is a normal part of everyday life and that intelligent decision-making depends on gathering evidence, evaluating risks, and remaining flexible as new information becomes available.

The chapter explained that uncertainty exists in many professions. Doctors often begin treatment before receiving every laboratory result. Emergency managers prepare for storms before knowing the exact forecast. Business leaders make investments without knowing future market conditions. Scientists conduct research while searching for answers that are still unknown.

Students learned that good decision-makers collect reliable information and carefully evaluate the quality of their sources. Reliable evidence leads to stronger decisions, while misinformation and unsupported claims can lead to poor judgment.

The chapter introduced the role of probability in estimating the likelihood of different outcomes. Instead of expecting certainty, intelligent systems use probability to compare possible futures and recommend actions based on the available evidence.

Students also explored important concepts such as risk assessment, trade-offs, multiple future scenarios, communication, experience, resilience, and ethical decision-making. These ideas help people and future AGI systems make responsible choices even when uncertainty cannot be completely eliminated.

Finally, the chapter emphasized that intelligence is not about always having perfect answers. True reasoning involves recognizing uncertainty, explaining confidence levels, adapting to new evidence, and making thoughtful decisions that balance safety, responsibility, and long-term success.

Chapter 10 Reflection

Life rarely provides complete certainty.

Every day we make decisions without knowing exactly what will happen tomorrow. We choose careers, plan vacations, prepare for weather changes, study for exams, invest in businesses, and solve problems while many questions remain unanswered.

The ability to make thoughtful decisions despite uncertainty is one of the greatest strengths of human intelligence.

This chapter reminds us that good decision-makers do not ignore uncertainty. Instead, they gather information, compare alternatives, evaluate risks, consider consequences, and remain willing to adjust their thinking when new evidence appears.

Artificial General Intelligence will also need these abilities. Future intelligent systems must learn to explain not only what they recommend but also how confident they are, what assumptions they made, and what additional information could improve their recommendations.

As students prepare for the future, they should remember that uncertainty is not something to fear. It is an opportunity to practice careful reasoning, strengthen critical thinking, and develop wise judgment.

The people who succeed are not those who know everything.

They are the people who continue learning, adapting, and making thoughtful decisions even when the future is uncertain.

Chapter 10 Worksheet

Name: ______________________________

Date: ______________________________

Part A – Vocabulary

Write your own definition for each term.

1. Uncertainty

____

____

2. Probability

____

____

3. Risk Assessment

____

____

4. Trade-Off

____

____

5. Confidence Level

6. Scenario Planning

Part B – Short Answer

1. Why is uncertainty a normal part of decision-making?

2. Why should decision-makers gather reliable information?

3. What role does probability play in reasoning?

4. Why is it important to evaluate risks before making decisions?

5. Why should future AGI systems explain how confident they are in their recommendations?

Part C – Decision-Making Activity

Imagine your community is preparing for a major storm.

Complete the following planning process.

Step 1 – What information would you collect?

Step 2 – What possible risks should be considered?

Step 3 – What are three possible actions?

1.
2.
3.

Step 4 – Which action would you recommend and why?

Step 5 – What new information might change your decision?

Part D – Critical Thinking

Imagine an AGI system is helping doctors during a disease outbreak.

Explain why each of the following is important.

Reliable Evidence

Probability

Risk Assessment

Communication

Ethical Decision-Making

Part E – Personal Reflection

Describe a difficult decision you made when you did not have all the information you wanted.

How did you decide what to do?

Chapter 10 Quiz

Name: ______________________________

Score: _________ /20

Multiple Choice

1. Decision-making under uncertainty means

A. Waiting until every answer is known.

B. Making thoughtful decisions with incomplete information.

C. Guessing without evidence.

D. Ignoring possible risks.

2. Why is reliable information important?

A. It increases uncertainty.

B. It improves decision quality.

C. It replaces reasoning.

D. It removes all risk.

3. Probability helps people

A. Guarantee future events.

B. Estimate how likely different outcomes are.

C. Avoid making decisions.

D. Ignore evidence.

4. Risk assessment involves

A. Ignoring possible problems.

B. Evaluating the likelihood and consequences of different outcomes.

C. Memorizing information.

D. Eliminating uncertainty completely.

5. Why should AGI communicate confidence levels?

A. To confuse people.

B. To help humans understand how certain or uncertain a recommendation is.

C. To replace human judgment.

D. To eliminate decision-making.

True or False

6. Every important decision can be made with complete certainty.

True / False

7. Good decision-makers evaluate multiple possible outcomes.

True / False

8. Ethical reasoning remains important during uncertain situations.

True / False

9. Future AGI systems should explain uncertainty clearly.

True / False

10. Experience helps improve future decision-making.

True / False

Short Answer

11. Explain why uncertainty is a normal part of life.

____

____

12. What is risk assessment?

____

____

13. Give one example of a trade-off.

____

____

14. Why should intelligent systems evaluate several possible futures?

____

____

15. What is the most important lesson you learned from this chapter?

Chapter 10 Answer Key

Multiple Choice

1. **B** – Making thoughtful decisions with incomplete information.
2. **B** – It improves decision quality.
3. **B** – Estimate how likely different outcomes are.
4. **B** – Evaluating the likelihood and consequences of different outcomes.
5. **B** – To help humans understand how certain or uncertain a recommendation is.

True or False

6. **False**
7. **True**
8. **True**
9. **True**
10. **True**

Short Answer (Sample Answers)

11. Uncertainty is a normal part of life because people often make decisions before all information is available. Conditions change, new evidence appears, and future events cannot always be predicted with complete accuracy.

12. Risk assessment is the process of identifying possible risks, estimating how likely they are to occur, and evaluating their potential consequences before making a decision.

13. Examples include spending money on new technology instead of other projects, choosing a longer but safer travel route, or investing time in additional education instead of entering the workforce immediately.

14. Evaluating multiple future scenarios helps intelligent systems prepare for different possibilities, reduce unexpected problems, and recommend more flexible and resilient solutions.

15. Answers will vary. Students should describe one important lesson, such as gathering reliable information, evaluating risks, using probability, communicating uncertainty honestly, or making ethical decisions despite incomplete information.

Extension Activity (Optional)

Choose a real-world decision currently facing your school, community, or the world. Examples include preparing for severe weather, planning transportation improvements, responding to a public health concern, or adopting a new technology. Create a decision-making report that identifies available evidence, possible risks, multiple future scenarios, trade-offs, ethical considerations, and your final recommendation. Then explain how a future AGI system could assist human decision-makers while ensuring that people remain responsible for the final decisions.

Chapter 11

Multi-Step Reasoning and Long-Term Planning

Imagine you are standing at the starting line of a marathon. You know the finish line is more than twenty-six miles away, but you also understand that you cannot reach it with one giant leap. Every mile depends on the one before it. You must pace yourself, stay hydrated, adjust to changing conditions, and continue moving forward even when the journey becomes difficult. Winning the race depends not on one single action but on thousands of small decisions made over many hours. Life works the same way. Building a successful career, earning a college degree, starting a business, designing a spacecraft, discovering a medical treatment, or preparing for the future all require long-term planning and multi-step reasoning. These abilities allow people to connect today's actions with tomorrow's goals. As Artificial General Intelligence (AGI) continues to develop, one of its greatest challenges will be learning how to think beyond the present moment, organize complex plans, adapt when conditions change, and pursue long-term objectives without losing sight of the final destination.

Many problems can be solved with a single decision. If a light is off, flipping the switch solves the problem immediately. However, most meaningful challenges are much more complex. Imagine planning the construction of a new hospital. Before the first patient ever receives care, many interconnected tasks must be completed. Community leaders identify the need for a hospital. Architects design the building. Engineers develop structural plans. Environmental experts evaluate the construction site. Government agencies issue permits. Construction teams build the facility. Medical equipment is installed. Doctors, nurses, and support staff are hired. Safety inspections are completed. Technology systems are tested. Emergency procedures are practiced. Every step depends on the successful completion of previous steps. This sequence illustrates multi-step reasoning, the ability to organize many connected decisions into one coordinated plan.

Multi-step reasoning begins by identifying a clear goal. Without a destination, planning becomes impossible. Consider a student who wants to become a physician. The long-term goal is clear, but achieving it requires many smaller objectives. The student must perform well in middle school, succeed in high school science and mathematics, graduate from college, attend medical school, complete clinical training, pass licensing examinations, and continue professional education throughout a medical career. Every stage prepares for the next. The student cannot skip directly to becoming a doctor. Long-term success depends on recognizing that large goals are achieved through many smaller accomplishments. Future AGI systems must develop similar planning abilities if they are to solve complex real-world problems.

One important characteristic of long-term planning is understanding **dependencies**. A dependency exists when one task cannot begin until another task has been completed. Imagine baking a cake. Ingredients must be gathered before mixing begins. Batter must be prepared before baking. The cake must cool before frosting can be applied. Ignoring these dependencies produces poor results. Engineers designing airplanes, scientists conducting experiments, teachers developing curriculum, and software developers creating computer programs all organize work according to similar sequences. AGI systems responsible for planning large projects will need to recognize these relationships automatically, ensuring that each step occurs in the proper order.

Another essential skill is breaking long-term goals into manageable stages. Large challenges often appear overwhelming when viewed all at once. However, dividing them into smaller milestones makes progress easier to measure. Consider the goal of writing a book. Rather than focusing on hundreds of pages, successful authors first develop an outline, write individual chapters, revise drafts, edit content, design illustrations, and prepare the final manuscript for publication. Completing one stage creates momentum for the next. This approach reduces stress while improving organization. Future AGI systems assisting researchers, educators, engineers, or business leaders may organize large projects into similar milestone-based plans that allow steady progress toward ambitious objectives.

Time management plays a central role in long-term planning. Every project has deadlines, priorities, and limited resources. Imagine organizing an international scientific conference. Invitations must be sent months in advance. Speakers confirm presentations. Travel arrangements are coordinated. Meeting rooms are reserved. Educational materials are prepared. Technical equipment is tested before participants arrive. Completing tasks at the correct time is just as important as completing them correctly. AGI systems designed to manage complex schedules must understand timing relationships while adjusting plans whenever unexpected delays occur.

Long-term planning also requires anticipating future obstacles. Experienced travelers preparing for a long journey pack extra supplies because they recognize that unexpected situations may arise. Engineers design backup systems into spacecraft because they understand that equipment failures are possible. Farmers prepare for changing weather conditions by developing irrigation plans and storing supplies. Successful planners do not assume everything will proceed perfectly. Instead, they identify possible risks and prepare alternative strategies. Future AGI systems must learn to anticipate uncertainty while recommending backup plans that improve resilience during changing circumstances.

Adaptation becomes especially important during long-term projects because the future rarely unfolds exactly as expected. Imagine a city planning to build a new public transportation system over ten years. Population growth, economic conditions, technological advances, environmental regulations, and community needs may all change during that period. Successful leaders continuously review progress, evaluate new information, and adjust plans accordingly. Remaining committed to the overall goal while adapting individual steps demonstrates intelligent planning. Future AGI systems must avoid rigid thinking by updating plans whenever changing conditions require new approaches.

One remarkable feature of human planning is the ability to balance **short-term actions** with **long-term consequences**. Students often choose to study for examinations instead of spending every evening on entertainment because they recognize the future benefits of education. Families save money for emergencies or college expenses rather than spending every dollar immediately. Governments invest in infrastructure projects that may not be completed for many years because future generations will benefit. These examples demonstrate delayed gratification, the willingness to accept smaller immediate rewards in exchange for greater long-term success. AGI systems supporting education, healthcare, environmental planning, or economic development must evaluate both immediate needs and future consequences before recommending actions.

Memory strengthens multi-step reasoning by allowing individuals to track progress across long periods. Imagine constructing a large suspension bridge over several years. Engineers must remember previous design decisions, completed inspections, material specifications, safety requirements, and construction milestones. Forgetting earlier decisions could lead to costly mistakes or dangerous failures. Human memory, written records, digital databases, and project management systems all help preserve continuity. Future AGI systems will require sophisticated memory structures capable of remembering previous decisions while explaining how earlier actions influence current recommendations.

Collaboration also becomes increasingly important as projects grow larger. No single individual possesses all the knowledge required to build hospitals, explore space, develop advanced medical treatments, or design global communication networks. Successful planning requires cooperation among specialists from many different fields. Architects collaborate with engineers. Doctors work alongside nurses, pharmacists, and researchers. Teachers coordinate with administrators, counselors, and families. Scientists share discoveries across international research teams. Future AGI systems may serve as collaborative partners by organizing information, monitoring progress, identifying potential conflicts, and supporting communication among diverse teams while respecting human leadership.

Monitoring progress represents another essential planning skill. Successful planners regularly compare current performance with original goals. A student reviews grades throughout the school year rather than waiting until the final examination. Business leaders monitor financial performance each quarter instead of waiting until the end of the year. Scientists evaluate research findings after each experiment before continuing additional studies. Continuous monitoring allows problems to be identified early when corrections are easier and less expensive. Future AGI systems will likely monitor complex projects in real time, identifying delays, recommending adjustments, and predicting future challenges before they become major obstacles.

One of the greatest strengths of human reasoning is learning from previous long-term projects. Engineers designing modern airplanes benefit from lessons learned through decades of aviation history. Medical researchers build upon discoveries made by earlier generations of scientists. Educators improve teaching methods by studying previous classroom experiences. Long-term planning becomes more effective because accumulated knowledge guides future decisions. AGI systems capable of lifelong learning may similarly improve planning by analyzing the successes and failures of previous projects while adapting strategies to new situations.

Ethics must remain central to long-term planning because today's decisions often influence future generations. Building factories without considering environmental consequences may create economic benefits today while causing ecological damage tomorrow. Developing powerful technologies without appropriate safeguards may create future risks. Responsible planning requires balancing immediate advantages with long-term responsibility. Future AGI systems must evaluate how decisions affect not only current users but also future communities, natural resources, and society as a whole. Ethical reasoning ensures that progress remains sustainable and beneficial.

One exciting possibility for AGI involves supporting humanity's largest long-term challenges. Climate change, renewable energy, disease prevention, food security, clean water, sustainable cities, and space exploration all require planning that extends across decades. These projects involve countless interconnected decisions made by governments, scientists, engineers, educators, businesses, and communities worldwide. AGI systems capable of organizing complex information, simulating future scenarios, coordinating resources, and adapting plans over time may become valuable partners in addressing these global challenges.

Students preparing for the future should recognize that long-term planning is one of the most valuable life skills they can develop. Every important achievement begins with a goal, followed by careful planning, steady effort, continuous learning, and thoughtful adaptation. Whether pursuing higher education, building a business, improving a community, conducting scientific research, or developing new technologies, success depends upon connecting many small actions into one meaningful journey. The ability to think beyond today's tasks while remaining focused on future objectives will become increasingly important in an AI-powered world.

Artificial General Intelligence represents much more than machines solving isolated problems. It represents intelligent systems capable of organizing extended sequences of reasoning, managing changing priorities, coordinating many interconnected tasks, and pursuing meaningful goals across long periods. These capabilities require memory, adaptability, communication, ethical reasoning, and continuous learning working together. Building such systems remains one of the most ambitious goals in artificial intelligence research.

As you continue your exploration of reasoning intelligence, remember that every great accomplishment in human history began with a vision that required patience, persistence, and thoughtful planning. Great cities were not built in a single day. Medical discoveries required years of research. Space missions demanded decades of preparation. Educational achievements grew through consistent effort over many years. The future will belong to those who can think several steps ahead while remaining flexible enough to adapt when circumstances change. By developing multi-step reasoning and long-term planning skills today, you are preparing not only to understand Artificial General Intelligence but also to become a thoughtful leader capable of shaping tomorrow's world with wisdom, responsibility, and purpose.

Learn AI. Understand AI. Shape the Future.
— Susie Hala, IntelliGloss Press

Chapter 11 Summary

Multi-Step Reasoning and Long-Term Planning

This chapter explained that many of life's most important goals cannot be achieved with a single decision. Instead, success depends on multi-step reasoning—the ability to organize many connected actions into a logical sequence that leads toward a long-term objective.

Students learned that large goals become manageable when they are divided into smaller milestones. Whether becoming a doctor, designing a bridge, building a hospital, conducting scientific research, or creating new technology, every achievement begins with careful planning and consistent progress.

The chapter introduced several important concepts that support long-term planning, including setting clear goals, understanding dependencies, organizing tasks into logical sequences, managing time effectively, monitoring progress, anticipating future challenges, and adapting when conditions change.

Students also discovered that successful planning requires balancing short-term actions with long-term consequences. Good decision-makers recognize that today's choices influence tomorrow's opportunities.

Another important lesson was the role of memory, collaboration, and continuous learning. Large projects often require teams of people working together while remembering previous decisions and improving plans as new information becomes available.

The chapter also emphasized the importance of ethical planning. Future AGI systems should consider how present decisions affect future generations, natural resources, and society as a whole.

Finally, students learned that long-term planning is one of the defining characteristics of intelligent reasoning. As Artificial General Intelligence continues to evolve, the ability to organize complex projects, adapt to changing environments, and pursue meaningful goals responsibly will become one of its most valuable capabilities.

Chapter 11 Reflection

Every great achievement begins with a single step.

A doctor begins as a student.

A bridge begins as a drawing.

A spacecraft begins as an idea.

A successful future begins with decisions made today.

This chapter reminds us that meaningful accomplishments require patience, planning, and perseverance. Multi-step reasoning teaches us that large goals are reached through many smaller decisions working together over time.

Artificial General Intelligence will also depend on this ability. Future intelligent systems must organize complex projects, remember previous decisions, adjust to changing conditions, and continue moving toward long-term objectives without losing sight of their purpose.

Students who develop strong planning skills today will be better prepared for tomorrow's opportunities. Learning how to organize tasks, solve problems step by step, work with others, and adapt to unexpected challenges will remain valuable in every profession.

Technology may become more intelligent, but thoughtful planning, ethical leadership, and responsible decision-making will always depend on people who understand the importance of looking beyond today.

The future is built one thoughtful decision at a time.

Chapter 11 Worksheet

Name: ______________________________________

Date: _______________________________________

Part A – Vocabulary

Write your own definition for each term.

1. Multi-Step Reasoning

---

2. Long-Term Planning

3. Dependency

4. Milestone

5. Adaptation

6. Monitoring Progress

Part B – Short Answer

1. Why is multi-step reasoning important?

2. What is the purpose of breaking large goals into smaller milestones?

3. Why must intelligent systems adapt when circumstances change?

4. How does monitoring progress improve long-term planning?

5. Why should future AGI systems consider ethical consequences while planning?

Part C – Planning Activity

Choose one long-term goal you would like to accomplish.

Examples:

- Graduate from college
- Start a business
- Become a teacher
- Become an engineer
- Learn a new language

Goal

Step 1

Step 2

Step 3

Step 4

Possible Challenges

How Will You Adapt?

Part D – Critical Thinking

Imagine an AGI system is helping build a new children's hospital.

Explain why each of the following is important.

Planning

Dependencies

Monitoring Progress

Adaptation

Ethical Responsibility

Part E – Personal Reflection

Describe a time when you worked toward a goal over several weeks or months.

What steps helped you succeed?

Chapter 11 Quiz

Name: ______________________________

Score: _________ /20

Multiple Choice

1. Multi-step reasoning helps people

A. Solve only simple problems.

B. Organize many connected decisions into a logical plan.

C. Avoid planning.

D. Ignore future goals.

2. A milestone is

A. A random event.

B. A smaller goal that marks progress toward a larger objective.

C. The final answer.

D. A mistake.

3. Why are dependencies important?

A. Some tasks must be completed before others can begin.

B. Every task is independent.

C. They eliminate planning.

D. They increase uncertainty.

4. Monitoring progress helps people

A. Ignore problems.

B. Identify challenges early and adjust plans.

C. Stop learning.

D. Avoid teamwork.

5. Long-term planning is important because

A. Meaningful goals usually require many connected steps.

B. Every goal can be completed immediately.

C. Planning is unnecessary.

D. Technology solves every problem automatically.

True or False

6. Large goals are easier to achieve when divided into smaller steps.

True / False

7. Future AGI systems should adapt when new information becomes available.

True / False

8. Ethical thinking should be part of long-term planning.

True / False

9. Collaboration often strengthens complex projects.

True / False

10. Multi-step reasoning only applies to engineering.

True / False

Short Answer

11. Explain multi-step reasoning.

____

____

12. Why is adaptation important during long-term projects?

____

____

13. Give one example of a dependency.

____

____

14. Why should AGI monitor progress during large projects?

____

____

15. What is the most important lesson you learned from this chapter?

____

____

Chapter 11 Answer Key

Multiple Choice

1. **B** – Organize many connected decisions into a logical plan.
2. **B** – A smaller goal that marks progress toward a larger objective.
3. **A** – Some tasks must be completed before others can begin.
4. **B** – Identify challenges early and adjust plans.
5. **A** – Meaningful goals usually require many connected steps.

True or False

6. **True**
7. **True**
8. **True**
9. **True**
10. **False**

Short Answer (Sample Answers)

11. Multi-step reasoning is the ability to solve complex problems by organizing many connected actions into a logical sequence that leads toward a long-term goal.

12. Adaptation allows people and intelligent systems to adjust plans when conditions change, new information becomes available, or unexpected challenges arise.

13. Example: A building's foundation must be completed before constructing the walls, or a student must graduate from high school before attending college.

14. Monitoring progress helps identify delays, measure success, improve efficiency, and make adjustments before small problems become major obstacles.

15. Answers will vary. Students should explain one important lesson from the chapter, such as breaking goals into smaller milestones, adapting to change, collaborating with others, or planning responsibly for the future.

Extension Activity (Optional)

Choose a real-world project such as preparing for college, organizing a community event, building a school garden, launching a small business, or planning a scientific research project. Create a complete long-term planning timeline that includes goals, milestones, dependencies, possible risks, backup plans, ethical considerations, and methods for monitoring progress. Then explain how a future AGI planning assistant could help organize the project while keeping humans responsible for the final decisions.

Chapter 12

Reasoning Across Multiple Domains

Imagine you are asked to solve a problem that has never existed before. A new disease appears that affects both human health and food production. Solving it requires knowledge of medicine, biology, agriculture, environmental science, economics, computer science, psychology, and public policy. No single subject provides all the answers. Success depends on bringing together knowledge from many different fields and understanding how they influence one another. This ability is called **reasoning across multiple domains**, and it represents one of the defining characteristics of human intelligence. People naturally combine information from different subjects to understand complex situations. Artificial General Intelligence (AGI) must eventually develop the same ability if it is to solve real-world problems responsibly. The future will not ask intelligent systems to solve isolated textbook exercises. It will ask them to address interconnected challenges where science, technology, society, economics, and ethics all influence the final decision.

Throughout history, education has been organized into individual subjects such as mathematics, science, history, language arts, geography, engineering, and the arts. This organization makes learning easier because students can focus on one discipline at a time. However, the real world rarely separates knowledge so neatly. Building a bridge requires mathematics to calculate structural strength, physics to understand forces, engineering to design the structure, environmental science to protect ecosystems, economics to manage costs, communication to coordinate construction teams, and government regulations to ensure public safety. Every major project combines many forms of knowledge. Human intelligence succeeds because it can move freely between these different domains while recognizing how they work together.

Consider the challenge of developing an electric vehicle. Engineers design motors and batteries. Chemists create advanced materials capable of storing energy safely. Computer scientists develop software that manages vehicle performance. Environmental scientists study how manufacturing affects natural resources. Economists analyze production costs and market demand. Designers create comfortable interiors and attractive exteriors. Government agencies establish safety regulations. Consumers evaluate affordability and convenience. A successful electric vehicle is not the product of one field alone. It is the result of experts reasoning across many disciplines while working toward a common goal. Future AGI systems must coordinate similar knowledge if they are to support complex innovation.

Healthcare offers another powerful example of multi-domain reasoning. Imagine a physician treating a patient with diabetes. Medical knowledge explains how the disease affects the body. Nutrition science helps develop healthy meal plans. Psychology supports motivation for long-term lifestyle changes. Exercise science recommends appropriate physical activity. Pharmacology guides medication management. Data science analyzes patient health records. Economics considers treatment affordability. Social work helps patients access community resources. Effective healthcare depends upon combining expertise from many fields rather than relying on one perspective. AGI systems supporting healthcare must integrate these diverse forms of knowledge while respecting the expertise of human professionals.

Education itself demonstrates the importance of interdisciplinary reasoning. A teacher introducing climate change may combine earth science to explain atmospheric processes, mathematics to interpret graphs and statistics, geography to examine global regions, history to study industrial development, economics to discuss energy systems, government to examine public policy, and language arts to strengthen communication skills through writing and discussion. Students gain deeper understanding because they see how knowledge from different subjects connects into one larger picture. Future AGI tutoring systems may personalize interdisciplinary learning by helping students discover these meaningful connections.

One important reason reasoning across multiple domains matters is that **complex problems rarely have simple causes**. Consider food insecurity in a growing city. Agriculture influences food production. Transportation affects food distribution. Economics determines affordability. Climate conditions influence harvests. Public policy shapes agricultural support programs. Technology improves farming efficiency. Education helps families make informed nutritional choices. Healthcare addresses the effects of poor nutrition. Solving food insecurity requires understanding the interactions among all these areas rather than focusing on only one. AGI systems capable of connecting these relationships may help leaders develop more effective long-term solutions.

Communication becomes especially important when specialists from different disciplines work together. Scientists, engineers, educators, business leaders, healthcare professionals, and policymakers often use specialized vocabulary unique to their fields. Successful collaboration requires translating technical knowledge into language everyone can understand. Human professionals regularly explain complex ideas to colleagues outside their specialties. Future AGI systems may serve as communication partners by helping different experts understand one another while preserving technical accuracy. This ability could improve teamwork across many industries.

Another valuable skill is recognizing that different fields often approach problems differently. Scientists rely heavily on experimentation and evidence. Historians examine documents and historical context. Engineers focus on design and practical application. Economists analyze incentives and resource allocation. Artists explore creativity and emotional expression. Each discipline contributes unique perspectives. Intelligent reasoning does not replace one approach with another. Instead, it combines multiple viewpoints to produce more complete understanding. AGI systems must appreciate these differences rather than assuming every problem should be solved using identical methods.

One fascinating example of interdisciplinary reasoning appears in space exploration. Sending astronauts to the Moon or Mars requires physics to calculate trajectories, engineering to build spacecraft, medicine to protect astronaut health, biology to study long-term effects of space travel, computer science to control navigation systems, chemistry to develop fuels, psychology to support crew well-being, communications technology to maintain contact with Earth, and international cooperation to coordinate global research efforts. Every successful mission depends on many disciplines working together toward one objective. Future AGI systems assisting space exploration must integrate all these forms of knowledge while adapting to changing conditions during missions.

Environmental sustainability also demands reasoning across multiple domains. Protecting forests involves ecology, economics, agriculture, law, education, public policy, engineering, and community engagement. Building renewable energy systems requires materials science, electrical engineering, environmental science, finance, manufacturing, transportation, and workforce development. Addressing climate change requires global cooperation among governments, businesses, educators, scientists, and citizens. These examples demonstrate that modern challenges cannot be solved by isolated expertise alone. AGI systems capable of interdisciplinary reasoning may help coordinate information while supporting collaborative decision-making.

Reasoning across domains also strengthens creativity. Many important innovations occur when ideas from one discipline inspire breakthroughs in another. Engineers studying bird flight developed improved aircraft designs. Medical researchers learned from nature when designing new surgical techniques. Computer scientists borrowed concepts from the human brain while developing artificial neural networks. Architects studied honeycombs to design stronger and lighter structures. These discoveries occurred because people recognized valuable connections across different areas of knowledge. Future AGI systems may accelerate innovation by identifying relationships that humans have not yet discovered.

Transfer learning plays an important role in interdisciplinary reasoning. Transfer learning means applying knowledge gained in one area to solve problems in another. A student who learns logical thinking in mathematics may apply those skills to computer programming. A musician may recognize patterns useful in language learning. A biology student studying ecosystems may better understand economic systems because both involve interconnected relationships. Human intelligence becomes stronger because knowledge rarely remains confined within one subject. AGI researchers hope future systems will transfer knowledge just as flexibly across many domains.

Data has become another bridge connecting disciplines. Hospitals analyze patient records to improve healthcare. Farmers use satellite imagery to improve crop production. Cities analyze traffic data to reduce congestion. Schools examine student performance to strengthen instruction. Businesses study customer behavior to improve services. Scientists analyze environmental measurements to predict climate trends. Data science supports nearly every profession by revealing patterns that guide decision-making. Future AGI systems must integrate information from many sources while protecting privacy, maintaining security, and ensuring ethical use of data.

Ethical reasoning becomes increasingly important as more disciplines interact. Imagine developing facial recognition technology. Computer science makes the technology possible. Engineering improves accuracy. Law establishes regulations. Ethics evaluates fairness. Psychology studies human behavior. Sociology examines community impact. Public policy determines appropriate use. A technically successful invention may still create serious problems if ethical considerations are ignored. Responsible AGI systems must evaluate not only whether something can be done but also whether it should be done. Interdisciplinary reasoning helps ensure that technology serves humanity responsibly.

One challenge facing future AGI involves resolving conflicts among competing goals. A city may want faster transportation, cleaner air, affordable housing, economic growth, and protected green spaces simultaneously. These objectives sometimes support one another but may also compete for limited resources. Intelligent reasoning requires balancing many priorities while understanding the consequences of different choices. Humans regularly negotiate these trade-offs through collaboration, discussion, and compromise. Future AGI systems should assist by organizing information, simulating possible outcomes, and explaining alternatives while leaving final decisions to human leaders.

Education is changing because future careers increasingly require interdisciplinary thinking. Employers seek individuals who can communicate across departments, analyze information from multiple perspectives, adapt to new technologies, and collaborate with people from diverse backgrounds. Students who understand only one discipline may struggle when facing problems requiring broader perspectives. Schools therefore increasingly emphasize critical thinking, collaboration, communication, creativity, and problem-solving that connects many subjects together. These skills prepare students not only for careers but also for thoughtful citizenship in a rapidly changing world.

Artificial General Intelligence represents an ambitious effort to build systems capable of integrating knowledge the way humans naturally do. Rather than performing one specialized task exceptionally well, AGI seeks to combine reasoning, memory, learning, communication, creativity, ethics, planning, and decision-making across countless domains. Achieving this goal requires more than faster computers or larger databases. It requires understanding how knowledge from different disciplines connects into one unified understanding of the world.

Students preparing for the future should recognize that the boundaries between subjects will continue becoming less important. Healthcare increasingly depends on artificial intelligence. Agriculture relies on satellite technology. Education incorporates data analytics. Transportation uses robotics and machine learning. Environmental science benefits from advanced computing. Every profession is becoming more interconnected. Those who learn to think across disciplines will be better prepared to solve tomorrow's challenges while leading innovation responsibly.

As you continue your journey through reasoning intelligence, remember that the world's greatest challenges do not belong to one subject alone. They belong to all of us. Solving them requires curiosity that reaches beyond traditional boundaries, communication that brings people together, and reasoning that connects ideas from many different fields. Artificial General Intelligence will one day help organize this knowledge, but human wisdom, collaboration, and ethical leadership will continue guiding its use. By learning to reason across multiple domains today, you are developing one of the most valuable abilities needed to build a future where technology and humanity work together to improve life for everyone.

Learn AI. Understand AI. Shape the Future.
— Susie Hala, IntelliGloss Press

Chapter 12 Summary

Reasoning Across Multiple Domains

This chapter explained that many of today's most important challenges cannot be solved by knowledge from a single subject. Instead, successful problem-solving requires reasoning across multiple domains by combining ideas from science, mathematics, engineering, healthcare, education, economics, technology, communication, ethics, and many other disciplines.

Students learned that while schools organize learning into separate subjects, the real world is highly interconnected. Building hospitals, designing electric vehicles, exploring space, improving education, protecting the environment, and advancing healthcare all require experts from many fields working together toward shared goals.

The chapter introduced the concept of interdisciplinary reasoning, which allows people and future Artificial General Intelligence (AGI) systems to connect knowledge from different disciplines to develop more complete and effective solutions.

Students also explored the importance of communication, collaboration, transfer learning, creativity, data analysis, and ethical reasoning. These skills help professionals understand one another, exchange ideas, and solve complex problems that no single field could solve alone.

Another important lesson was that interdisciplinary thinking strengthens innovation. Many scientific discoveries and technological advances occurred because someone recognized useful connections between different areas of knowledge.

Finally, the chapter emphasized that future AGI systems must reason across many domains rather than specializing in only one task. The ability to integrate knowledge, explain complex ideas, support collaboration, and evaluate ethical consequences will be essential for intelligent systems working alongside humans.

Chapter 12 Reflection

The world does not divide problems into school subjects.

Climate change is not only science.

Healthcare is not only medicine.

Building a bridge is not only engineering.

Teaching children is not only education.

Every important challenge connects many different areas of knowledge.

This chapter reminds us that true intelligence comes from seeing relationships that cross traditional boundaries. The greatest innovators throughout history learned to combine ideas from different fields to create new discoveries that improved society.

Artificial General Intelligence must also learn this ability. Future intelligent systems will need to understand how science, technology, economics, ethics, communication, and human behavior work together instead of treating them as separate topics.

As students prepare for the future, they should remember that curiosity should never stop at the edge of one subject. Every new skill strengthens another. Every new perspective expands understanding.

Learning across many disciplines prepares us not only for future careers but also for thoughtful leadership in a world where cooperation, creativity, and responsible decision-making matter more than ever.

The future belongs to those who can connect ideas, work with others, and see the bigger picture.

Chapter 12 Worksheet

Name: ______________________________________

Date: ____

Part A – Vocabulary

Write your own definition for each term.

1. Interdisciplinary Reasoning

____

____

2. Domain

____

____

3. Collaboration

____

____

4. Transfer Learning

____

____

5. Data Integration

6. Ethical Reasoning

Part B – Short Answer

1. Why is reasoning across multiple domains important?

2. Why do real-world problems require knowledge from many disciplines?

3. How does collaboration improve problem-solving?

4. What is transfer learning?

5. Why must future AGI systems understand many different domains?

Part C – Interdisciplinary Activity

Choose one of the following challenges.

- Build a new hospital
- Reduce pollution

• Improve public transportation

• Design a Mars mission

List at least five different fields that would be involved.

Field 1

Field 2

Field 3

Field 4

Field 5

Explain how these fields work together.

Part D – Critical Thinking

Imagine an AGI system is helping a city build a new renewable energy system.

Explain why each area is important.

Engineering

Environmental Science

Economics

Government Policy

Ethics

Part E – Personal Reflection

Describe a school project where you used knowledge from more than one subject.

How did combining different subjects improve your work?

Chapter 12 Quiz

Name: ________________________________

Score: _________ /20

Multiple Choice

1. Reasoning across multiple domains means

A. Studying only one subject.

B. Combining knowledge from different disciplines to solve problems.

C. Ignoring other viewpoints.

D. Memorizing information only.

2. Which project requires many different fields of knowledge?

A. Building a hospital

B. Space exploration

C. Environmental protection

D. All of the above

3. Why is collaboration important?

A. It combines different knowledge and perspectives.

B. It eliminates communication.

C. It removes creativity.

D. It replaces planning.

4. Transfer learning means

A. Moving to another classroom.

B. Applying knowledge from one area to another.

C. Forgetting previous knowledge.

D. Ignoring experience.

5. Why is interdisciplinary reasoning important for AGI?

A. It allows intelligent systems to connect knowledge from many different fields.

B. It increases computer speed only.

C. It eliminates uncertainty.

D. It replaces human expertise.

True or False

6. Most real-world problems involve only one academic subject.

True / False

7. Data can connect many different disciplines.

True / False

8. Ethical reasoning should be included in interdisciplinary problem-solving.

True / False

9. Future AGI systems should communicate effectively with experts from different fields.

True / False

10. Creativity often grows by connecting ideas from different domains.

True / False

Short Answer

11. Explain interdisciplinary reasoning.

12. Why do large projects require many specialists?

13. Give one example of transfer learning.

14. Why should AGI understand ethics as well as technology?

15. What is the most important lesson you learned from this chapter?

Chapter 12 Answer Key

Multiple Choice

1. **B** – Combining knowledge from different disciplines to solve problems.
2. **D** – All of the above.
3. **A** – It combines different knowledge and perspectives.
4. **B** – Applying knowledge from one area to another.
5. **A** – It allows intelligent systems to connect knowledge from many different fields.

True or False

6. **False**
7. **True**
8. **True**
9. **True**
10. **True**

Short Answer (Sample Answers)

11. Interdisciplinary reasoning is the ability to combine knowledge, skills, and ideas from multiple subjects or fields to better understand and solve complex problems.

12. Large projects require many specialists because each discipline contributes unique expertise. Working together produces stronger, safer, and more effective solutions than any one field could achieve alone.

13. Examples include applying mathematical reasoning to computer programming, using biology to inspire engineering designs, or using psychology to improve educational methods.

14. AGI should understand ethics as well as technology so its recommendations are not only technically effective but also fair, responsible, transparent, and beneficial to individuals and society.

15. Answers will vary. Students should describe one important lesson from the chapter, such as connecting ideas across disciplines, collaborating with experts, using transfer learning, or considering ethics during problem-solving.

Extension Activity (Optional)

Choose a current global challenge such as climate change, clean energy, food security, disease prevention, cybersecurity, or space exploration. Create an interdisciplinary project plan that identifies at least eight different fields of expertise needed to address the challenge. Explain the role of each discipline and describe how a future AGI system could help experts organize information, improve collaboration, simulate possible solutions, and support ethical decision-making while keeping humans responsible for final choices.

Chapter 13

Self-Reflection and Metacognition: Thinking About Thinking

Imagine taking an important test at school. After receiving your grade, you do something that many successful learners naturally do. Instead of simply celebrating a high score or feeling disappointed by a low one, you begin asking yourself questions. Which study methods worked best? Which questions were most difficult? Did you manage your time wisely? What should you change before the next exam? At that moment, you are doing something extraordinary. You are not only thinking—you are thinking about your own thinking. This ability is called **metacognition**, and it is one of the most powerful forms of human reasoning. It allows people to examine how they learn, evaluate the quality of their decisions, recognize mistakes, improve strategies, and become better problem-solvers over time. As researchers work toward Artificial General Intelligence (AGI), one of the greatest challenges is teaching intelligent systems to evaluate their own reasoning instead of simply producing answers. Self-reflection may become one of the defining characteristics that separates truly intelligent systems from machines that merely calculate.

Human beings constantly monitor their own thinking, often without realizing it. A reader notices that a paragraph did not make sense and decides to read it again. A driver recognizes becoming tired and chooses to stop for a break. A basketball player realizes a shooting technique is not working and adjusts their form during the game. A scientist questions whether an experiment contains errors before announcing conclusions. These examples demonstrate self-monitoring, the ability to observe one's own mental processes while they are happening. Rather than continuing automatically, people evaluate their progress and make adjustments when necessary. This ability greatly improves learning because it prevents repeated mistakes while encouraging continuous improvement.

Metacognition can be divided into two closely related parts. The first involves **awareness** of how we think. People recognize their strengths, weaknesses, habits, and preferred learning styles. Some students remember information best by reading. Others learn through discussion, hands-on activities, diagrams, or teaching concepts to classmates. Understanding personal learning strategies allows individuals to select methods that help them succeed more efficiently. The second part involves **regulation**, the ability to change thinking when necessary. Awareness identifies what is happening, while regulation determines what should happen next. Together these abilities create intelligent learning that continuously improves over time.

One of the greatest benefits of self-reflection is recognizing mistakes before they become larger problems. Imagine an engineer designing a bridge. Before construction begins, the engineer carefully reviews calculations, checks measurements, and asks colleagues to examine the design. Discovering an error during planning is far less costly than discovering it after construction has begun. Students benefit from the same principle. Reviewing homework before submitting assignments often reveals small mistakes that can easily be corrected. Writers revise drafts multiple times before publishing books. Doctors review medical information before confirming difficult diagnoses. Successful professionals in every field rely upon self-reflection because careful review improves the quality of their work.

Learning improves dramatically when individuals ask themselves thoughtful questions. Instead of simply asking, "Did I get the right answer?" successful learners ask deeper questions. Why did I choose this approach? Could another method work better? What evidence supports my conclusion? Did I overlook important information? These questions encourage deeper reasoning by examining the process rather than focusing only on the final result. Future AGI systems may require similar internal questioning to evaluate the quality of their recommendations before presenting them to human users.

Consider how experienced chess players think during competition. Rather than making the first move that appears reasonable, they often pause to examine several possibilities. They predict how opponents might respond, identify weaknesses in their own plans, and reconsider decisions before acting. This internal conversation allows players to improve decision quality without requiring outside assistance. Researchers hope future AGI systems will develop comparable abilities by reviewing possible solutions internally before selecting the most appropriate recommendation.

Reflection also strengthens **critical thinking** because it encourages healthy skepticism toward one's own conclusions. Human beings naturally make assumptions, but thoughtful individuals regularly examine whether those assumptions remain valid. Scientists repeat experiments to verify discoveries. Journalists confirm information through multiple sources. Historians compare documents from different perspectives. Judges review evidence carefully before reaching legal decisions. These professionals understand that confidence should be supported by careful reasoning rather than certainty alone. Future AGI systems should similarly evaluate the reliability of their conclusions while identifying situations where additional information is needed.

Another important aspect of metacognition involves recognizing **uncertainty**. Sometimes people know that they understand a topic well. Other times they realize their knowledge remains incomplete. This awareness influences decision-making. A physician may consult a specialist when facing an unfamiliar medical condition. A teacher may seek additional training before introducing new technology into the classroom. A business leader may request expert advice before entering a new market. Recognizing limitations demonstrates wisdom rather than weakness. AGI systems capable of estimating their own confidence levels may become more trustworthy because they can explain when additional evidence or human expertise is necessary.

Feedback plays an essential role in self-reflection. Imagine learning to play a musical instrument. A teacher provides guidance, but improvement depends on the student's willingness to listen, evaluate performance, and adjust technique. Athletes study recordings of competitions to improve future performance. Public speakers watch presentations to strengthen communication skills. Pilots review flight simulations after training exercises. Every profession benefits from thoughtful analysis of previous performance. Future AGI systems may similarly compare expected outcomes with actual results, learning continuously from both successes and mistakes.

Memory provides the foundation for meaningful self-reflection. Without remembering previous experiences, improvement becomes difficult because lessons cannot accumulate over time. Students remember effective study habits from earlier courses. Doctors recall previous patient cases when treating similar illnesses. Engineers remember design challenges encountered during earlier projects. These memories become valuable resources that strengthen future reasoning. AGI systems capable of lifelong learning must preserve experiences in ways that support continuous improvement rather than simply storing isolated facts.

Self-reflection also encourages **adaptability**. Suppose a teacher notices that students appear confused during a science lesson. Rather than continuing exactly as planned, the teacher changes instructional methods by using demonstrations, diagrams, or small-group discussions. This flexibility results from observing outcomes and adjusting strategies accordingly. Businesses adapt products to changing customer needs. Scientists revise theories when new evidence appears. Emergency responders adjust plans as disasters evolve. Successful reasoning depends upon recognizing when previous approaches no longer produce the best results. AGI systems must similarly remain flexible while updating strategies whenever circumstances change.

One remarkable feature of human intelligence is the ability to separate emotions from careful analysis while still learning from emotional experiences. A student disappointed by a poor examination score may initially feel frustrated. Through reflection, however, the student recognizes that stronger study habits rather than discouragement offer the best path forward. Emotional awareness combined with thoughtful reasoning promotes resilience. Although AGI systems may not experience emotions exactly as humans do, they may benefit from computational methods that evaluate confidence, uncertainty, priorities, and outcomes while remaining objective during decision-making.

Collaboration often improves self-reflection because other people notice things we may overlook ourselves. Teachers provide constructive feedback to students. Coaches identify athletic techniques requiring improvement. Research teams review one another's experiments before publication. Businesses conduct project evaluations after completing major initiatives. Different perspectives strengthen reasoning by revealing blind spots and encouraging more complete analysis. Future AGI systems may support collaborative reflection by organizing information, identifying inconsistencies, and presenting alternative viewpoints for human consideration.

Ethics represents another essential part of self-reflection. Responsible individuals ask not only whether a decision was effective but also whether it was fair, honest, respectful, and beneficial to others. Business leaders evaluate how decisions affect employees and customers. Scientists consider the social consequences of new discoveries. Teachers reflect upon whether instructional practices support every student fairly. Physicians examine whether treatment decisions respect patient dignity. Future AGI systems should similarly evaluate recommendations using ethical principles alongside technical accuracy. Self-reflection without ethics risks improving efficiency while overlooking human well-being.

Education increasingly emphasizes metacognitive skills because students who understand how they learn often become more successful throughout life. Instead of memorizing information temporarily, they develop strategies for continuous improvement. They plan before beginning assignments, monitor progress while working, evaluate results afterward, and apply lessons to future challenges. These habits strengthen independence because students become active participants in their own learning rather than passive receivers of information. As AI technologies continue advancing, the ability to learn effectively may become even more valuable than memorizing facts that computers can retrieve instantly.

Researchers developing AGI recognize that self-reflection may become one of the final steps toward creating truly adaptive intelligence. Current AI systems often generate answers rapidly but may not always evaluate the quality of their own reasoning. Future AGI systems may include internal reasoning processes that review conclusions, identify possible errors, estimate confidence levels, compare alternative solutions, and revise recommendations before presenting final responses. These capabilities could improve reliability while building greater trust between humans and intelligent systems.

The future workplace will increasingly reward individuals capable of learning continuously. Technologies will change. Careers will evolve. New scientific discoveries will reshape industries. Those who regularly reflect upon their thinking, improve their strategies, and remain open to new knowledge will adapt more successfully than those who rely solely on previous habits. Metacognition therefore becomes not only a learning skill but also a lifelong survival skill in a rapidly changing world.

Artificial General Intelligence represents an ambitious effort to build systems capable of learning, reasoning, adapting, and improving over time. Yet one of the most important lessons from human intelligence is that progress comes not only from thinking harder but also from thinking more wisely. Self-reflection transforms experience into understanding by encouraging careful examination of both successes and failures. It allows intelligence to grow continuously rather than remaining fixed.

As you continue exploring reasoning intelligence, remember that some of the most important conversations you will ever have are the conversations you have with yourself. Asking thoughtful questions, examining your own reasoning, learning from mistakes, remaining open to improvement, and acting with integrity are habits that strengthen every area of life. Future AGI systems may one day learn to evaluate their own reasoning, but human beings already possess this extraordinary ability. By developing strong metacognitive skills today, you are preparing yourself to become not only a better student but also a wiser thinker, a more effective problem-solver, and a responsible leader in the Age of Artificial General Intelligence.

Learn AI. Understand AI. Shape the Future.
— Susie Hala, IntelliGloss Press

Chapter 13 Summary

Self-Reflection and Metacognition: Thinking About Thinking

This chapter explored one of the highest forms of human reasoning: **metacognition**, or thinking about our own thinking. Students learned that intelligent people do more than solve problems—they evaluate how they solve problems and continually improve their reasoning.

The chapter explained that metacognition has two major parts: **awareness** and **regulation**. Awareness helps people recognize how they learn, think, and make decisions. Regulation allows them to change their strategies when they discover a better approach.

Students learned that self-reflection helps identify mistakes before they become larger problems. Engineers review designs before construction begins, scientists examine research before publishing results, teachers evaluate lesson effectiveness, and students improve by reviewing assignments and correcting errors.

Another important lesson was that asking thoughtful questions strengthens reasoning. Questions such as *Why did I choose this solution?*, *Could there be a better approach?*, and *What evidence supports my conclusion?* help develop deeper understanding and better decision-making.

The chapter also explained how memory, feedback, adaptability, collaboration, and ethical thinking contribute to continuous learning. Successful learners improve because they reflect on previous experiences and apply those lessons to future challenges.

Finally, students discovered that future AGI systems may eventually include forms of self-evaluation that allow them to review their reasoning, estimate confidence levels, recognize uncertainty, and improve future decisions. However, ethical judgment and responsible human oversight will remain essential.

Metacognition allows intelligence to grow throughout life, making it one of the most valuable reasoning skills anyone can develop.

Chapter 13 Reflection

Some of the most important questions we ask are not directed toward other people.

They are questions we ask ourselves.

Did I make the best decision?

What could I improve?

What did I learn from this experience?

These questions are signs of true intelligence because they show a willingness to grow.

This chapter reminds us that learning is not simply collecting information. Learning becomes powerful when we examine our own thinking, recognize our strengths and weaknesses, and make thoughtful improvements over time.

Artificial General Intelligence will also need this ability. Future intelligent systems must evaluate their own reasoning, recognize uncertainty, and improve continuously instead of simply producing answers.

As students prepare for an AI-powered future, one of their greatest advantages will be the uniquely human ability to reflect on experiences, learn from mistakes, and make ethical choices.

People who continue asking thoughtful questions will continue growing throughout their lives.

The strongest minds are not those that never make mistakes.

They are the minds that learn from every experience.

Chapter 13 Worksheet

Name: ______________________________________

Date: ____

Part A – Vocabulary

Write a definition for each term.

1. Metacognition

2. Self-Reflection

3. Self-Monitoring

4. Feedback

5. Adaptability

6. Confidence Level

Part B – Short Answer

1. What is metacognition?

2. Why is self-reflection important?

3. How does feedback improve learning?

4. Why should intelligent systems recognize uncertainty?

5. How can self-reflection improve future decision-making?

Part C – Thinking About Thinking Activity

Choose a recent assignment, project, or test.

Complete the reflection.

Goal

What went well?

What challenges did you experience?

What would you do differently next time?

What did you learn about yourself?

Part D – Critical Thinking

Imagine an AGI system is helping scientists conduct medical research.

Explain why each of the following is important.

Self-Evaluation

Feedback

Confidence Levels

Ethical Reflection

Continuous Learning

Part E – Personal Reflection

Describe a mistake that helped you become better at something.

How did reflecting on the experience help you improve?

Chapter 13 Quiz

Name: ________________________________

Score: _________ /20

Multiple Choice

1. Metacognition means

A. Memorizing information.

B. Thinking about your own thinking.

C. Avoiding questions.

D. Ignoring mistakes.

2. Self-reflection helps people

A. Improve future decisions.

B. Eliminate learning.

C. Stop asking questions.

D. Ignore feedback.

3. Feedback is valuable because it

A. Prevents improvement.

B. Helps identify strengths and weaknesses.

C. Eliminates reasoning.

D. Replaces experience.

4. Why should AGI evaluate its own reasoning?

A. To improve future performance.

B. To replace human judgment.

C. To ignore mistakes.

D. To avoid learning.

5. Ethical reflection helps ensure decisions are

A. Faster only.

B. Fair, responsible, and respectful.

C. Random.

D. Based only on technology.

True or False

6. Metacognition involves thinking about how we think.

True / False

7. Reflection can help identify mistakes before they become larger problems.

True / False

8. Good learners adjust their strategies when necessary.

True / False

9. Future AGI systems may benefit from evaluating their own reasoning.

True / False

10. Self-reflection has no connection to ethical decision-making.

True / False

Short Answer

11. Explain metacognition in your own words.

---

12. Why is self-monitoring important?

---

13. Give one example of self-reflection.

---

14. Why should intelligent systems estimate confidence levels?

---

15. What is the most important lesson you learned from this chapter?

Chapter 13 Answer Key

Multiple Choice

1. **B** – Thinking about your own thinking.
2. **A** – Improve future decisions.
3. **B** – Helps identify strengths and weaknesses.
4. **A** – To improve future performance.
5. **B** – Fair, responsible, and respectful.

True or False

6. **True**
7. **True**
8. **True**
9. **True**
10. **False**

Short Answer (Sample Answers)

11. Metacognition is the ability to think about, evaluate, and improve your own thinking and learning processes.

12. Self-monitoring helps people recognize mistakes, measure progress, adjust strategies, and improve their performance before problems become more serious.

13. Examples include reviewing a test after receiving the grade, evaluating a presentation to improve future speaking skills, reflecting on a sports performance, or revising a written assignment before submitting it.

14. Confidence levels help intelligent systems communicate how certain they are about their conclusions, allowing people to better judge when additional information or human expertise is needed.

15. Answers will vary. Students should explain one important lesson from the chapter, such as learning from mistakes, improving through self-reflection, recognizing uncertainty, or strengthening reasoning through metacognition.

Extension Activity (Optional)

Keep a **Thinking Journal** for one week. Each day, record one important decision you made. Describe how you reached the decision, what evidence you considered, what uncertainties existed, and what you learned afterward. At the end of the week, write a one-page reflection explaining how your thinking changed over time. Then describe how a future AGI system could use a similar self-evaluation process to improve its reasoning while remaining transparent, ethical, and under human oversight.

Chapter 14

Ethical Reasoning and Responsible Intelligence

Imagine you are riding in a self-driving vehicle when an unexpected situation occurs. A large tree suddenly falls across the road during a storm. At the same moment, another vehicle approaches from the opposite direction, and several pedestrians are standing nearby waiting to cross the street. The intelligent system controlling the vehicle has only a fraction of a second to respond. It must quickly analyze the environment, predict possible outcomes, evaluate risks, protect human life, and make the safest possible decision. This situation illustrates one of the greatest challenges in the future of Artificial General Intelligence (AGI). Intelligence alone is not enough. A system may process information rapidly, recognize patterns, and solve complicated mathematical problems, but if it cannot make responsible decisions that consider fairness, safety, honesty, and human well-being, it cannot truly serve society. This is where ethical reasoning becomes essential. Ethical reasoning is the ability to evaluate actions based not only on whether they are effective but also on whether they are morally responsible and beneficial to others.

Throughout history, every major technological advancement has created new opportunities as well as new responsibilities. The invention of electricity transformed daily life but required safety standards to prevent injuries. The automobile revolutionized transportation but introduced traffic laws, driver's education, and road safety regulations. The internet connected billions of people but also created challenges involving privacy, cybersecurity, misinformation, and digital responsibility. Artificial intelligence is following the same path. As intelligent systems become increasingly capable, society must ensure that technological progress remains guided by human values rather than technical ability alone.

Ethics has been part of human civilization for thousands of years. Families teach children to tell the truth, respect others, share fairly, and take responsibility for their actions. Schools encourage honesty, kindness, and academic integrity. Communities develop laws to protect people and promote cooperation. Although cultures may differ in traditions and customs, nearly every society recognizes the importance of fairness, trust, compassion, and respect. Ethical reasoning allows individuals to apply these values when making decisions, especially during difficult situations where there may not be one obvious answer.

One of the first principles of ethical reasoning is recognizing that every decision affects other people. Imagine a company developing facial recognition technology. Engineers may focus on improving technical accuracy, but ethical reasoning asks additional questions. How will personal information be protected? Could the technology be misused? Will it treat all individuals fairly? What safeguards are necessary to prevent discrimination? These questions extend beyond engineering into law, public policy, psychology, and human rights. Future AGI systems must similarly evaluate the broader consequences of their recommendations rather than focusing only on technical performance.

Fairness is one of the most important ethical principles in both human society and artificial intelligence. Fairness means treating people equitably while avoiding unjust discrimination. Consider a school using an intelligent system to recommend scholarships. If the system unknowingly favors certain groups because of biased historical data, deserving students may lose important educational opportunities. Even though the computer followed its programming correctly, the outcome would still be unfair. Researchers therefore devote significant effort to identifying and reducing bias in AI systems. Future AGI must continuously examine its reasoning to ensure that decisions promote equal opportunity rather than reinforcing historical inequalities.

Bias often develops unintentionally because intelligent systems learn from existing information. If historical data reflects past inequalities, AI systems trained on that information may unknowingly repeat similar patterns. Imagine an employment system trained using decades of hiring records from a period when certain qualified individuals had fewer opportunities. Without careful oversight, the system may continue recommending similar hiring patterns even though society has changed. Ethical reasoning requires recognizing these hidden influences while actively seeking more balanced and representative information. Human oversight remains essential because ethical decisions cannot rely solely on historical data.

Honesty and transparency also play essential roles in responsible intelligence. People are more likely to trust recommendations when they understand how decisions were made. Imagine a doctor receiving treatment recommendations from an AGI medical assistant. Rather than simply providing an answer, the system should explain the medical evidence, confidence level, possible alternatives, and remaining uncertainties. Transparent reasoning allows physicians to evaluate recommendations thoughtfully while maintaining responsibility for patient care. Similarly, educators, business leaders, engineers, and government officials should understand the reasoning behind intelligent recommendations before making important decisions.

Privacy has become another major ethical consideration in the digital age. Every day people generate enormous amounts of personal information through smartphones, wearable devices, online learning platforms, healthcare records, financial transactions, and internet activity. This information can improve services, personalize education, strengthen medical research, and increase convenience. However, collecting information also creates responsibilities. Personal data should be protected from unauthorized access, misuse, or unnecessary collection. Future AGI systems must balance the benefits of information analysis with respect for individual privacy and personal rights.

Accountability is another cornerstone of ethical reasoning. When important decisions affect people's lives, someone must remain responsible for those decisions. Imagine an AGI system assisting judges by analyzing legal documents. Although the system may organize evidence efficiently, final legal judgments should remain under human authority because legal decisions involve ethical, cultural, and societal considerations beyond computational analysis. Likewise, autonomous medical systems, financial systems, military technologies, and educational tools require clear human oversight. AGI should support human decision-making rather than replacing human responsibility.

Ethical reasoning also involves considering **long-term consequences** rather than focusing only on immediate results. Suppose a company develops an inexpensive manufacturing process that increases production but generates harmful environmental pollution. Short-term profits may improve, but future communities could experience damaged ecosystems, poorer health, and higher cleanup costs. Responsible decision-making requires balancing present benefits with future responsibilities. Future AGI systems must evaluate environmental sustainability, resource conservation, and long-term social well-being alongside immediate efficiency.

Healthcare provides powerful examples of ethical reasoning in action. Physicians frequently face difficult decisions involving treatment options, patient preferences, limited medical resources, and uncertain outcomes. Ethical principles such as respect for patient autonomy, fairness, compassion, honesty, and informed consent guide these decisions. AGI systems supporting healthcare must recognize these ethical foundations while providing recommendations that assist rather than replace professional medical judgment. Protecting human dignity should remain central to every healthcare decision.

Education also depends upon ethical reasoning. Imagine an AGI tutoring system helping millions of students worldwide. The system should provide equal educational opportunities regardless of income, location, language, or background. It should encourage learning rather than replacing independent thinking. Student information should remain secure, and recommendations should support teachers instead of undermining their professional expertise. Responsible educational technology strengthens human learning while preserving meaningful relationships between students and educators.

Another important ethical principle is **beneficence**, which means acting in ways that promote well-being and improve people's lives. Intelligent systems should be designed with the purpose of helping individuals, families, communities, and society. Whether supporting healthcare, education, transportation, environmental protection, or scientific research, AGI should seek outcomes that benefit humanity while reducing harm whenever possible. Designers and researchers therefore carry tremendous responsibility because the goals built into intelligent systems influence future behavior.

Closely related to beneficence is the principle of **non-maleficence**, often summarized as "do no harm." Before implementing new technologies, researchers carefully evaluate possible risks. Engineers test safety systems extensively before releasing products. Pharmaceutical companies conduct years of clinical trials before new medicines become available. Responsible innovation requires identifying potential dangers early while developing safeguards that reduce unintended consequences. Future AGI systems should similarly evaluate risks before recommending actions, especially when decisions affect human safety or well-being.

Ethical reasoning becomes even more important during uncertain situations. Imagine emergency responders using AGI after a major earthquake. Resources may be limited while many communities require assistance simultaneously. Decisions involving rescue operations, medical care, transportation, and communication require balancing urgency, fairness, available information, and changing conditions. Ethical reasoning helps guide these difficult choices by emphasizing human dignity, transparency, and responsible prioritization rather than simple efficiency alone.

Global cooperation will play an increasingly important role in shaping ethical AI. Artificial intelligence does not stop at national borders. Technologies developed in one country may quickly influence people worldwide. Governments, universities, businesses, researchers, and international organizations increasingly collaborate to establish shared principles for responsible AI development. Although countries may differ in regulations and cultural traditions, many agree that AI should respect human rights, protect privacy, promote fairness, maintain transparency, and remain under meaningful human oversight. Future AGI will likely operate within international frameworks encouraging responsible innovation across many societies.

Students preparing for future careers should recognize that ethical reasoning will become valuable in every profession, not only technology. Business leaders must make responsible financial decisions. Engineers design safe infrastructure. Healthcare professionals protect patient welfare. Teachers promote fairness in education. Scientists conduct research honestly. Journalists report information responsibly. Public officials serve communities ethically. Regardless of career choice, ethical reasoning strengthens leadership because people trust leaders who demonstrate integrity, accountability, and respect for others.

Artificial General Intelligence represents one of humanity's most ambitious technological goals. Yet its greatest success will not be measured only by faster calculations, larger databases, or more powerful algorithms. It will be measured by whether these systems improve human life while respecting the values that define civilization. Intelligence without ethics can become dangerous. Ethics without intelligence may struggle to solve complex challenges. Together, reasoning and responsibility create the foundation for trustworthy intelligent systems.

As you continue your exploration of reasoning intelligence, remember that every important decision carries both technical and human consequences. The smartest solution is not always the most responsible solution. True intelligence asks not only **Can we do this?** but also **Should we do this?**, **Who will be affected?**, **Is it fair?**, and **Will it improve people's lives?** These questions have guided responsible leadership throughout history, and they will become even more important as Artificial General Intelligence continues to evolve. By developing ethical reasoning today, you are preparing to help ensure that the intelligent technologies of tomorrow remain tools that serve humanity with wisdom, fairness, compassion, and responsibility.

Learn AI. Understand AI. Shape the Future.
— Susie Hala, IntelliGloss Press

Chapter 14 Summary

Ethical Reasoning and Responsible Intelligence

This chapter explored one of the most important topics in Artificial General Intelligence (AGI): ethical reasoning. Students learned that intelligence alone is not enough. Truly responsible intelligence must also consider fairness, honesty, safety, privacy, accountability, and the well-being of others.

The chapter explained that every major technological advancement brings both opportunities and responsibilities. As AI systems become more powerful, ethical reasoning helps ensure that technology improves people's lives instead of creating unnecessary harm.

Students learned that ethical reasoning requires asking important questions before making decisions. Instead of asking only, "Can this be done?" responsible thinkers also ask, "Should it be done?", "Who might be affected?", "Is it fair?", and "What are the long-term consequences?"

The chapter introduced several key ethical principles, including fairness, transparency, privacy, accountability, beneficence (doing good), and non-maleficence (avoiding harm). These principles help guide responsible decision-making across many professions.

Students also discovered that AI systems can unintentionally inherit bias from historical data. Future AGI systems must therefore be carefully designed, monitored, and evaluated to reduce unfair outcomes while respecting human rights and equal opportunity.

Another important lesson was that humans must remain responsible for important decisions. AGI should support human reasoning by providing information, analysis, and recommendations, but people should continue making final decisions in areas such as healthcare, education, law, public safety, and government.

The chapter concluded by emphasizing that the future success of AGI will depend not only on technical excellence but also on ethical leadership. Responsible intelligence combines knowledge with wisdom, fairness, compassion, and accountability.

Chapter 14 Reflection

Technology changes quickly.

Values should not.

Throughout history, every new invention has challenged society to think carefully about how it should be used. Electricity, automobiles, airplanes, computers, and the internet all improved human life, but each also required responsibility, safety, and ethical leadership.

Artificial General Intelligence will be no different.

Future intelligent systems may help doctors save lives, teachers educate millions of students, scientists solve difficult problems, and engineers design remarkable technologies. Yet none of these achievements will matter if ethical principles are ignored.

This chapter reminds us that intelligence is not measured only by knowledge or speed. True intelligence also includes fairness, honesty, compassion, transparency, and respect for human dignity.

As future leaders, students should remember that technology is a tool. It reflects the values of the people who create and use it.

The future will need people who are not only intelligent but also wise.

Knowledge creates possibilities.

Ethics determines how those possibilities are used.

Chapter 14 Worksheet

Name: ______________________________

Date: _______________________________

Part A – Vocabulary

Write a definition for each term.

1. Ethical Reasoning

2. Fairness

3. Transparency

4. Accountability

5. Privacy

6. Bias

Part B – Short Answer

1. Why is ethical reasoning important for AGI?

2. What is algorithmic bias?

3. Why should humans remain responsible for important decisions?

---

4. Why is transparency important?

---

5. How can ethical reasoning improve technology?

Part C – Ethics in Action

Read each situation and explain the ethical issues involved.

Situation 1

An AGI system helps hospitals decide which patients receive limited medical equipment.

What ethical principles should guide the decision?

Situation 2

A school uses AGI to recommend scholarships.

How can fairness be protected?

Situation 3

A company collects personal information from customers.

How should privacy be protected?

Part D – Critical Thinking

Imagine an AGI system is helping a city improve public transportation.

Explain why each ethical principle is important.

Fairness

Transparency

Accountability

Privacy

Human Oversight

Part E – Personal Reflection

Describe a time when you had to make a difficult decision that affected someone else.

How did you try to make the decision fairly?

Chapter 14 Quiz

Name: ______________________________

Score: _________ /20

Multiple Choice

1. Ethical reasoning helps people

A. Ignore consequences.

B. Make responsible decisions that consider others.

C. Memorize information.

D. Increase computer speed.

2. Fairness means

A. Treating people equitably and avoiding unjust discrimination.

B. Ignoring differences.

C. Making random decisions.

D. Eliminating technology.

3. Transparency means

A. Keeping every decision secret.

B. Explaining how decisions are made.

C. Avoiding communication.

D. Hiding information.

4. Why should humans remain responsible for important decisions?

A. Because many important decisions involve ethics, values, and human judgment.

B. Because computers never calculate.

C. Because technology cannot help people.

D. Because AI cannot analyze information.

5. Which ethical principle focuses on protecting personal information?

A. Privacy

B. Speed

C. Automation

D. Efficiency

True or False

6. Intelligence alone is enough to create responsible AGI.

True / False

7. AI systems can unintentionally learn bias from historical data.

True / False

8. Ethical reasoning includes considering long-term consequences.

True / False

9. Future AGI systems should support human decision-making rather than replace it completely.

True / False

10. Accountability is an important ethical principle.

True / False

Short Answer

11. Explain ethical reasoning in your own words.

12. Why is fairness important in AI?

13. Give one example of transparency.

14. Why should AGI protect privacy?

15. What is the most important lesson you learned from this chapter?

Chapter 14 Answer Key

Multiple Choice

1. **B** – Make responsible decisions that consider others.
2. **A** – Treating people equitably and avoiding unjust discrimination.
3. **B** – Explaining how decisions are made.
4. **A** – Because many important decisions involve ethics, values, and human judgment.
5. **A** – Privacy.

True or False

6. **False**
7. **True**

8. **True**
9. **True**
10. **True**

Short Answer (Sample Answers)

11. Ethical reasoning is the process of making decisions that consider fairness, honesty, responsibility, safety, respect, and the well-being of others instead of focusing only on technical success.

12. Fairness helps ensure that AI systems treat people equitably, reduce discrimination, provide equal opportunities, and avoid biased decision-making.

13. Examples include an AI system explaining why it recommended a medical treatment, a bank describing why a loan application was approved or denied, or a school explaining how scholarship decisions were made.

14. Protecting privacy helps safeguard personal information, maintain trust, prevent misuse of data, and respect the rights of individuals.

15. Answers will vary. Students should describe one important lesson from the chapter, such as the importance of fairness, transparency, accountability, privacy, reducing bias, or keeping humans responsible for important decisions.

Extension Activity (Optional)

Choose one AI application currently used in society, such as healthcare, education, transportation, banking, cybersecurity, or law enforcement. Create an **Ethics Review Report** that identifies the benefits of the technology, possible ethical concerns, the people who may be affected, and recommendations for improving fairness, transparency, accountability, privacy, and human oversight. Conclude by explaining how these ethical principles could help future AGI systems earn public trust while serving society responsibly.

Chapter 15

Human Reasoning and Artificial General Intelligence Working Together

Imagine walking into a hospital twenty years from now. A patient arrives with a rare illness that has puzzled doctors around the world. Within seconds, an advanced Artificial General Intelligence (AGI) system reviews millions of medical research papers, analyzes the patient's medical history, compares genetic information, studies similar cases from many countries, evaluates possible treatments, and presents several recommendations to the medical team. The physicians carefully examine the information, discuss the patient's personal circumstances, consider family preferences, weigh ethical concerns, and choose the treatment they believe offers the greatest chance of success. In this future hospital, the remarkable achievement is not that humans or machines worked alone. The true achievement is that they worked together. This vision represents one of the most important ideas in the future of Artificial General Intelligence. Rather than replacing human intelligence, AGI has the potential to become a powerful partner that strengthens human reasoning, expands knowledge, and helps solve challenges that neither humans nor machines could solve alone.

Throughout history, people have created tools that extend human abilities. The telescope allowed astronomers to observe distant galaxies beyond the reach of the human eye. The microscope revealed invisible microorganisms that transformed medicine and biology. Calculators improved mathematical accuracy. Computers accelerated scientific research and engineering design. The internet connected billions of people and made knowledge available almost instantly. None of these inventions replaced human intelligence. Instead, they expanded what people could accomplish. AGI may become the next great tool in this long history of innovation, not by replacing human reasoning, but by enhancing it.

Human intelligence possesses remarkable strengths that have developed over thousands of years. People understand emotions, appreciate culture, build relationships, demonstrate compassion, exercise moral judgment, and adapt creatively to unfamiliar situations. Human beings recognize humor, understand personal experiences, appreciate art, and make decisions influenced by empathy and shared values. These qualities allow people to lead families, teach students, comfort patients, inspire communities, and solve problems that require emotional understanding alongside logical reasoning. These uniquely human abilities will remain essential even as AGI becomes increasingly capable.

Artificial General Intelligence, however, may excel in areas where humans face natural limitations. Intelligent systems may analyze enormous amounts of information within seconds, recognize subtle patterns hidden across millions of documents, simulate thousands of possible solutions to complex problems, remember vast amounts of knowledge without forgetting important details, and perform repetitive analytical tasks with remarkable consistency. These capabilities can significantly assist scientists, educators, engineers, healthcare professionals, and business leaders who must process more information than any individual could manage alone.

The greatest opportunities emerge when these complementary strengths are combined. Consider education. A teacher understands the personalities, emotions, motivations, and learning styles of individual students. An AGI tutoring system may analyze learning progress, identify knowledge gaps, recommend personalized practice activities, and provide immediate feedback. Together, the teacher and the intelligent system create a richer educational experience than either could provide independently. The teacher supplies encouragement, inspiration, ethical guidance, and human connection, while the AGI provides detailed analysis and personalized academic support. Collaboration creates stronger outcomes than competition.

Healthcare offers another powerful example of partnership. Physicians bring years of clinical experience, ethical judgment, communication skills, and compassion to patient care. Future AGI systems may rapidly analyze medical literature, identify uncommon disease patterns, compare treatment options, predict medication interactions, and monitor patient recovery continuously. Doctors remain responsible for discussing treatment choices with patients, respecting personal values, explaining risks, and making final medical decisions. AGI becomes a trusted assistant that strengthens professional judgment rather than replacing it.

Scientific research may experience similar transformation. Modern researchers already work with enormous collections of scientific publications, experimental results, satellite observations, genomic databases, and environmental measurements. No individual scientist can personally study every relevant document. AGI systems capable of organizing this information, identifying hidden relationships, suggesting new research directions, and simulating experiments could accelerate discovery across medicine, physics, chemistry, biology, environmental science, and many other fields. Human scientists would continue asking meaningful questions, designing experiments, evaluating evidence, and determining how discoveries should benefit society.

Engineering projects also demonstrate the power of collaboration. Imagine designing a sustainable city for future generations. Human architects understand community needs, cultural values, public spaces, and aesthetic beauty. Civil engineers design transportation systems and infrastructure. Environmental scientists protect ecosystems. Economists evaluate long-term financial sustainability. Urban planners coordinate growth. Future AGI systems may analyze traffic patterns, simulate energy consumption, optimize resource distribution, and predict future population changes. Together, humans and AGI could design cities that are safer, healthier, and more sustainable than ever before.

Business and entrepreneurship will also evolve through human-AI collaboration. Successful business leaders understand customer relationships, company culture, employee motivation, and long-term organizational vision. AGI systems may analyze market trends, forecast demand, optimize supply chains, evaluate financial risks, and identify emerging opportunities. Human leaders remain responsible for setting organizational values, inspiring employees, building trust with customers, and making ethical business decisions. Data-driven analysis combined with human leadership creates stronger organizations capable of adapting to rapidly changing markets.

One of the greatest strengths of human reasoning is creativity. Artists, musicians, writers, inventors, and designers constantly produce original ideas inspired by imagination, emotion, experience, and curiosity. AGI may assist by generating alternative designs, exploring creative possibilities, analyzing historical influences, and suggesting unexpected combinations of ideas. However, human creativity gives meaning to artistic expression because it reflects lived experiences, cultural identity, and personal values. The partnership between human imagination and computational exploration may open entirely new forms of artistic and scientific innovation.

Communication will become increasingly important as humans collaborate with intelligent systems. Successful partnerships require clear explanations, shared understanding, and mutual trust. Future AGI systems should communicate recommendations transparently by explaining reasoning, confidence levels, assumptions, and possible alternatives. Likewise, people must learn how to ask thoughtful questions, evaluate AI-generated information critically, and understand both the capabilities and limitations of intelligent technologies. Effective communication strengthens collaboration while preventing misunderstanding and overreliance.

Trust represents another essential element of successful partnerships. Trust is earned through reliability, honesty, consistency, and accountability. Human professionals must trust that AGI systems produce accurate analyses while understanding situations where uncertainty remains. At the same time, AGI systems should be designed to support human authority rather than encouraging blind dependence. Trust grows when intelligent systems acknowledge limitations, explain uncertainty openly, and encourage independent human evaluation instead of unquestioning acceptance.

Human oversight remains fundamental in every high-impact application of AGI. Imagine intelligent systems assisting judges, military leaders, healthcare providers, financial institutions, or emergency managers. These fields involve decisions affecting human rights, public safety, personal dignity, and societal values. Although AGI may provide valuable information, final authority should remain with accountable human decision-makers. Human oversight ensures that ethical principles, compassion, legal responsibility, and cultural understanding remain central to important decisions.

Collaboration also requires recognizing the limitations of both humans and machines. Human beings sometimes become tired, distracted, emotional, or influenced by cognitive biases. Intelligent systems may process information rapidly yet misunderstand cultural context, emotional meaning, or ethical complexity. Effective teamwork acknowledges these differences while allowing each partner to compensate for the other's limitations. Human wisdom complements computational precision, creating stronger overall performance than either could achieve independently.

Learning will become increasingly collaborative as well. Students may work alongside AGI learning assistants that provide personalized instruction while teachers encourage curiosity, teamwork, creativity, and critical thinking. Professionals may use AGI mentors to stay current with rapidly changing scientific knowledge while continuing to develop practical experience through real-world applications. Lifelong learning will become a partnership between human curiosity and intelligent educational technology.

Ethical reasoning remains essential throughout every human-AGI partnership. Technology should strengthen human dignity rather than diminish it. Intelligent systems should increase educational opportunity rather than widen inequality. Medical technology should improve patient care while respecting privacy and informed consent. Business innovation should promote economic growth while treating employees and customers fairly. Human values provide the moral foundation upon which technological progress should be built. AGI must always remain aligned with these principles if it is to earn public trust.

One exciting possibility involves AGI helping humanity address global challenges requiring unprecedented cooperation. Climate change, sustainable energy, disease prevention, food security, disaster response, space exploration, clean water, and environmental conservation all involve enormous amounts of information spread across many scientific disciplines. Human experts working together with AGI systems may coordinate knowledge more effectively, identify innovative solutions, simulate future outcomes, and accelerate progress while maintaining ethical oversight. Such partnerships could improve the lives of billions of people around the world.

Students entering tomorrow's workforce should prepare for careers where collaboration with intelligent systems becomes a normal part of daily life. Instead of competing against AI, future professionals will increasingly compete based on how effectively they work with AI. Critical thinking, communication, ethical reasoning, adaptability, creativity, leadership, and emotional intelligence will become even more valuable because these human abilities complement advanced computational reasoning. Those who understand both technology and humanity will become leaders in every profession.

Artificial General Intelligence is often described as one of the most important technological developments in history. Yet its greatest achievement may not be building machines that think like humans. Its greatest achievement may be helping humans think more effectively together. By expanding access to knowledge, strengthening problem-solving, supporting scientific discovery, improving education, advancing healthcare, and encouraging global collaboration, AGI has the potential to become one of humanity's greatest partners rather than one of its greatest competitors.

As you approach the final chapter of this book, remember that the future of reasoning intelligence is not a story about humans versus machines. It is a story about humans and intelligent machines working together with shared purpose. Technology will continue advancing, but wisdom, compassion, creativity, integrity, and ethical leadership will remain uniquely human responsibilities. The strongest future will be built not by choosing between human intelligence and Artificial General Intelligence, but by combining the best qualities of both. By preparing yourself to become a thoughtful collaborator with intelligent systems, you are preparing to lead confidently in a future where partnership, responsibility, and lifelong learning define success.

Learn AI. Understand AI. Shape the Future.
— Susie Hala, IntelliGloss Press

Chapter 15 Summary

Human Reasoning and Artificial General Intelligence Working Together

This chapter explored how humans and Artificial General Intelligence (AGI) can work together to solve complex problems and improve life around the world. Students learned that AGI is not intended to replace human intelligence but to become a powerful partner that strengthens human decision-making, creativity, and problem-solving.

The chapter explained that throughout history, people have developed tools that extend human abilities. Telescopes, microscopes, computers, and the internet all expanded what people could accomplish. AGI represents the next step in this long tradition by helping humans analyze information, discover patterns, and solve increasingly complex challenges.

Students learned that humans and AGI each have unique strengths. Human beings contribute creativity, empathy, ethical judgment, communication, cultural understanding, and emotional intelligence. AGI contributes rapid information processing, large-scale data analysis, pattern recognition, memory, and the ability to evaluate many possible solutions quickly.

The chapter demonstrated how this partnership could improve many professions. Teachers and AGI tutors can personalize education. Doctors and AGI systems can improve patient care. Scientists and AGI can accelerate research. Engineers can design safer infrastructure with AGI support, while business leaders can use AGI to improve planning and decision-making.

Students also learned that successful collaboration depends on trust, communication, transparency, accountability, and human oversight. Important decisions involving healthcare, education, law, public safety, and government should always include responsible human leadership.

Finally, the chapter emphasized that the future belongs to people who learn how to work effectively with intelligent technologies. Students who develop critical thinking, creativity, ethical reasoning, adaptability, and communication skills will be well prepared to lead in an AI-powered world where humans and AGI work together to solve problems that neither could solve alone.

Chapter 15 Reflection

The future is not a competition between people and intelligent machines.

It is a partnership.

Throughout history, every major invention has helped people accomplish more than they could alone. Artificial General Intelligence has the potential to become another remarkable tool—but only if it is guided by responsible human leadership.

This chapter reminds us that technology does not replace human qualities such as compassion, integrity, creativity, wisdom, and ethical judgment. Instead, it can strengthen our ability to solve difficult problems when these uniquely human qualities remain at the center of every decision.

Doctors will continue caring for patients.

Teachers will continue inspiring students.

Scientists will continue asking new questions.

Engineers will continue designing better solutions.

AGI will become a powerful assistant, helping professionals work more efficiently while allowing people to focus on leadership, relationships, innovation, and responsible decision-making.

The future will reward those who know how to combine human strengths with intelligent technology.

The best results will come from collaboration—not competition.

When people and technology work together with wisdom and purpose, extraordinary things become possible.

Chapter 15 Worksheet

Name: ______________________________

Date: ______________________________

Part A – Vocabulary

Write your own definition for each term.

1. Collaboration

____

____

2. Human Oversight

____

____

3. Artificial General Intelligence (AGI)

____

____

4. Transparency

5. Emotional Intelligence

6. Partnership

Part B – Short Answer

1. Why is collaboration between humans and AGI important?

2. What strengths do humans contribute that AGI does not fully replace?

3. What strengths does AGI contribute?

4. Why should humans remain responsible for important decisions?

5. Why is communication important in human-AGI partnerships?

Part C – Real-World Applications

Choose one profession below.

• Teacher

• Doctor

• Engineer

• Scientist

• Business Leader

Complete the chart.

How could AGI help?

What should humans continue to do?

Why is teamwork important?

Part D – Critical Thinking

Imagine your city introduces AGI to improve emergency response services.

Explain why each of the following is important.

Human Leadership

Transparency

Ethical Decision-Making

Communication

Public Trust

Part E – Personal Reflection

Describe one way you think people and AGI could work together to improve your school or community.

Explain why your idea would benefit others.

Chapter 15 Quiz

Name: ________________________________

Score: _________ /20

Multiple Choice

1. The main idea of this chapter is that

A. Humans should compete against AGI.

B. Humans and AGI can work together to solve complex problems.

C. AGI should replace all human workers.

D. Technology eliminates the need for human reasoning.

2. Which is a uniquely human strength?

A. Empathy

B. Ethical judgment

C. Creativity

D. All of the above

3. AGI is especially good at

A. Processing large amounts of information.

B. Remembering large collections of data.

C. Finding patterns.

D. All of the above.

4. Why is human oversight important?

A. Important decisions involve ethics, values, responsibility, and accountability.

B. Computers cannot process information.

C. Technology should never be used.

D. AGI never makes recommendations.

5. Successful human-AGI partnerships require

A. Trust and communication.

B. Transparency and accountability.

C. Ethical leadership.

D. All of the above.

True or False

6. AGI should completely replace human decision-making.

True / False

7. Human creativity and emotional intelligence remain valuable in the future.

True / False

8. Communication strengthens collaboration.

True / False

9. AGI can support scientific research and education.

True / False

10. Responsible human leadership remains essential.

True / False

Short Answer

11. Explain why collaboration between humans and AGI is valuable.

12. Name two human strengths that AGI complements.

13. Give one example of AGI helping a professional.

14. Why should trust be part of every human-AGI partnership?

15. What is the most important lesson you learned from this chapter?

Chapter 15 Answer Key

Multiple Choice

1. **B** – Humans and AGI can work together to solve complex problems.
2. **D** – All of the above.
3. **D** – All of the above.
4. **A** – Important decisions involve ethics, values, responsibility, and accountability.
5. **D** – All of the above.

True or False

6. **False**
7. **True**
8. **True**
9. **True**
10. **True**

Short Answer (Sample Answers)

11. Collaboration combines the strengths of humans and AGI. AGI can quickly analyze information and identify patterns, while humans contribute creativity, empathy, ethical judgment, communication, and leadership. Working together often produces better decisions than either could achieve alone.

12. Possible answers include empathy, creativity, emotional intelligence, ethical reasoning, cultural understanding, leadership, communication, compassion, and critical thinking.

13. Examples include:

- A doctor using AGI to analyze medical research before choosing a treatment.
- A teacher using AGI to personalize lessons for students.
- An engineer using AGI to test bridge designs.
- A scientist using AGI to analyze research data.
- A business leader using AGI to forecast market trends.

14. Trust allows people to use AGI confidently while understanding how recommendations are made. Transparent communication, reliable performance, accountability, and human oversight help build and maintain that trust.

15. Answers will vary. Students should explain one key lesson from the chapter, such as the importance of collaboration, keeping humans responsible for major decisions, combining human and AGI strengths, or using technology ethically to improve society.

Extension Activity (Optional)

Imagine it is the year **2045** and you are leading a team where humans and AGI work together every day. Choose a profession such as education, healthcare, engineering, agriculture, law, environmental science, or space exploration. Write a two-page plan describing how humans and AGI share responsibilities, communicate effectively, protect ethical values, solve problems together, and improve people's lives. Conclude by explaining why human leadership, compassion, and responsibility remain essential even in a world with highly advanced AGI.

Chapter 16

The Future of Reasoning Intelligence: Preparing for an AGI World

Imagine waking up twenty years from now. Your morning begins with an intelligent personal assistant that has already organized your schedule, monitored your health, adjusted your home's energy use to save electricity, translated messages from friends living around the world, and suggested new learning opportunities based on your interests. Your school or workplace uses advanced Artificial General Intelligence (AGI) systems that help teachers personalize lessons, assist doctors in discovering new treatments, support engineers designing safer cities, and help scientists solve environmental challenges that once seemed impossible. Intelligent systems are no longer unusual tools used only by experts. They have become trusted partners that assist people in nearly every area of daily life. Yet as remarkable as this future may appear, one important truth remains unchanged: the future will still depend on human reasoning. Technology may become increasingly powerful, but wisdom, ethics, creativity, leadership, compassion, and responsibility will continue to guide how that technology is used. The purpose of this final chapter is not simply to imagine the future of AGI. It is to prepare you to become one of the people who will help shape that future.

Throughout this book, you have explored many dimensions of reasoning intelligence. You learned that reasoning involves much more than finding correct answers. It includes logical thinking, problem-solving, common sense, analogical reasoning, decision-making under uncertainty, long-term planning, interdisciplinary thinking, self-reflection, ethical judgment, and collaboration. Together, these abilities create a form of intelligence that allows people to understand the world, adapt to change, solve unfamiliar problems, and improve continuously through experience. These same capabilities represent many of the goals researchers hope to achieve while developing Artificial General Intelligence.

One of the most important lessons in the study of AGI is that intelligence is not a single skill. Imagine a talented musician who performs beautifully but struggles to solve mathematical problems. Imagine an excellent engineer who finds public speaking difficult. Imagine a gifted writer who has little experience in chemistry. Human intelligence is wonderfully diverse. Every individual develops unique combinations of abilities, interests, and experiences. AGI researchers hope to build systems capable of performing well across many different domains instead of specializing in only one task. This broad adaptability distinguishes AGI from today's narrow AI systems and represents one of the greatest scientific challenges of our time.

As intelligent technology becomes more capable, lifelong learning will become increasingly important. Previous generations often learned one profession and remained in similar careers throughout their working lives. The future may be very different. New technologies will emerge continuously. Entire industries will evolve. Some jobs will change dramatically while new careers appear that do not yet exist today. Success will depend less on memorizing information and more on learning how to learn. Students who remain curious, adaptable, and willing to develop new skills throughout life will be better prepared for these changes than those who expect education to end after graduation.

Curiosity has always been one of humanity's greatest strengths. Every scientific discovery began with someone asking a question. Why do planets move? How do diseases spread? Can machines learn? Is there life beyond Earth? These questions inspired generations of researchers to investigate the unknown. Artificial General Intelligence will likely answer many questions, but it will also create entirely new ones. Curious people will continue driving progress because every answer leads to additional opportunities for exploration. The future belongs to those who never stop asking thoughtful questions.

Critical thinking will become even more valuable in an age filled with intelligent technology. AGI systems may provide recommendations, summarize information, generate reports, and analyze enormous amounts of data. However, people must continue evaluating evidence independently rather than accepting every recommendation automatically. Responsible citizens ask questions such as: Is this information reliable? What evidence supports this conclusion? Are there alternative explanations? Could bias influence the results? These habits protect society from misinformation while strengthening informed decision-making. Intelligent technology becomes most valuable when paired with thoughtful human evaluation.

Communication skills will remain essential regardless of technological advancement. Throughout history, progress has depended on people sharing ideas clearly and respectfully. Scientists explain discoveries to colleagues. Teachers inspire students through effective communication. Engineers present designs to communities. Healthcare professionals discuss treatment options with patients. Business leaders motivate employees toward shared goals.

Future AGI systems may translate languages instantly and summarize complex information, but human communication involves trust, empathy, encouragement, and relationship-building that extend beyond exchanging facts. Strong communication strengthens collaboration between people and intelligent systems alike.

Creativity will continue shaping the future because innovation requires imagination. While AGI may generate many possible solutions to difficult problems, humans will continue defining meaningful goals, exploring new possibilities, appreciating beauty, and expressing personal experiences through art, music, literature, design, and invention. Creativity allows society to move beyond existing knowledge by imagining what does not yet exist. Every important invention, scientific breakthrough, artistic masterpiece, and social improvement began with someone willing to think differently. Technology expands creative possibilities, but human imagination gives those possibilities purpose.

Ethics becomes increasingly important as technological power grows. Earlier chapters explained that intelligence without ethical guidance can produce harmful consequences. Future AGI systems may assist governments, hospitals, schools, businesses, transportation networks, and scientific laboratories. Every one of these applications influences people's lives. Responsible leadership requires asking difficult ethical questions before implementing powerful technologies. Are decisions fair? Is privacy protected? Are vulnerable populations respected? Does technology strengthen communities? Human values provide the moral compass that keeps technological progress aligned with society's highest ideals.

One exciting possibility involves AGI helping humanity solve challenges that no single nation or profession can address alone. Climate change, renewable energy, clean water, disease prevention, disaster response, sustainable agriculture, cybersecurity, and space exploration require cooperation among scientists, engineers, educators, healthcare professionals, governments, businesses, and citizens around the world. Future AGI systems may organize enormous collections of information, identify meaningful connections, simulate future scenarios, and recommend possible solutions. Yet success will still depend upon people choosing to cooperate across cultures, disciplines, and generations.

The workplace of the future will likely emphasize skills that complement intelligent technology. Routine tasks may become increasingly automated, allowing people to spend more time solving complex problems, leading teams, developing creative ideas, mentoring others, and building meaningful relationships. Employers will increasingly value adaptability, emotional intelligence, ethical reasoning, communication, collaboration, leadership, and lifelong learning. These qualities allow people to work effectively with advanced technologies while contributing uniquely human strengths that machines cannot easily replicate.

Education itself will continue evolving. Students may receive personalized instruction from intelligent tutoring systems capable of adjusting lessons to individual learning styles and progress. Teachers will spend more time mentoring, encouraging curiosity, facilitating discussions, and helping students develop higher-order reasoning skills. Classrooms may become places where students learn not only facts but also how to evaluate information, collaborate effectively, solve authentic problems, and make responsible decisions in partnership with intelligent technologies. Education will increasingly prepare students for continuous learning rather than one-time career preparation.

Leadership in the AGI era will require wisdom as much as knowledge. Great leaders listen carefully, consider different perspectives, communicate honestly, accept responsibility, encourage collaboration, and remain committed to serving others. Future leaders will make decisions involving technologies more powerful than any previous generation has experienced. Their success will depend not only on technical understanding but also on integrity, humility, fairness, and courage. These qualities cannot simply be programmed into machines; they must be developed within people.

One encouraging truth is that every student has the ability to strengthen reasoning intelligence. Every time you solve a difficult problem, ask thoughtful questions, revise your work, consider another person's perspective, learn from mistakes, or explore a new subject, your reasoning abilities become stronger. Intelligence is not fixed. It grows through effort, experience, curiosity, reflection, and continuous learning. The future of AGI should therefore inspire students not to fear technology but to become stronger thinkers themselves.

Researchers continue working toward AGI because they believe intelligent systems can help humanity accomplish extraordinary things. They hope to accelerate medical discoveries, improve educational opportunities, strengthen environmental protection, support scientific research, reduce accidents, improve accessibility for people with disabilities, and solve complex global challenges. These goals demonstrate that technology reaches its greatest value when it serves human needs rather than existing for its own sake. Every technological breakthrough should ultimately improve people's lives.

As you finish this book, remember that the future is not something that simply happens. The future is something people create through their choices, ideas, values, and actions. Every engineer designing safer transportation systems, every scientist searching for medical breakthroughs, every teacher inspiring students, every entrepreneur building innovative businesses, every policymaker creating responsible regulations, and every student preparing for tomorrow contributes to shaping the future of intelligence. Artificial General Intelligence will become one of history's most important technologies, but humanity will remain responsible for determining how it is developed and used.

Perhaps the most important lesson of all is that intelligence reaches its highest purpose when it improves the lives of others. Knowledge becomes meaningful when it solves problems. Creativity becomes valuable when it inspires hope. Leadership becomes powerful when it serves communities. Technology becomes remarkable when it reflects human compassion, fairness, and responsibility. Whether you become a scientist, teacher, engineer, healthcare professional, artist, entrepreneur, public servant, or community leader, your reasoning abilities will influence the people around you every day.

The story of Artificial General Intelligence has not yet been fully written. You are part of the generation that will witness many of its greatest discoveries and perhaps contribute to them. Some of you may design intelligent systems. Others may create ethical guidelines that protect society. Some may discover new scientific breakthroughs with the assistance of AGI. Others may teach future generations how to use intelligent technologies responsibly. Whatever path you choose, remember that the future will always need thoughtful people who combine knowledge with wisdom, innovation with integrity, and intelligence with compassion.

This book began by asking how intelligent systems think, solve problems, and make better decisions. It ends with an even more important question: **How will you use your own reasoning intelligence to shape the future?** The answer to that question belongs to you. Continue asking questions. Continue learning. Continue thinking critically. Continue acting ethically. Continue working with others. Most importantly, continue believing that intelligence achieves its greatest purpose when it helps build a better world for everyone.

The future of reasoning intelligence has already begun.

Now it is your turn to help write the next chapter.

Learn AI. Understand AI. Shape the Future.
— Susie Hala, IntelliGloss Press

Chapter 16 Summary

The Future of Reasoning Intelligence: Preparing for an AGI World

This final chapter brought together the major ideas explored throughout the book and looked ahead to the future of Artificial General Intelligence (AGI). Students learned that AGI has the potential to become one of the most important technologies in human history, but its success will depend on responsible human leadership, ethical decision-making, and lifelong learning.

The chapter reviewed the many forms of reasoning intelligence discussed throughout the book, including logical reasoning, problem-solving, common sense, analogical reasoning, decision-making under uncertainty, long-term planning, interdisciplinary thinking, self-reflection, ethical reasoning, and collaboration. Together, these abilities create a strong foundation for understanding both human intelligence and future AGI.

Students also learned that the future workplace will increasingly value skills that complement intelligent technology. Creativity, communication, critical thinking, adaptability, emotional intelligence, leadership, and ethical reasoning will become even more valuable as AGI systems assist people in education, healthcare, engineering, science, business, and many other professions.

The chapter emphasized that lifelong learning will become essential because technology continues to evolve rapidly. Students who remain curious, flexible, and willing to learn new skills throughout their lives will be well prepared for future opportunities.

Another important lesson was that AGI should be viewed as a partner rather than a replacement for human intelligence. While AGI may analyze enormous amounts of information and solve complex problems, humans continue to provide wisdom, empathy, compassion, ethics, creativity, and responsible leadership.

Finally, the chapter reminded students that the future is created by the decisions people make today. Every student has the opportunity to contribute to the responsible development of Artificial General Intelligence by becoming a thoughtful learner, an ethical leader, and a lifelong problem-solver dedicated to improving the lives of others.

Chapter 16 Reflection

The future has always belonged to people who continue learning.

Every generation has faced new discoveries that changed the world. Electricity transformed cities. Airplanes connected continents. Computers reshaped communication. The internet changed how people share knowledge.

Artificial General Intelligence may become the next great transformation.

But no matter how advanced technology becomes, one truth remains the same:

People will decide how technology is used.

This chapter reminds us that intelligence is not measured only by how much we know. It is measured by how wisely we use our knowledge, how fairly we treat others, how responsibly we solve problems, and how courageously we prepare for tomorrow.

The future will need scientists who ask meaningful questions.

Teachers who inspire curiosity.

Engineers who design responsibly.

Doctors who care for people with compassion.

Leaders who place ethics above convenience.

Students who never stop learning.

Artificial General Intelligence may help humanity solve many difficult problems, but the character of the people who guide that technology will determine whether it becomes one of history's greatest achievements.

The future is not waiting for someone else.

The future is waiting for you.

Chapter 16 Worksheet

Name: ______________________________

Date: ______________________________

Part A – Vocabulary

Write your own definition for each term.

1. Artificial General Intelligence (AGI)

2. Lifelong Learning

3. Critical Thinking

4. Leadership

5. Collaboration

6. Ethical Responsibility

Part B – Short Answer

1. Why is lifelong learning important in an AGI world?

2. What human qualities will remain valuable even as AGI becomes more capable?

3. Why should AGI be viewed as a partner instead of a replacement?

4. Why are ethics important in the future of AI?

5. How can today's students help shape tomorrow's world?

Part C – Future Planning Activity

Imagine yourself twenty years from now.

Complete the following plan.

Career You Hope to Have

How Could AGI Help You?

What Human Skills Will You Continue Developing?

How Will You Use Technology Responsibly?

Part D – Critical Thinking

Imagine your community is introducing AGI into schools, hospitals, businesses, and transportation systems.

Explain why each of the following remains important.

Human Leadership

Ethical Decision-Making

Communication

Creativity

Continuous Learning

Part E – Final Reflection

After reading this book, describe the three most important lessons you learned about Artificial General Intelligence and reasoning intelligence.

Lesson 1

Lesson 2

Lesson 3

____

How will these lessons influence your future?

____
____
____

Chapter 16 Quiz

Name: ______________________________

Score: _________ /20

Multiple Choice

1. One of the main ideas of this chapter is that

A. Learning ends after graduation.

B. Lifelong learning is essential in an AGI world.

C. AGI replaces all human thinking.

D. Technology eliminates leadership.

2. Which human quality will remain valuable?

A. Creativity

B. Ethical reasoning

C. Compassion

D. All of the above

3. AGI should be viewed primarily as

A. A replacement for people.

B. A partner that supports human intelligence.

C. A competitor.

D. A threat to education.

4. Why is critical thinking important?

A. It helps people evaluate information and make thoughtful decisions.

B. It replaces communication.

C. It eliminates uncertainty.

D. It prevents learning.

5. Who is responsible for how AGI is developed and used?

A. Humans.

B. Computers alone.

C. Robots only.

D. Nobody.

True or False

6. Lifelong learning will become less important in the future.

True / False

7. Human leadership remains essential in an AGI-powered world.

True / False

8. Ethical reasoning should guide technological progress.

True / False

9. Communication and collaboration will continue to be valuable workplace skills.

True / False

10. Students can help shape the future of Artificial General Intelligence.

True / False

Short Answer

11. Explain why lifelong learning is important.

12. Name three human qualities that AGI complements.

13. Give one example of humans and AGI working together.

14. Why should ethics guide future AI development?

15. What is the most important lesson you learned from this entire book?

Chapter 16 Answer Key

Multiple Choice

1. **B** – Lifelong learning is essential in an AGI world.
2. **D** – All of the above.
3. **B** – A partner that supports human intelligence.

4. **A** – It helps people evaluate information and make thoughtful decisions.
5. **A** – Humans.

True or False

6. **False**
7. **True**
8. **True**
9. **True**
10. **True**

Short Answer (Sample Answers)

11. Lifelong learning is important because technology, careers, and society continue to change. People who keep learning can adapt to new challenges, develop new skills, and work effectively with emerging technologies such as AGI.

12. Possible answers include creativity, empathy, ethical reasoning, communication, leadership, emotional intelligence, compassion, critical thinking, cultural understanding, and collaboration.

13. Examples include:

- Teachers using AGI to personalize lessons while providing encouragement and mentorship.
- Doctors using AGI to analyze medical research while making final treatment decisions.
- Engineers using AGI to simulate designs before construction.
- Scientists using AGI to organize research data and identify new discoveries.

14. Ethics ensures that AI technologies are used fairly, responsibly, transparently, and for the benefit of individuals and society while protecting privacy, safety, and human rights.

15. Answers will vary. Students should describe one or more important ideas from the book, such as the importance of reasoning intelligence, ethical AI, lifelong learning, collaboration between humans and AGI, or preparing for future careers.

Final Book Extension Activity

My AGI Future Portfolio

Using everything you learned in this book, create a personal **AGI Future Portfolio**.

Include the following sections:

- My Dream Career
- How AGI Could Help Me
- Human Skills I Will Continue Developing
- My Ethical Responsibilities
- My Lifelong Learning Plan
- Three Global Problems I Would Like to Help Solve
- My Vision for Human and AGI Collaboration in 2050
- A personal commitment statement describing how you will use reasoning intelligence, ethical leadership, creativity, and compassion to make a positive difference in your school, community, and the world.

This portfolio serves as a capstone project that encourages students to apply the concepts from the entire book while envisioning their role in shaping a future where humans and Artificial General Intelligence work together responsibly.

Teacher's Guide

AGI: Reasoning Intelligence

How Intelligent Systems Think, Solve Problems, and Make Better Decisions

By Susie Hala
IntelliGloss Press
IntelliGloss AI Education Series
Module 2: Artificial General Intelligence (AGI)

Welcome to the Teacher's Guide

Artificial General Intelligence (AGI) is one of the most exciting and important topics students will encounter during their education. While today's Artificial Intelligence systems perform specific tasks, AGI represents the next stage of intelligent systems—machines capable of reasoning, learning, adapting, and solving problems across many different situations.

This book introduces students to the foundations of reasoning intelligence using clear, age-appropriate language that makes complex ideas understandable without sacrificing academic quality. Rather than focusing on programming or advanced mathematics, this textbook develops the reasoning skills that students will need to understand, evaluate, and responsibly work alongside future intelligent systems.

This guide provides educators with lesson goals, discussion ideas, classroom activities, assessment suggestions, and extension projects that encourage students to become thoughtful, ethical, and informed users of future AI technologies.

Purpose of This Book

The purpose of this book is to help students understand:

- How reasoning differs from memorization.
- How intelligent systems solve problems.
- Why common sense matters in intelligence.
- How logical thinking supports good decisions.
- Why creativity and analogical reasoning drive innovation.
- How intelligent systems make decisions under uncertainty.

- Why long-term planning is essential.
- How reasoning connects multiple academic disciplines.
- Why self-reflection improves learning.
- How ethics guides responsible AI development.
- Why humans and AGI work best as partners.
- How students can prepare for an AGI-powered future.

The emphasis is on understanding **how to think**, not simply **what to think**.

Learning Objectives

By completing this book, students should be able to:

- Explain the difference between narrow AI and AGI.
- Describe several forms of reasoning.
- Analyze problems using logical thinking.
- Recognize the importance of common sense.
- Explain analogical reasoning.
- Evaluate uncertainty and risk.
- Create long-term plans.
- Connect knowledge across multiple disciplines.
- Reflect on their own thinking.
- Evaluate ethical AI decisions.
- Explain why human oversight remains important.
- Describe future careers involving AGI.
- Apply reasoning skills to real-world situations.

Target Audience

This book is appropriate for:

- Grades 6–12
- Career Technical Education (CTE)
- STEM Programs
- Computer Science Courses
- Technology Education
- Artificial Intelligence Electives
- Digital Literacy
- Future Ready Programs
- Honors Programs
- Gifted Programs
- Homeschool Programs

- Teacher Professional Development

Suggested Course Length

This book works well as:

- 16-week semester course (one chapter per week)
- 8-week accelerated course
- Professional development workshop
- AI summer program
- Technology enrichment course
- Independent study

Chapter 1 — What Is Reasoning Intelligence?

Students explore reasoning as the foundation of intelligent behavior and learn why reasoning is central to AGI.

Chapter 2 — Logical Thinking

Students examine logical reasoning, structured thinking, and evidence-based decision-making.

Chapter 3 — Problem-Solving Strategies

Students learn systematic approaches to solving simple and complex problems.

Chapter 4 — Learning From Experience

Students discover how experience improves reasoning and supports continuous learning.

Chapter 5 — Pattern Recognition

Students examine how recognizing meaningful patterns supports prediction and decision-making.

Chapter 6 — Causal Reasoning

Students learn to distinguish correlation from causation and analyze cause-and-effect relationships.

Chapter 7 — Inference and Evidence

Students evaluate evidence, draw conclusions, and understand uncertainty in reasoning.

Chapter 8 — Common Sense Reasoning

Students explore everyday reasoning, context, and practical decision-making.

Chapter 9 — Analogies and Creative Reasoning

Students discover how comparisons and creativity help solve unfamiliar problems.

Chapter 10 — Decision-Making Under Uncertainty

Students learn to evaluate risks, probabilities, and incomplete information responsibly.

Chapter 11 — Multi-Step Reasoning and Long-Term Planning

Students examine planning, sequencing, dependencies, and strategic thinking.

Chapter 12 — Reasoning Across Multiple Domains

Students learn how combining knowledge from different disciplines strengthens problem-solving.

Chapter 13 — Self-Reflection and Metacognition

Students develop awareness of their own thinking and strategies for continuous improvement.

Chapter 14 — Ethical Reasoning and Responsible Intelligence

Students explore fairness, transparency, accountability, privacy, bias, and responsible AI.

Chapter 15 — Humans and AGI Working Together

Students examine collaboration between people and intelligent systems across many professions.

Chapter 16 — Preparing for an AGI World

Students synthesize the entire book and explore future careers, lifelong learning, and responsible leadership.

Teaching Strategies

This textbook is designed to encourage active learning.

Recommended instructional approaches include:

- Classroom discussions
- Think-Pair-Share activities
- Small-group collaboration
- Case studies
- Problem-based learning
- Debate and discussion
- Reflection journals
- Research projects
- Student presentations
- Career exploration
- Current events connected to AI

Encourage students to explain *why* they reached an answer rather than simply giving the answer.

Classroom Discussion Questions

Examples include:

- What makes reasoning different from memorization?
- Can intelligence exist without ethics?
- Should AI always explain its decisions?
- Can creativity be taught?
- Why is common sense difficult for computers?
- What responsibilities come with powerful technology?
- How can humans and AGI work together responsibly?
- What skills will employers value most in an AI-powered economy?
- How should society prepare for AGI?

Assessment Suggestions

Evaluate student learning through a variety of methods.

Possible assessments include:

- Chapter quizzes
- Reflection journals

- Group presentations
- Classroom debates
- Research papers
- Case-study analyses
- AI ethics essays
- Future career reports
- Team projects
- Capstone presentations

Assessment should emphasize reasoning, communication, creativity, and ethical judgment in addition to factual knowledge.

Cross-Curricular Connections

This book integrates naturally with many subjects.

Science

- Scientific reasoning
- Observation
- Experimentation
- Evidence

Mathematics

- Logic
- Probability
- Data interpretation
- Decision analysis

Language Arts

- Critical reading
- Persuasive writing
- Communication
- Research

Social Studies

- Ethics
- Public policy
- Government
- Global cooperation

Technology

- AI systems
- Robotics
- Automation
- Data science

Career Education

- Future careers
- Workforce readiness
- Leadership
- Innovation

Classroom Projects

Possible projects include:

- Design an ethical AGI assistant.
- Create an AI career portfolio.
- Research current AI applications.
- Compare human and machine reasoning.
- Build a decision-making flowchart.
- Analyze an AI ethics case study.
- Create a future smart city proposal.
- Interview professionals who use AI.
- Develop classroom AI guidelines.
- Present a solution to a real-world problem using human-AGI collaboration.

Capstone Project

My Reasoning Intelligence Portfolio

Students create a portfolio demonstrating what they learned throughout the course.

Suggested sections include:

- My definition of reasoning intelligence
- My strongest reasoning skill
- A problem I solved using structured reasoning
- An ethical AI case study
- Human strengths that AGI complements

- My future career and AGI
- My lifelong learning plan
- My personal AI ethics pledge
- My vision for AGI in my community
- Final reflection

Differentiated Instruction

Support diverse learners by:

- Using visual organizers
- Providing guided notes
- Allowing collaborative learning
- Offering multiple project formats
- Encouraging peer teaching
- Connecting lessons to students' interests
- Breaking complex concepts into smaller parts
- Using real-world examples

Students can demonstrate learning through writing, presentations, artwork, multimedia, discussions, or projects.

Digital Citizenship Connections

Encourage students to:

- Verify information before sharing.
- Protect personal information online.
- Respect intellectual property.
- Recognize AI-generated content responsibly.
- Evaluate sources critically.
- Understand algorithmic bias.
- Use AI ethically for learning.
- Balance technology with independent thinking.

Preparing Students for the Future

One of the greatest lessons in this book is that future success will depend on more than technical knowledge.

Students should continue developing:

- Critical thinking
- Creativity
- Communication
- Collaboration
- Ethical reasoning
- Adaptability
- Emotional intelligence
- Curiosity
- Leadership
- Lifelong learning

These human strengths will remain valuable regardless of how advanced AGI becomes.

Final Message to Educators

Artificial General Intelligence will influence nearly every profession represented in today's classrooms. The students reading this book will become tomorrow's teachers, engineers, healthcare professionals, scientists, entrepreneurs, artists, policymakers, researchers, and community leaders.

Our responsibility is not simply to teach students about AI.

Our responsibility is to help students become thoughtful thinkers, ethical decision-makers, compassionate leaders, and lifelong learners who can guide powerful technologies with wisdom and integrity.

Reasoning is more than solving problems.

Reasoning is learning how to improve the world.

Thank you for investing in your students and preparing them for a future where human intelligence and Artificial General Intelligence work together to build safer, smarter, and more compassionate communities.

Learn AI. Understand AI. Shape the Future.

— Susie Hala
IntelliGloss Press

GLOSSARY

Letter A

1. Access Time

The amount of time it takes for an AI system or computer to locate and retrieve data from memory or storage. Access time affects how quickly megabytes of data can be used during AI processing.

2. Activation Data

Intermediate data generated inside an AI model while it is running. Activation data is stored temporarily in memory and often measured in megabytes during model execution.

3. Adaptive Storage

A storage approach that automatically adjusts how data is stored or moved based on usage patterns. In AI systems, adaptive storage helps manage large volumes of megabytes efficiently.

4. Algorithmic Data Size

The total amount of data an algorithm needs to operate effectively. In AI, this size is often measured in megabytes or larger units, depending on model complexity.

5. Allocation (Memory Allocation)

The process of assigning a specific number of megabytes in memory or storage for an AI task, model, or dataset.

6. Analytics Dataset

A structured collection of data used for analysis or AI training. The size of an analytics dataset is commonly measured in megabytes, gigabytes, or more.

7. Annotation Storage

The space required to store labels, tags, or explanations added to AI training data. These annotations contribute additional megabytes to total dataset size.

8. Artificial Neural Network (ANN) Size

The total memory footprint of a neural network, including weights, biases, and parameters. ANN size is often described in megabytes when discussing model efficiency.

9. Asset Compression

The process of reducing the number of megabytes required to store AI-related files such as models, images, or datasets without losing essential information.

10. Available Memory

The amount of free memory, measured in megabytes, that an AI system can still use to load data, run models, or perform computations.

ANI (Artificial Narrow Intelligence)

Artificial Narrow Intelligence refers to AI systems designed to perform **one specific task or a narrow set of tasks** rather than general intelligence. ANI systems rely on data stored and processed in memory and storage measured in **megabytes, gigabytes, or more**. Examples include image recognition, speech-to-text, recommendation systems, and chatbots. ANI does not understand beyond its training scope, but it can process large amounts of data efficiently within its defined function.

Letter B

1. Bandwidth

The amount of data that can be transferred between systems in a given time. In AI systems, bandwidth determines how quickly megabytes of data can move between storage, memory, and processors.

2. Batch Processing

A method where AI systems process large groups of data all at once instead of one item at a time. Batch processing often involves handling many megabytes of data in a single operation.

3. Binary Encoding

The process of representing information using binary values (0s and 1s). All megabytes of AI data are ultimately stored and transmitted using binary encoding.**4. Bit Depth**

The number of bits used to represent a single piece of data, such as a pixel or audio sample. Higher bit depth increases data quality but also increases the number of megabytes required.

5. Bitmap Data

A type of image data where each pixel is stored as a set of bits. Bitmap images can quickly grow in size, consuming large numbers of megabytes in AI vision systems.

6. Buffer Memory

Temporary memory used to hold data while it is being transferred or processed. Buffers store data in chunks measured in megabytes to keep AI systems running smoothly.

7. Bulk Data Storage

Large-scale storage designed to hold massive datasets used for AI training or analysis. Bulk storage capacity is measured in megabytes, gigabytes, or larger units.

8. Byte Stream

A continuous flow of bytes transmitted or processed by a system. AI applications often analyze byte streams that accumulate into megabytes of data.

9. Bytecode

An intermediate form of program code that is easier for machines to execute than human-written code. Bytecode files occupy storage space measured in megabytes.

10. Byzantine Fault Tolerance (BFT)

A system property that allows AI or distributed systems to continue functioning even when some components fail or act unpredictably. Implementing BFT requires additional data handling and storage overhead measured in megabytes.

Letter C

1. Cache Memory

A small, high-speed memory area that stores frequently used data so the processor can access it faster. Cache helps reduce the time needed to move megabytes of data from main memory or storage.

2. Capacity Planning

The process of estimating how much memory and storage an AI system will need. Capacity planning ensures there are enough megabytes available to handle data, models, and future growth.

3. Checkpoint File

A saved snapshot of an AI model during training. Checkpoint files are stored in memory or storage and often consume many megabytes so training can resume without starting over.

4. Chunking

The practice of breaking large datasets into smaller pieces. Chunking helps AI systems process megabytes of data more efficiently by handling them in manageable parts.

5. Cloud Storage

A method of storing data on remote servers accessed through the internet. Cloud storage manages files measured in megabytes and allows AI systems to scale beyond local hardware limits.

6. Compression

The process of reducing the size of data so it uses fewer megabytes. Compression helps AI systems store, transfer, and process data more efficiently.

7. Compute Load

The amount of processing work required to run an AI task. Compute load often increases as the number of megabytes being processed grows.

8. Context Window

The amount of data an AI model can consider at one time. Context windows consume memory measured in megabytes, especially in language and vision models.

9. Corpus

A large collection of text or data used to train AI models. A corpus is usually measured in megabytes or larger units depending on its size.

10. CUDA Memory

Specialized memory used by GPUs to accelerate AI computations. CUDA memory holds model data and intermediate results measured in megabytes during processing.

Letter D

1. Data Allocation

The process of assigning a specific amount of memory or storage for data use. In AI systems, data allocation determines how many megabytes are reserved for datasets, models, or tasks.

2. Data Buffer

A temporary storage area that holds data while it is being transferred or processed. Data buffers manage megabytes of information to keep AI systems running smoothly.

3. Data Compression

A technique used to reduce the size of data so it consumes fewer megabytes. AI systems use data compression to save storage space and speed up data transfer.

4. Data Footprint

The total amount of data an AI system uses, including datasets, models, and temporary files. A data footprint is measured in megabytes, gigabytes, or more.

5. Data Loader

A software component that loads data into memory for AI training or inference. Data loaders handle batches of data measured in megabytes.

6. Data Migration

The process of moving data from one storage system to another. During AI system upgrades, data migration may involve transferring large numbers of megabytes.

7. Data Throughput

The rate at which data is processed or transferred by a system. Higher throughput allows AI systems to move more megabytes efficiently.

8. Dataset Size

The total amount of data in a dataset used for AI training or testing. Dataset size is commonly measured in megabytes or larger units.

9. Deep Learning Model Size

The amount of memory required to store a deep learning model, including its parameters and weights. Model size is often described in megabytes to assess efficiency.

10. Disk Storage

Long-term storage used to save files, datasets, and AI models. Disk storage capacity and usage are measured in megabytes, gigabytes, or terabytes.

Letter E

1. Edge Computing

A computing approach where data is processed closer to where it is generated rather than sent to a central server. Edge computing reduces how many megabytes must be transferred over networks.

2. Embedding Size

The amount of memory required to store vector representations used by AI models. Embedding size is often measured in megabytes and affects model performance and storage needs.

3. Encoded Data

Data that has been converted into a specific format for storage or transmission. Encoded data occupies megabytes depending on the encoding method used.

4. Encoding Scheme

A rule set that defines how data is represented digitally, such as text or images. Different encoding schemes can increase or reduce the number of megabytes required.

5. Encrypted Storage

Storage that protects data by converting it into a secure format. Encryption may slightly increase the number of megabytes used due to added security information.

6. End-to-End Data Pipeline

The full path data takes from collection to processing and storage. Each stage of the pipeline manages data volumes measured in megabytes.

7. Energy Efficiency (AI Systems)

A measure of how much energy an AI system uses to process data. Systems that move and store fewer megabytes are often more energy efficient.

8. Execution Memory

The memory required while a program or AI model is running. Execution memory usage is tracked in megabytes during runtime.

9. External Storage

Storage devices located outside a computer, such as USB drives or external hard drives. External storage capacity is measured in megabytes and larger units.

10. Extracted Features

Important data patterns identified by AI models during processing. Extracted features are stored temporarily or permanently in memory measured in megabytes.

Letter F

1. Feature Map

A structured output produced by AI models, especially in image and signal processing. Feature maps are stored in memory and can consume significant megabytes during computation.

2. Feature Scaling

The process of adjusting data values to a consistent range before training an AI model. Feature scaling affects how efficiently megabytes of data are processed and stored.

3. File Allocation Table (FAT)

A file system structure that tracks where files are stored on a disk. FAT helps manage how megabytes are organized and retrieved from storage.

4. File Compression Format

A standardized way to reduce file size so it uses fewer megabytes. Compression formats help AI systems store and transfer data efficiently.

5. File System Cache

A temporary memory area that stores frequently accessed files. File system caches reduce repeated access to storage and manage megabytes more efficiently.

6. Floating-Point Data

Numerical data that includes decimal values and is commonly used in AI calculations. Floating-point data requires more bits per value, increasing memory usage measured in megabytes.

7. Frame Buffer

A region of memory that stores image or video frames before they are displayed or processed. Frame buffers often consume large numbers of megabytes in AI vision systems.

8. Fragmentation

A condition where data is stored in scattered locations instead of one continuous block. Fragmentation can reduce storage efficiency even when megabytes appear available.

9. Free Memory

The amount of unused memory available for programs or AI tasks. Free memory is measured in megabytes and determines how much additional data can be loaded.

10. Full Dataset Load

The act of loading an entire dataset into memory at once. This approach can require large amounts of megabytes and is common in AI training scenarios.

Letter G

1. Garbage Collection

An automatic memory-management process that frees memory no longer in use. Garbage collection helps reclaim megabytes so AI programs can continue running efficiently.

2. Generalization Data

Data used to test how well an AI model performs on new, unseen inputs. Storing and evaluating generalization data requires additional megabytes beyond training data.

3. Gigabyte (GB)

A larger unit of data measurement equal to 1,024 megabytes (or commonly approximated as 1,000 MB). Gigabytes are used when datasets or models grow beyond megabyte scale.

4. Graph Data Structure

A way of organizing data using nodes and connections. Graph-based AI systems store graph data in memory and storage measured in megabytes.

5. GPU Memory

Specialized memory used by graphics processing units to accelerate AI workloads. GPU memory holds model parameters and data batches measured in megabytes.

6. Gradient Data

Numerical values calculated during AI training to update model parameters. Gradient data is stored temporarily in memory and contributes to overall megabyte usage.

7. Granularity

The level of detail at which data is stored or processed. Finer granularity often increases the number of megabytes required.

8. Greedy Algorithm

An algorithm that makes the best immediate choice at each step. Greedy algorithms may reduce memory usage by limiting how many megabytes of data must be stored at once.

9. Ground Truth Data

Correct, labeled data used to train or evaluate AI systems. Ground truth datasets are stored in files measured in megabytes or larger units.

10. Growth Rate (Data)

The speed at which data size increases over time. In AI systems, a high data growth rate means storage needs measured in megabytes can expand quickly.

Letter H

1. Hard Disk Capacity

The total amount of data a hard disk can store. Capacity is measured in megabytes and larger units.

2. Hardware Acceleration

The use of specialized hardware to speed up AI processing. Acceleration often reduces how long megabytes of data stay in memory.

3. Hash Table

A data structure that stores information for fast lookup. Hash tables occupy memory measured in megabytes in large AI systems.

4. Hierarchical Storage

A storage design that uses multiple layers such as RAM, disk, and cloud. Each layer manages data measured in megabytes.

5. High-Dimensional Data

Data with many features or variables. High-dimensional datasets often require large numbers of megabytes.

6. Host Memory

Main system memory used by the CPU. Host memory stores AI data and models measured in megabytes.

7. Hybrid Storage

A combination of different storage types working together. Hybrid storage systems manage megabytes across multiple devices.

8. Hyperparameter Storage

Memory used to store configuration values for AI models. These settings are saved in files measured in megabytes.

9. Hyperscale Data

Extremely large datasets used by major AI systems. Hyperscale data is tracked from megabytes up to much larger units.

10. Heuristic Data

Information used by AI systems to guide decision-making. Heuristic data contributes to the overall data size in megabytes.

Letter I

1. Image Dataset Size

The total amount of storage required for image data. Size is measured in megabytes or more.

2. Inference Memory

The memory used when an AI model is making predictions. Inference memory usage is tracked in megabytes.

3. Input Buffer

A temporary area where incoming data is stored. Input buffers hold megabytes before processing begins.

4. Intermediate Data

Data produced during processing steps. Intermediate data can significantly increase memory usage in megabytes.

5. Index File

A file that helps locate data quickly. Index files use additional megabytes to improve performance.

6. Information Density

The amount of useful data stored within a given size. Higher density means more information per megabyte.

7. Initialization Data

Data loaded when an AI system starts. Initialization data occupies memory measured in megabytes.

8. In-Memory Processing

Processing data directly in RAM instead of storage. This approach uses large amounts of memory measured in megabytes.

9. Input Feature Size

The amount of data required to represent input features. Feature size affects how many megabytes are needed.

10. Instruction Cache

A small memory area that stores frequently used instructions. Instruction caches manage small but critical megabytes.

Letter J

1. Job Queue

A list of tasks waiting to be processed. Job queues may store task data measured in megabytes.

2. Joint Dataset

A dataset created by combining multiple sources. Joint datasets often increase total size in megabytes.

3. JSON Data Size

The amount of storage required for data stored in JSON format. JSON files can grow quickly in megabytes.

4. Jitter Buffer

A temporary storage area that smooths data flow. Jitter buffers store megabytes during real-time processing.

5. Job Scheduler

A system that decides when tasks run. Schedulers manage memory and data measured in megabytes.

6. Just-in-Time Processing

Processing data only when needed. This approach can reduce how many megabytes are stored at once.

7. Joint Memory Allocation

Memory shared across multiple AI tasks. Joint allocation must carefully manage available megabytes.

8. Java Bytecode Size

The storage size of compiled Java programs. Bytecode files occupy megabytes on disk.

9. Job Metadata

Information describing AI tasks. Metadata adds additional megabytes to total system storage.

10. Junction Storage Point

A logical link between storage locations. Junctions help organize data measured in megabytes.

Letter K

1. Kernel Memory

Memory reserved for core system operations. Kernel memory usage is tracked in megabytes.

2. Key-Value Store

A data storage method that pairs keys with values. Large key-value stores consume many megabytes.

3. Knowledge Base Size

The total amount of stored knowledge in an AI system. Size is measured in megabytes or larger units.

4. K-Means Dataset Size

The amount of data used in clustering algorithms. Dataset size affects memory usage in megabytes.

5. Keras Model Size

The storage required for AI models built with Keras. Model size is measured in megabytes.

6. Keyframe Data

Important frames selected from video data. Keyframe storage contributes to total megabyte usage.

7. Kernel Cache

A cache used by the operating system kernel. Kernel caches store frequently used data in megabytes.

8. Knowledge Graph Storage

Memory used to store relationships between data points. Knowledge graphs require significant megabytes.

9. Kinetic Data Stream

Continuously changing data from sensors or systems. These streams generate growing megabytes over time.

10. K-Nearest Neighbor Memory Usage

The memory required by nearest-neighbor algorithms. Memory use increases as datasets grow in megabytes.

Letter L

1. **Latency**
   The delay between requesting data and receiving it. Latency affects how quickly megabytes move through AI systems.
2. **Layer Output Size**
   The amount of data produced by a neural network layer. Output size is measured in megabytes during processing.
3. **Load Balancing**
   Distributing work across systems so no single device is overloaded. Balancing helps manage megabytes efficiently.
4. **Local Storage**
   Data stored on a device rather than the cloud. Local storage capacity is measured in megabytes.
5. **Log File Size**
   The amount of storage used by system logs. Logs can accumulate many megabytes over time.
6. **Loss History Data**
   Stored values showing how model error changes during training. Loss history consumes megabytes.

7. **Low-Precision Data**
   Data stored using fewer bits per value. Low-precision formats reduce megabyte usage.
8. **Labeled Dataset**
   Data that includes tags or labels for AI training. Labels increase total dataset size in megabytes.
9. **Linear Model Size**
   The storage required for a linear AI model. Size is measured in megabytes.
10. **Load Time**
    The time required to bring data or models into memory. Load time depends on megabytes involved.

Letter M

1. **Memory Allocation**
   Assigning a specific amount of memory for tasks. Allocation is tracked in megabytes.
2. **Memory Footprint**
   The total memory an AI program uses. Footprint is measured in megabytes.
3. **Metadata Size**
   The storage used by descriptive information about data. Metadata adds extra megabytes.
4. **Mini-Batch Size**
   The amount of data processed at once during training. Batch size affects megabyte usage.
5. **Model Checkpoint Size**
   The storage required for saved training states. Checkpoints often consume many megabytes.
6. **Model Compression**
   Reducing model size while preserving performance. Compression lowers megabytes required.
7. **Model Parameters**
   Values learned by an AI model. Parameter storage contributes to total megabytes.
8. **Memory Bandwidth**
   The rate at which memory transfers data. Bandwidth affects how fast megabytes move.
9. **Multimodal Dataset**
   Data combining text, images, audio, or video. Multimodal data uses large megabytes.
10. **Mutable Data**
    Data that changes during processing. Mutable data can increase temporary megabyte usage.

Letter N

1. **Network Bandwidth**
   The capacity of a network connection. Bandwidth controls how many megabytes can be transferred.

2. **Neural Network Size**
   The total storage required for a neural network. Size is measured in megabytes.
3. **Node Memory**
   Memory available on a computing node. Node memory limits megabytes per task.
4. **Normalization Data**
   Values used to scale data consistently. Normalization adds to dataset megabytes.
5. **Non-Volatile Memory**
   Memory that retains data without power. Capacity is measured in megabytes.
6. **Numerical Precision**
   The detail level of stored numbers. Higher precision increases megabytes.
7. **Noise Data**
   Unwanted or random information in datasets. Noise increases data size in megabytes.
8. **Neural Activation Size**
   Memory used to store neuron outputs. Activation size is measured in megabytes.
9. **Network Transfer Size**
   The amount of data sent across a network. Transfer size is tracked in megabytes.
10. **Node Cache**
    Temporary storage on a node for faster access. Cache size uses megabytes.

Letter O

1. **Object Storage**
   A storage method that manages data as objects. Capacity is measured in megabytes.
2. **Offline Dataset**
   Data stored locally rather than streamed. Offline datasets occupy megabytes.
3. **On-Device Storage**
   Storage located on the AI device itself. On-device capacity is measured in megabytes.
4. **Operational Memory**
   Memory used during active AI operations. Usage is tracked in megabytes.
5. **Optimization Data**
   Information used to improve model performance. Optimization data uses megabytes.
6. **Output Buffer**
   Temporary storage for results before delivery. Buffers hold megabytes.
7. **Overhead Data**
   Extra data required for system operation. Overhead increases total megabytes.
8. **Object Detection Output Size**
   The amount of data produced by detection models. Output size is measured in megabytes.
9. **Online Storage**
   Storage accessible via the internet. Online storage limits are measured in megabytes.
10. **Open Dataset Size**
    The storage footprint of publicly available datasets. Size is measured in megabytes.

Letter P

1. **Parameter Count**
   The total number of model values. Count correlates with megabytes required.
2. **Persistent Storage**
   Long-term storage that retains data. Capacity is measured in megabytes.
3. **Pipeline Buffer**
   Temporary storage between processing stages. Buffers manage megabytes in motion.
4. **Preprocessing Data**
   Data created while preparing datasets. Preprocessing adds megabytes.
5. **Precision Reduction**
   Lowering numeric detail to save space. Reduction decreases megabyte usage.
6. **Prediction Output Size**
   The amount of data produced by model predictions. Size is measured in megabytes.
7. **Primary Memory**
   Main system memory used for processing. Capacity is measured in megabytes.
8. **Processing Overhead**
   Extra resources needed during computation. Overhead increases megabyte usage.
9. **Profiling Data**
   Information collected to analyze performance. Profiling data uses megabytes.
10. **Paged Memory**
    Memory divided into fixed-size blocks. Paging manages megabytes efficiently.

Letter Q

1. **Quantization**
   A technique that reduces numerical precision to lower memory usage. Quantization helps AI models use fewer megabytes.
2. **Query Cache**
   Stored results from previous searches or requests. Query caches save megabytes by avoiding repeated computation.
3. **Query Latency**
   The time it takes to retrieve data after a request. Latency depends on how many megabytes must be accessed.
4. **Queue Buffer**
   A temporary holding area for data waiting to be processed. Buffers store megabytes in order.
5. **Quick Access Memory**
   Memory designed for fast retrieval. It handles megabytes needed immediately by AI tasks.
6. **Quantitative Dataset**
   Data made up of numerical values. These datasets are stored and measured in megabytes.
7. **Query Result Size**
   The amount of data returned from a query. Result size is measured in megabytes.

8. **Quorum Storage**
   A distributed storage method requiring agreement across systems. Data is replicated in megabytes.
9. **Quality Metrics Data**
   Information used to measure model performance. Metrics consume storage in megabytes.
10. **Quantized Model Size**
    The reduced size of an AI model after quantization. Size is typically measured in megabytes.

Letter R

1. **RAM Usage**
   The amount of active memory in use. RAM usage is tracked in megabytes.
2. **Read Throughput**
   The speed at which data is read from storage. Throughput affects how fast megabytes are accessed.
3. **Real-Time Processing**
   Processing data immediately as it arrives. Real-time systems manage megabytes continuously.
4. **Recursive Memory Use**
   Memory consumption during repeated function calls. Usage accumulates in megabytes.
5. **Redundant Storage**
   Extra copies of data kept for reliability. Redundancy increases total megabytes stored.
6. **Resource Allocation**
   Assigning system resources like memory and storage. Allocation is measured in megabytes.
7. **Runtime Memory**
   Memory required while a program is running. Runtime memory usage is tracked in megabytes.
8. **Raw Dataset Size**
   The size of unprocessed data. Raw datasets often require many megabytes.
9. **Read-Only Memory Footprint**
   The storage space used by non-modifiable data. Footprint is measured in megabytes.
10. **Retrieval Speed**
    How quickly stored data can be accessed. Speed depends on the number of megabytes involved.

Letter S

1. **Sample Size**
   The number of data examples used in AI training. Larger samples increase megabytes.

2. **Scalable Storage**
   Storage that grows with demand. Scalability supports increasing megabytes.
3. **Serialized Data Size**
   The storage size of data converted into a transferable format. Size is measured in megabytes.
4. **Shared Memory**
   Memory accessible by multiple processes. Shared memory usage is tracked in megabytes.
5. **Snapshot Size**
   The storage required for saved system states. Snapshots consume megabytes.
6. **Sparse Data Representation**
   A storage method that saves space when data contains many empty values. Sparsity reduces megabytes.
7. **Storage Capacity**
   The total amount of data a system can store. Capacity is measured in megabytes or more.
8. **Streaming Data Buffer**
   Temporary storage for incoming data streams. Buffers handle megabytes in motion.
9. **System Cache**
   Memory that stores frequently used data. Caches manage megabytes for faster access.
10. **Synchronization Data**
   Information used to keep systems aligned. Sync data adds to total megabytes.

Letter T

1. **Temporary Storage**
   Short-term storage used during processing. Temporary storage holds megabytes briefly.
2. **Tensor Size**
   The memory required to store multidimensional data structures. Tensor size is measured in megabytes.
3. **Throughput Rate**
   The amount of data processed per unit time. Rate is often described in megabytes per second.
4. **Training Dataset Size**
   The total amount of data used to train AI models. Size is measured in megabytes.
5. **Transfer Buffer**
   Temporary memory used during data movement. Buffers hold megabytes during transfer.
6. **Transactional Storage**
   Storage that ensures data consistency. Transactions add overhead measured in megabytes.
7. **Thread Memory Usage**
   Memory consumed by execution threads. Usage is tracked in megabytes.
8. **Token Storage Size**
   The memory required to store processed tokens. Token data uses megabytes.
9. **Time-Series Data Size**
   The storage footprint of data collected over time. Size increases in megabytes.

10. **Training Checkpoint Size**
    The storage required for saved training states. Checkpoints are measured in megabytes.

Letter U

1. **Unified Memory**
   A memory system shared between CPU and GPU. Unified memory manages data in megabytes efficiently across processors.
2. **Upload Size**
   The amount of data sent to storage or the cloud. Upload size is measured in megabytes.
3. **User Data Storage**
   Storage allocated for user-generated files. Capacity is tracked in megabytes.
4. **Utilization Rate**
   The percentage of memory or storage currently in use. Utilization reflects how many megabytes are occupied.
5. **Uncompressed Data Size**
   The size of data before compression. Uncompressed data often uses more megabytes.
6. **Update Payload**
   Data sent during software or model updates. Payload size is measured in megabytes.
7. **Uptime Storage Logs**
   Logs recorded while systems run continuously. Logs accumulate megabytes over time.
8. **Unified Dataset**
   A dataset combined from multiple sources. Size is measured in megabytes.
9. **User Session Memory**
   Memory allocated for active users. Session memory uses megabytes dynamically.
10. **Usage Quota**
    A storage limit set for users or systems. Quotas are defined in megabytes or larger units.

Letter V

1. **Validation Dataset Size**
   The amount of data used to evaluate AI models. Size is measured in megabytes.
2. **Vector Embedding Size**
   The memory required to store numerical representations of data. Size is measured in megabytes.
3. **Virtual Memory**
   A system that extends RAM using disk storage. Virtual memory is managed in megabytes.
4. **Volatile Memory**
   Memory that loses data when power is off. Capacity is measured in megabytes.
5. **Video Dataset Size**
   The storage required for video data. Video datasets consume many megabytes.

6. **Versioned Storage**
   Storage that keeps multiple file versions. Versioning increases megabyte usage.
7. **Vision Model Size**
   The memory footprint of computer vision models. Size is measured in megabytes.
8. **Vector Database Storage**
   Storage used for similarity search data. Vector databases consume large megabytes.
9. **Virtualized Storage**
   Storage abstracted from physical hardware. Capacity is tracked in megabytes.
10. **Volume Capacity**
    The total size of a storage volume. Capacity is measured in megabytes or more.

Letter W

1. **Weight Parameters**
   Learned values in AI models. Weight storage contributes to megabytes used.
2. **Working Memory**
   Memory actively used during processing. Working memory usage is measured in megabytes.
3. **Write Throughput**
   The speed at which data is written to storage. Throughput affects megabytes per second.
4. **Warm Cache**
   Cached data that is already loaded. Warm caches reduce repeated megabyte transfers.
5. **Workflow Data Size**
   The total data used across an AI workflow. Size is measured in megabytes.
6. **Web Dataset Size**
   The storage required for web-based data. Size is tracked in megabytes.
7. **Weight Compression**
   Reducing model weight size to save memory. Compression lowers megabytes used.
8. **Window Size (AI Context)**
   The amount of data processed at once. Window size affects memory megabytes.
9. **Writable Storage**
   Storage that allows data modification. Capacity is measured in megabytes.
10. **Workload Memory Demand**
    The memory required for tasks. Demand is expressed in megabytes.

Letter X

1. **X-Axis Data Size**
   Data stored along one dimension of a dataset. Size contributes to megabytes used.
2. **XML Data Size**
   The storage footprint of XML-formatted data. XML files often use many megabytes.

3. **XOR Encoding**
   A binary operation used in data processing. Encoded data occupies megabytes.
4. **Execution Context Size**
   Memory required during task execution. Size is measured in megabytes.
5. **External Dataset Size**
   The size of data sourced externally. External datasets add megabytes.
6. **Expanded Memory Use**
   Memory growth during processing. Expansion increases megabytes consumed.
7. **Experimental Dataset**
   Data used for testing AI models. Size is measured in megabytes.
8. **Extraction Buffer**
   Temporary storage during data extraction. Buffers store megabytes briefly.
9. **Extended Storage Capacity**
   Additional storage added to a system. Capacity is measured in megabytes.
10. **Explainability Data Size**
    Data used to explain AI decisions. Explainability outputs consume megabytes.

Letter Y

1. **Yield Data Size**
   The amount of useful output data produced. Yield is measured in megabytes.
2. **Yearly Data Growth**
   Annual increase in stored data. Growth is tracked in megabytes.
3. **YAML File Size**
   The storage footprint of YAML configuration files. Size is measured in megabytes.
4. **Y-Axis Feature Size**
   Feature data along a dataset dimension. Size contributes to megabytes.
5. **Young Generation Memory**
   Memory area for newly created data. Usage is measured in megabytes.
6. **Yield Optimization Data**
   Data used to improve output efficiency. Stored in megabytes.
7. **YourAIStudyBuddy Dataset Size**
   The total data used by AI study tools. Size is measured in megabytes.
8. **Yottabyte Reference Scale**
   A conceptual upper scale of data measurement. Used for comparison beyond megabytes.
9. **Yield Metrics Storage**
   Storage used for performance metrics. Metrics consume megabytes.
10. **Yoked Memory Allocation**
    Linked memory regions used together. Allocation is measured in megabytes.

Letter Z

1. **Zero-Copy Memory**
   A method that avoids duplicating data. Zero-copy reduces megabytes in motion.
2. **Zipped Dataset Size**
   The storage size after compression. Zipped files use fewer megabytes.
3. **Zettabyte Scale (Reference)**
   A large-scale data concept. Used to compare growth beyond megabytes.
4. **Zone-Based Storage**
   Storage divided into regions. Zones manage megabytes efficiently.
5. **Z-Score Normalization Data**
   Statistical values used in preprocessing. Data adds megabytes.
6. **Zero Padding**
   Adding placeholder data to inputs. Padding increases memory megabytes.
7. **Zoomed Feature Maps**
   Scaled representations in vision models. Stored in megabytes.
8. **Zonal Cache**
   Cache divided by region. Cache size is measured in megabytes.
9. **Zero-Day Model Update Size**
   The storage required for emergency updates. Size is measured in megabytes.
10. **Zipped Model Archive**
    Compressed AI model files. Archives reduce megabytes required.

NOTE:

NOTE:

NOTE:

www.ingramcontent.com/pod-product-compliance
Lightning Source LLC
LaVergne TN
LVHW070524061126
851857LV00024B/2141
9781972925300